Eleanor of Aquitaine

Eleanor of Aquitaine

Queen and Legend

D. D. R. OWEN

BLACKWELL
Publishers

First published 1993
Reprinted 1993, 1994
First published in paperback 1996
Reprinted 1998

Blackwell Publishers Ltd
108 Cowley Road
Oxford OX4 1JF, UK

Blackwell Publishers Inc.
350 Main Street
Malden, Massachusetts 02148 , USA

British Library Cataloguing in Publication Data
A CIP catalogue record for this book is available from the British Library.

Library of Congress Cataloging-in-Publication Data
Owen, D. D. R. (Douglas David Roy)
        Eleanor of Aquitaine : queen and legend / D. D. R. Owen.
            p.   cm.
        Includes bibliographical references and index.
        ISBN 0-631-17072-3 (acid-free paper) (Hbk)—ISBN 0-631-20101-7 (Pbk)
            1.   Eleanor of Aquitaine, Queen, consort of Henry II, King of
    England, 1122?–1204. 2. Great Britain–History–Henry II, 1154–1189.
    3. France–Queens–Biography.
    I. Title.
    DA209.E6095 1993
    942.03'1'092–dc20
    [B]   92-28890
                                                                                              CIP

Typeset in 11 on 13pt Sabon
by TecSet Ltd, Wallington, Surrey
Printed in Great Britain by
Athenæum Press Ltd, Gateshead, Tyne & Wear

This book is printed on acid-free paper

Contents

Plates

The author and publishers are grateful to the following for supplying photographs and for their kind permission to reproduce them:

Plate 1 Bibliothèque Nationale and Photographie Giraudon, Paris; *Plate 2* The Metropolitan Museum of Art, The Cloisters Collection Purchase, 1934 (34.115.4ab); *Plate 3* Archives Nationales and Photographie Giraudon, Paris; *Plate 4* By permission of the British Library, London; *Plate 5* © Insel Verlag, Frankfurt, 1988; *Plate 6* © Roger-Viollet, Paris; *Plate 7* © Michael Holford; *Plate 8* Society of Antiquaries of London; *Plate 9* Photographie Giraudon, Paris; *Plate 10* © Roger-Viollet, Paris; *Plate 11* The Dean

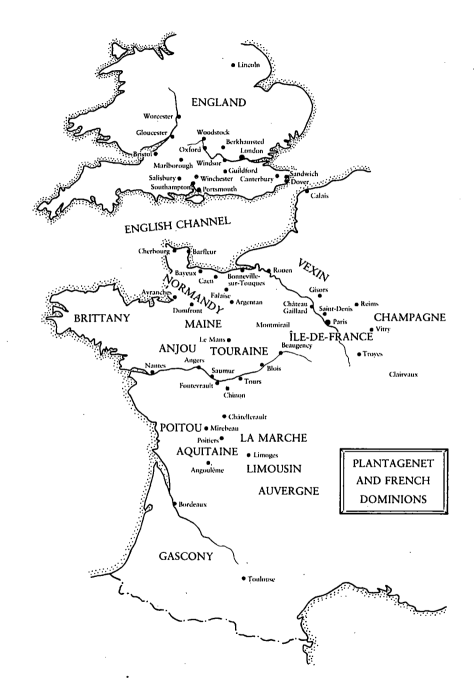

Lincoln

ENGLAND

Worcester
Gloucester   Woodstock
                            Berkhamsted
Bristol   Oxford   London
Marlborough   Windsor
Salisbury   Winchester   Canterbury   Sandwich
Southampton   Portsmouth   Dover
                                          Calais

ENGLISH CHANNEL

Cherbourg   Barfleur
                                    Rouen   VEXIN
    Bayeux   Caen   Bonneville-
                     sur-Touques   Gisors
Avranches   Falaise   Château   Saint-Denis   Reims
NORMANDY   Argentan   Gaillard
    Domfront   Paris
BRITTANY   MAINE   Montmirail   ÎLE-DE-FRANCE   CHAMPAGNE
                                                            Vitry
            Le Mans   Beaugency
    ANJOU   TOURAINE   Troyes
        Angers
Nantes   Saumur   Blois   Clairvaux
    Fontevrault   Tours
            Chinon

            Châtellerault
POITOU   Mirebeau
    Poitiers   LA MARCHE
    AQUITAINE   Limoges
        Angoulême   LIMOUSIN

                    AUVERGNE

    Bordeaux

                                        ┌─────────────────┐
                                        │   PLANTAGENET   │
                                        │   AND FRENCH   │
                                        │   DOMINIONS   │
                                        └─────────────────┘

    GASCONY

                    Toulouse

THE FAMILY OF ELEANOR OF AQUITAINE

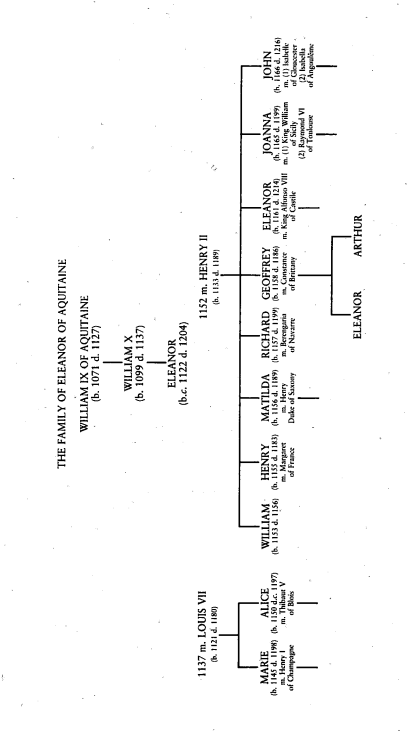

WILLIAM IX OF AQUITAINE
(b. 1071 d. 1127)

WILLIAM X
(b. 1099 d. 1137)

ELEANOR
(b.c. 1122 d. 1204)

1137 m. LOUIS VII
(b. 1121 d. 1180)

1152 m. HENRY II
(b. 1133 d. 1189)

MARIE
(b. 1145 d. 1198)
m. Henry I
of Champagne

ALICE
(b. 1150 d.c. 1197)
m. Thibaut V
of Blois

WILLIAM
(b. 1153 d. 1156)

HENRY
(b. 1155 d. 1183)
m. Margaret
of France

MATILDA
(b. 1156 d. 1189)
m. Henry
Duke of Saxony

RICHARD
(b. 1157 d. 1199)
m. Berengaria
of Navarre

GEOFFREY
(b. 1158 d. 1186)
m. Constance
of Brittany

ELEANOR
(b. 1161 d. 1214)
m. King Alfonso VIII
of Castile

JOANNA
(b. 1165 d. 1199)
m. (1) King William
of Sicily
(2) Raymond VI
of Toulouse

JOHN
(b. 1166 d. 1216)
m. (1) Isabelle
of Gloucester
(2) Isabella
of Angoulême

ELEANOR

ARTHUR

Acknowledgements

I am much indebted to friends and colleagues too numerous to mention for their encouragement and advice on this project. My labours have been greatly eased by the unstinted help of the staff of the St Andrews University Library; and the resulting text has benefited from the patient scrutiny of my wife Berit. But my first debt of gratitude is owed to the editors of Blackwell Publishers for proposing this fascinating subject and for their care in ushering it into print.

D.D.R.O.

Introduction

As if to taunt us quietly, the effigy of Queen Eleanor at Fontevrault
holds an open book, whereas her stone lips are closed for all time.
If only we could unseal them and persuade them to tell some of the
secrets they are guarding! So much information, public in its day,
is now past recovery; and there is far more, surely the most
interesting, that only Eleanor herself could tell. Yet even if we
could raise her ghost, I wonder if the memory of the dead would
not prove as fallible as our own and apt to impose in retrospect on
her life's deeds a pattern they never really possessed? The ghost
might continue faithful to some role adopted by the person in life
and persist in the same delusions. Would Eleanor really have been
able to explain the deep motivation behind a great deal of her
behaviour? How far was she in control of the varied roles she
played in the course of her long life, and how far did she slip into
them unawares? The question is unanswerable; but we shall do
well to bear it in mind as we follow her through times of fortune
and misfortune.

One can imagine, masked behind those calm features, Eleanor's
last thoughts as she looked back over her life and saw it as the
lustrous end of a golden strand of history such as might have been
woven by a poet of her time into an inspiring ancestral romance.
She may even at an early age already have sensed the part she was
to play in bringing her family destiny to its culmination and
consummation. The idea is appealing: more so than the thought of
her dying a disillusioned woman, saddened by a sense of ultimate
failure. And it is a view encouraged as much by her life's whole
context as by its bald facts. In giving these, so far as they can be
ascertained from contemporary sources, I shall have an eye to

1

what they may suggest of Eleanor's character, while treating with caution its assessment by possibly biased observers and trying to avoid the pitfall of making it correspond to any preconceived image.

Having attempted to sift fact from fiction, I shall see how, even in her own day, she caught the imagination of commentators and writers ready to spice the truth or even totally ignore it for the sake of a good story. So there was spun a web of legend that became elaborated over the centuries. Truth was, in any case, infinitely malleable in the Middle Ages, and liable especially to be adapted to the patterns of popular fiction. The legend of Eleanor may, then, owe some debt to the literary culture within which its creators worked. Is it possible that her own outlook was to some degree the product of that culture? The matter is certainly worth considering. Whilst on the one hand, as will be seen, the medieval mind was apt to envisage real events in terms of favourite fictions, people also felt the urge on occasion to make life imitate art by acting in the manner of the heroes and heroines of legend.

After seeing her through the public eye of the legend-mongers, I shall look at the possibility of catching her by surprise, masquerading under an assumed identity in some of the literary compositions of her time. For it is not inconceivable that their authors used her on occasion as a model in order to give the ring of truth to their fictional characters. As my particular concern is more with Eleanor the woman than Eleanor the politician, this approach could prove worthwhile if it gives some oblique insight into the way in which she was perceived by her contemporaries or near-contemporaries. Others have dealt comprehensively with the complex tapestry of characters and events through which her own life was threaded. Much of this detail I shall take for granted in order to keep the spotlight more constantly on her; and I leave to those more competent than I the delicate operation of political analysis and appraisal, while reserving most of my speculation for the latter part of the study. But I shall begin with a glance at the family background which may have had a formative influence on her personality.

1

Lineage

Roland replies: 'May it never please God
That blame should fall on my kinsfolk through me,
Or fair France ever lapse in infamy!'[1]

Roland's idealism was not misplaced in an age which laid so much
stress on the acquisition and inheritance of landed property within
the feudal structure; and it was into a world where family and
territorial loyalties were strong that Eleanor was born. There is no
certainty as to the date and place of the event, though it is most
commonly thought to have taken place in 1122, either in Poitiers
or in the castle of Belin near Bordeaux. By that time the *Song of
Roland* had been circulating in the form most familiar to us for
about a generation; and there is no doubt that his legend was by
now widely known in the whole of France and beyond. Bordeaux
has a special place in the story in that we are assured by the poet
that Charlemagne himself, as he returned from Spain, left his dead
nephew's horn in the church there:

Then Charles came to the city of Bordeaux;
Upon noble Saint Seurin's altar there
He placed the oliphant filled with gold coins:
Pilgrims may see it when they pass that way.[2]

Doubtless Eleanor, as a child, would have had her imagination
fired by the heroism of Roland at Roncevaux and by the ideals on
which it was founded. She might even have seen in him, mistakenly, a distant kinsman, since her family claimed descent from
Charlemagne.

Eleanor's childhood informed by song of Roland?

3

Their land of Aquitaine had been established by the Romans as a province of Gaul, extending eventually from the Pyrenees to the Loire. An independent duchy under the Merovingians, it was turned by Charlemagne, before he took the imperial title, into a sub-kingdom for his infant son Louis, who received its crown from the pope in 781. Its administration Charles entrusted to nine lords, one of whom, having failed in his duty, was replaced in 789 by William, Count of Toulouse. Four years later this stalwart suffered a gallant defeat at the hands of marauding Saracens in the vicinity of Carcassonne. But that turned out to be their last incursion across the Pyrenees; and William's reputation was paradoxically enhanced. The heroic count is remembered by legend as William of Orange and his disastrous battle as Aliscans, a second Roncevaux. And by the end of the twelfth century a whole cycle of chansons de geste, the epic poems performed in castle hall and market-place by itinerant jongleurs, had accumulated round his own name and those of his kinsmen. William ended his days peacefully having withdrawn to the abbey of Gellone, near Montpellier, renamed Saint-Guilhem-le-Désert after his canonization in 1066. The monks there wrote a Latin life in his celebration at about the time of Eleanor's birth. It has been claimed in the past that memories of one or more of Eleanor's forebears may have been fused into his legend; but be that as it may, William of Orange is another larger-than-life character who must have frequented the landscape of her childhood imagination.

As the Carolingian dynasty fell into decline, so did the territorial integrity of Aquitaine. It remained a kingdom until 877, but in name only, becoming politically fragmented and forming the stage for a tug-of-war between the counts of Poitiers and of Toulouse, who each aspired to the by then hollow title of Duke of Aquitaine. In 951, however, it passed to a man of some substance, William I of Poitiers, known as the Tow-Headed ('Tête d'Étoupes'), who was blessed with real ability as well as a strong-minded Norman wife, Adela. Both were noted for their practical piety; and William eventually retired to a monastery, but not before starting (though in title he was the third) the direct line of dukes from which Eleanor was to issue.

His successors were not lacking in character,[3] William IV of Aquitaine, Strong-Arm ('Fierebras', interestingly enough one of the sobriquets of the legendary William of Orange), did not share his father's temperate ways. His over-indulgence in the chase and in women gave offence to his spirited wife Emma, the sister of the king, Hugh Capet. The upshot was two lengthy separations and ultimately his own taking refuge from the sins of the world in the religious life, leaving his young son in Emma's care. This was Duke William V, the Great, who reigned from 993 to 1030 and whose character seems to bear the imprint of that of his mother. She was to remain a figure of authority in his court until her death in 1004.

Not only did William the Great show considerable skill and diplomacy in the government of his lands, forming important bonds and alliances beyond their borders, but he is also given the credit for effecting in his court at Poitiers the fruitful union of northern learning with the less strait-laced southern civilization. Well schooled himself and familiar with the intellectual life of centres such as Blois, Tours and Chartres, he took real pleasure, we are told by a contemporary, in burning the midnight candle over a book. Before his day the south had a bright but rather thin veneer of culture when compared with the less elegant life of the north where, however, the Latin learning of the emerging schools had deeper roots. Now Poitiers acquired its own cathedral school, the only one of note south of the Loire. William himself, who showed genuine interest in religious affairs, enjoyed the friendship of such luminaries as the erudite Fulbert of Chartres and Odilo of Cluny, promoter of the 'Truce of God'. His piety, moreover, took him quite frequently to Rome. At the same time he was far from being an ascetic, enjoying the good life himself and gaining a wide reputation for the bountiful hospitality of his court. By the end of his long reign, indeed, Poitiers was setting the standard, material and intellectual, for all the southern courts. A centre of lay and clerical culture, it was for its period a thoroughly civilized place; and so it remained until Eleanor's day.

On William's death in 1030, the succession passed to his son by his first marriage, William the Fat, fourth Count of Poitiers and sixth Duke of Aquitaine. Eight years later he in turn was followed, though for only a few months, by a son whom William the Great had had by his second wife; and on that young man's premature death, the offspring of a third marriage took over with the title of William V of Poitiers and VII of Aquitaine. His mother was a formidable lady, Agnes of Burgundy, who was by now remarried to the Count of Anjou, but continued to impose her considerable authority on affairs in Poitou throughout the reign of this son and, after his death in 1058, during some ten years of that of her second son, Gui-Geoffrey-William (William VI and VIII). Aquitaine was by now a power to be reckoned with and internally secure to the extent that its new ruler was able to look beyond its borders for military adventure, notably against the Moors in Spain. There he captured Barbastro, the scene of one of the more exotic episodes in a chanson de geste of the following century.

In his anxiety for an heir, Duke William VIII also took a third wife, having renounced her barren predecessor. His choice fell on a girl twenty-five years younger than himself to whom, however, he was related within the prohibited degrees of consanguinity. The union had the desired effect in producing in 1071 a son; but the child could not be considered legitimate before the marriage had been put on a proper footing by the pope. A visit by William to Rome, where he appears to have had some indirect influence, sufficed for the purpose. Innocent though the child was of this initial offence, he was destined to cause much arching of papal brows in later years, when courting scandal became for him almost a way of life. For this was the notorious William VII of Poitiers or IX of Aquitaine, the first known troubadour and grandfather of Eleanor. In his case, ancestral memories would have taken second place in Eleanor's mind to direct, and no doubt vivid, recollection, since he reigned from 1086 until his death in 1127, when she was about five years old.

It is worth pausing here to reflect on the perhaps surprisingly active role played by women in the Poitiers/Aquitaine line. The third Duke William, it has been suggested, was rather under the thumb of his pious spouse Adela. His son's wife Emma, when faced with her husband's philanderings, was no patient Griselda, but took matters into her own hands and showed as much zeal in taking revenge on his mistress as she commonly devoted to charitable works. (The latter included the foundation of the abbey of Bourgueil in Touraine.) Emma, as we have seen, played a vital part in the formative years of the future William the Great and during the first decade of his reign. Of this count's three wives, the first was reputedly a witch and is said to have made the first advances to him when his prisoner; but she is a shadowy figure beside the energetic and durable Agnes, whose influence reached from the German imperial court, where her daughter by William was empress, to the English circles of Emma of Normandy, mother of Edward the Confessor, with whom she was associated in various pious projects. She herself was co-founder with her second husband of the great abbey at Vendôme, consecrated in the presence of the French king, and in 1068 entered a convent in Saintes, which she had established for daughters of the nobility.

These noble ladies of the Aquitaine dynasty show an impressive range of active virtues. By no means cloistered in the narrow confines of the court, they were ready to apply their initiative to public as well as domestic matters, and commonly expressed their religious faith in practical ways, through gifts and foundations. In an age when ancestral memories were passed down the generations often in embroidered form and largely by word of mouth, it is likely that the young Eleanor's daydreams were frequently visited by one or other of her spirited ancestresses. We can imagine, though, with what special awe she came to learn of the rumbustious doings of her talented but reprobate grandfather.

Born in 1071 and Duke in his fifteenth year, William IX had one brief and inauspicious marriage before, in 1094, taking as his second wife Philippa or Mahaut, daughter of the Count of Toulouse. Two years later we find him entertaining Pope Urban II, who was travelling his lands seeking recruits for the First Crusade. But William had other matters on his mind, it seems; and before long he seized the opportunity to appropriate his wife's native territories as well as to campaign for William Rufus in Normandy. In 1101, however, he took it into his head to lead an army to the Holy Land and Jerusalem, now in Christian hands; and to this end he found it politic to surrender the county of Toulouse. His expedition, though, proved a military fiasco, and his future crusading ventures were to be limited to an occasional foray against the Moors in Spain. His main deeds of arms were henceforth devoted to more domestic squabbles and defences of his lands against unruly vassals.

It was not as a warrior that William was to be chiefly remembered. His thirteenth-century Provençal biographer wasted no words:

The Count of Poitiers was one of the most courtly men in the world and one of the greatest deceivers of women. He was a fine knight at

arms, liberal in his attentions to ladies, and an accomplished
composer and singer of songs. For a long time he roved the world,
bent on the deception of ladies. He had a son who took to wife the
Duchess of Normandy,[4] by whom he had a daughter [i.e. Eleanor]
who was married to King Henry of England and was the mother of
the Young King, of Richard and of Count Geoffrey of Brittany.[5]

William's reputation as a womanizer was already of long standing; and we shall later see it put to oblique literary use in a satirical
romance.[6] It seems to have been reinforced, if not acquired, after
his return from his crusading adventure, and to have gone hand in
hand with the deployment of those talents for erotic verse that
have gained for him the name of the first of the troubadours. It is
more than likely indeed that the few surviving poems commonly
attributed to him along with others now lost helped to colour the
image even his contemporaries had of him.[7] Some speak of his
robust chivalry and magnanimity; but monkish voices, Ordericus
Vitalis and William of Malmesbury among them, deplore his
human weaknesses. According to the latter he plunged himself,
once back from Jerusalem, into a slough of vice and gave himself
over to frivolous versifying to the merriment of his companions.
Another censures him as the enemy of all modesty and holiness.

His relationship with the Church was more equivocal than that
of some of his forebears. He was twice excommunicated, as
William of Malmesbury tells us. The first time, in 1114 for some
unknown offence, was by the Bishop of Poitiers, from whom he
vainly demanded absolution at the point of his sword within the
cathedral itself. The second was occasioned by his liaison with the
Viscountess of Châtellerault, which also appears to have caused a
temporary breach with his son in sympathy with his affronted
mother Philippa. Tradition has it that William installed his
mistress (named Dangerosa in one document) in the new Maubergeonne tower of his palace at Poitiers, whence she became known
as 'la Maubergeonne'. If we believe William of Malmesbury, never
one to pass over a little scandal, he even had her portrait painted
on his shield. In the face of such blatant adultery on the part of her
husband, Philippa withdrew perhaps in late 1115 to the abbey of
Fontevrault, which was to become so closely associated with
Eleanor and the Plantagenets.

The establishment of the community and then the order of Fontevrault was a significant event in the cultural and social history of the Middle Ages. Its founder was Robert d'Arbrissel, a Breton wandering scholar of ascetic leanings who, after a period of eremitical existence with a band of followers, was recognized by Urban II as a peripatetic apostolic preacher. Women in particular were attracted by his views and his personality; and in 1100 he was granted land within Duke William's domains to establish a church and community dedicated to the Virgin. What emerged was a double order of monks and nuns, housed in separate convents but living under the rule, remarkably for the time, of a single abbess. Already by Robert's death in 1117, Fontevrault was being favoured as a retreat by various noble ladies, including William's first wife as well as the spurned Philippa. It is interesting, in anticipation of one of Eleanor's reputed exploits, to learn of the retirement to a daughter-house of the noted Angevin beauty Isabelle de Montfort, whom Ordericus Vitalis describes as having once played the role of a true Amazon, riding armed into battle like some figure from Classical mythology.

William's fantasy, as reported of course by William of Malmesbury, of establishing at Niort a convent of prostitutes may have been his way of poking fun at the pious idealism of Fontevrault. There is certainly, in his verse, jesting at the expense of women, and often in the crudest of terms, as if to prove his point that he was a past-master in the art of loving. Sometimes they figure as the actual or potential objects of his lust: fine horses to be mounted, or captives chafing under jealous guard. Their nature, though, rebels against constraint; and he records with relish his seduction by two ladies whose only care was to avoid disclosure. And a curse on those who prefer monks to lusty knights!

So run his more bawdy songs. Yet in others we have our first glimpse in literature of that new, more reverent attitude to women which was to characterize the poetry of the troubadours and profoundly influence the subsequent depiction of sexual relationships. This is the phenomenon loosely known as courtly love. In these poems William's lady is as aloof as she is desirable. In one case her coolness suggests she would become a nun: but what advantage could she reap if he, too, then took to the cloister? Elsewhere he clings to the memory of past joy in the hope that some day it may be repeated. But the lover must be patient and, as he waits for favours, behave with courtesy to all about him. His one aspiration is that joy which his lady alone can give: she has the power to kill or cure, to make a base man courtly, to bestow eternal youth; and in her hands alone lies his salvation. Then, in what is presumably the last of his poems, the tone changes once more; for though he has known the joys of chivalry and love, he must soon leave Poitou for that last exile which is death. As he begs pardon from his fellows and from Jesus, his one remaining care is for the welfare of his son, left behind in a hostile world.

On his death in 1127, his lands and titles passed to this son, who had been born to Philippa in 1099 and was destined, as William X, to rule for ten years as the last in this line of Dukes of Aquitaine. His father the troubadour had earlier, with dubious tact, arranged for him to marry Aenor, the legitimate daughter of that very Viscountess of Châtellerault whom he now flaunted as his mistress, 'la Maubergeonne'; and it was of this union that Eleanor had been born. The troubadour's fears for the security of his son's inheritance turned out to be well founded; for his reign was plagued by unrest in his territories and an embroilment with his own bishops, which led to his excommunication, as well as to a dramatic confrontation with the irate Bernard of Clairvaux. This took place on William's own lands at Parthenay and, according to Bernard's biographer, left him in a state of collapse at the prelate's feet. Perhaps it was a kind of stroke he had suffered. It was not, however, fatal, unlike the sudden illness which ended his days at the shrine of St James of Compostela, whither he had journeyed on Easter pilgrimage in 1137.

Duke William X had not inherited his father's poetic talent; but it does appear that his court was frequented by some of the early troubadours, including Cercamon and Marcabru, who both composed elegies on his death. So it can be assumed that its thriving literary culture persisted. It is likely, too, that professional storytellers passed that way, to compete with the singers of songs. And their fare may well have included samples of the legendary Matter of Britain before this was incorporated in the north in the great romances of Tristan or of King Arthur and his knights. Several later writers were to mention a mysterious Welsh *fabulator* named Breri or Bleheris (Bleddri), said by one to have spun his tales for the Count of Poitiers. Marcabru, in his lament for William,

Eleanor's Birth

St Bernard

complains that with the Poitevin gone, he will himself be lost like Arthur, implying that even at this early date the legendary king's name would be familiar to his public. At about the same time, Cercamon is found holding up Tristan as a model of fidelity.[8] The adolescent Eleanor's ears would not have been closed to any of this; and we can imagine her captivated by the exciting new vogues in poetry and story-telling that were being enthusiastically exploited at her father's court.

These were indeed exciting times on several grounds. It was a moment in history when Western civilization was feeling the need for a reassessment, a redefinition of some of its basic principles regarding the nature of man, his place and function in creation, his social organization and responsibilities, his proper conduct in all his various activities. A quest had begun which was to be pursued, and with some confidence, throughout the coming decades; and its product was what has become known as the Twelfth-Century Renaissance.[9] Prefiguring, in a sense, the post-medieval Renaissance, its causes, substance and impact are likewise open to fine analysis and debate. It too embraced an awareness of a debt to Classical Antiquity, though lacking the later age's historical perspective. It looked for further inspiration to the early Christian Fathers in its search for an authority which nevertheless left room for interpretation by theologians moved by a spirit of enquiry. There was not simply a wish to consolidate the inheritance from the past, but a desire to refashion it. At the same time the developing schools produced almost a surfeit of well-trained clerks equipped to wrestle with the complexities of civil and canon law as well as more mundane administrative duties in lay or clerical establishments.

A current of idealism manifested itself in various ways. One thinks in religious matters not only of that underlying the Crusades but also of the maturing fruits of the Cluniac reforms (Cluny itself had been founded in 910 by one of the early dukes of Aquitaine) and of the flourishing of the Cistercian order under the austere mystic Bernard of Clairvaux. In the secular sphere we find in, for instance, the chansons de geste a celebration of the ideals of service and loyalty within feudal relationships which still seemed to offer the prospect, however distant, of just and ordered government. Even warfare and its ravages were under scrutiny,

Changing Times

Crusades
Cluny
Clairvaux
Cistercian

and various peace movements had ephemeral existence beside the more widely practised stipulations of the Truce of God, which banned hostilities at certain closely defined times.

In fact the feudal system had developed as an essentially practical defence against political anarchy; and it already carried the seeds of its own decline as the idea of the nation-state began to emerge and the towns grew in wealth and power. Whereas the great courts flourished and could afford to foster the chivalric ideal, the lesser nobility found themselves under increasing pressures, not least economic. But that was a social problem which Eleanor would never have to confront. She would have enjoyed the growing material comforts as castles were reconstructed to serve as much as residences as fortresses, developing trade brought luxuries from the East or other distant parts, and tastes were refined in social behaviour as well as such practical matters as female dress.

No doubt as a young girl she would have thrilled more to a new delicacy for the table or gown for her wardrobe than to a new proposition from a theologian. She would scarcely have been aware of the gradual shifting, in broad terms, from the general to the individual, the progressive focusing on personal feelings, personal conduct, which can be seen in retrospect as a product of the 'Twelfth-Century Renaissance' and its new learning. Some aspects of that learning, however, would not have passed her by, even at an early age, reaching as it did beyond the cloister to the life of the courts. Centred on the great cathedral schools and culminating in the emergence of the universities, it spread widely, if selectively, throughout the clerical and secular worlds. Libraries expanded, and even Latin books were not confined to the shelves of the religious houses, whilst the growing number of vernacular manuscripts catered for the tastes of the laity; and in the more enlightened courts reading became a leisure activity.

In a way, Eleanor and modern European literature grew up together. At the beginning of her century books were rare and contained for the most part pious and didactic works, a few annals perhaps and possibly a Classical text or two, all in Latin. By the end of her life, she would have had access to a vastly increased store of Latin writings, including some in verse and prose with scarcely a whiff of the monastery about them; but in addition there would be others in the vernacular tongue offering a range of

material from saints' lives and rhymed sermons to collections of
bawdy tales, from the songs of the troubadours and northern
trouvères to versions of Virgil and Ovid, and from lengthy
chansons de geste to the especially fashionable romances of the
Arthurian world.

troubadour

All this new literature held a mirror to, while helping to
promote, new norms of behaviour for the society of the courts.
The knights were expected to be devotees of chivalry in all senses
of the term, tempering the epic ideal of honour with a magnanimity rarely found in the early chansons de geste. Nobility was a
matter of conduct, not merely of rank; and all social relationships
should be governed by the practice of what the French called
courtoisie. For the man this entailed a modest civility, generosity
in thought and deed, especially in support of the weak or
oppressed, frankness and total reliability in his dealings with his
fellows. Ideally, the courtly experience should be completed and
enhanced by a worthy love relationship, with each partner showing a faithful devotion, and both deriving from it increased virtue
and merit.

Chivalry courtesy civility

Traditionally the men of the Church had held woman in
contempt as the cause of Adam's fall. Had not Tertullian described
her as 'ianua Diaboli', the gateway for the Devil? Among the old
warrior nobility she had been prized chiefly as the provider of
offspring and of a handy dowry in the event of a suitable marriage
of convenience. Only exceptionally, as in the cases of some of
those worthy ladies of Aquitaine, would she play a major role in
events, and then largely as a manipulator of husbands and sons in
what was essentially a man's world. So now her role and nature as
woman was ripe for reappraisal; and this, as we have seen, was
already happening in the very homeland of Eleanor. On the one
hand, Robert d'Arbrissel and his followers were raising her status
within the Church itself, affording her some of the honour due to
the Virgin as her earthly symbol and representative. On the other,
William IX had launched in his verse the poetic conceit of the
domna-figure, an object of reverence as well as desire for the lover,
the source of all goodness who could, at her pleasure, grant or
withhold that ultimate joy to which he aspired.

women's role

The young Eleanor must have sensed that she was living at the
dawning of a new age vibrant with exciting possibilities.

2

Life

QUEEN OF FRANCE

Having lost a young brother in infancy and being the elder of two sisters, Eleanor suddenly found herself in that momentous year of 1137 sole heiress to the great estates of Poitou and Aquitaine, held in fief from the French crown. Her father had died at Easter, leaving her ward of the ailing Capetian King Louis the Fat; and ironically her new-found dignity made her, on one of the rare occasions in her life, a mere pawn in the political game. For Louis, more able in mind than in body, saw in her the means of vastly increasing the domains under direct control of the monarchy. An arranged marriage to his own heir, the sixteen-year-old Louis, was the master-move already planned; but now it would have to be made promptly, before it could be blocked by any potential rival. So with an impressive escort he hustled the prince south from Paris to make Eleanor his bride at a July wedding in Bordeaux. Adroit as his move was, its sequel would be beyond his control. For before the royal couple returned to his capital at the end of the summer, he was in his tomb, and they made their entry as King and Queen of France.

Much has been written, and not only by modern historians, of the character of the young Louis.[1] Brought up in anticipation of some high office in the Church but now, because of the untimely death of his elder brother, thrust upon the throne as Louis VII, he found himself in a position for which he was psychologically unprepared and, moreover, in the company of a lively wife from a very different background and even younger than himself. As for Eleanor, she came as a stranger to the court in Paris, a less

14

convivial place no doubt than sunny Poitiers. One can imagine her prey to conflicting emotions: excitement tempered by homesickness, natural pride by curiosity verging on bewilderment. The whole situation, indeed, was likely to generate psychological problems for both herself and the unpredictable Louis, docile and impetuous by turns. Their marriage, however, does at least appear to have fostered in the adolescent king a genuine love for his wife.

One wonders what Eleanor's feelings were towards him and whether they could have been coloured by a chanson de geste of the day with William of Orange in the heroic role, but which seems to contain some mischievous contemporary relevance. This was *Le Couronnement de Louis* (*The Crowning of Louis*),[2] the Louis in question being Charlemagne's son and reluctant successor. It told how the timorous lad, about to be invested with the crown in his father's lifetime, had to be forced by William to receive it. Is it pure coincidence that the boy's namesake, Eleanor's husband, had himself, as an eleven-year-old child, been prematurely invested with the French crown by his own father, Louis VI? If, as is commonly supposed, the chanson de geste was composed soon after that ceremony of 1131,[3] contemporaries could hardly have been blind to the parallels between epic and reality. So the poet's mockery of the future Louis the Pious, portrayed as a pusillanimous and cringing milksop, must have turned people's thoughts to the pious Louis Capet, recently become or soon to be their own king. Was he also measured in the poet's sights? And what would Eleanor's reaction have been on hearing a jongleur uttering Charlemagne's denunciation of his 'craven heir', or William's 'Ah, wretched, cowardly and besotted king!'? Would she have thought the less of her consort? Or might she have pictured herself in the loyal, protective role that the heroic count continued to play in the song despite his inner contempt?

Although we have no record of the literary entertainment enjoyed at the royal court at this period, and there is reason to suppose that Louis's own interests lay more in the current theological disputes, it would be surprising if Eleanor's ears were barred to the songs and legends purveyed by itinerant jongleurs when there were no court poets to hand. But we are left to guess how far her tastes, nurtured in the now rarely visited Poitou, were humoured in the more earnest atmosphere of Paris.

Paris

Religion
Scholarship

Becket

St Bernard

Not that Paris was by any means a lifeless place.[4] By this time it had come fully to deserve its status as capital city, one token of which was the royal palace on the Ile de la Cité, where Eleanor doubtless spent much of her time. It was also a thriving commercial centre, its tradesmen largely occupying the right bank of the busy Seine. But no less significant was its pre-eminence by the middle of the twelfth century in the sphere of religious scholarship and debate. Louis had himself studied in the school of Notre-Dame. On the left bank, still the haunt of scholars, were the abbeys of Sainte-Geneviève and Saint-Victor as well as Saint-Germain-des-Prés, though the latter was somewhat in eclipse. These were all centres of learning, not to mention the individual schools set up by masters eager to attract students to their more modest establishments. Ambitious young men flocked there to deepen their theological knowledge or sharpen their skills in dialectic: Peter Lombard, the young Thomas Becket, John of Salisbury for a decade from 1136, and many another drawn by the fame of such masters as the mystic Hugh of Saint-Victor or anxious to taste the heady unorthodoxies of Abelard, when his stormy career took him back to Paris (John of Salisbury heard him lecturing on the Montagne Sainte-Geneviève in 1136). These theologian-philosophers were waging their verbal battles in the war between nominalists and realists, pitching their camps with those like Abelard of rationalist inclination or with the advocates of faith and contemplation who rallied to the banner of Bernard of Clairvaux.

As well as theological disputation, poetic composition and experimentation seems to have flourished beside the Seine at this time in the hands of such exponents as Adam of Saint-Victor and Abelard himself.[5] Whilst their surviving Latin verse is pious in content, it would be surprising if some of the more worldly, even scurrilous, lyrics in the learned tongue were not circulating among the student fraternity, though most that have come down are anonymous and undatable.

Although the emergence of the University as such was still a few decades away, its foundations were being laid by the growth of the schools and the prestige they brought to Paris as a citadel of clerical scholarship and culture. How far Eleanor participated in this intellectual ferment is impossible to say; but there is no reason to suppose that it left her entirely untouched. She would have brought with her the fruits of her schooling in the south, which were surely not negligible. One is tempted, and not wholly unreasonably, to ascribe to her the accomplishments of Philomena as elaborated by a French poet of her own day, probably the débutant Chrétien de Troyes, in a re-working of Ovid's tale.[6]

The young princess's peerless beauty is depicted in lavish but entirely conventional terms (medieval rhetorical training encouraged tedious identikit portraits, and we have no reliable description of Eleanor's own appearance). Then we learn of Philomena's expertise at chess, backgammon and other dice games as well as at hawking, a favourite pastime. Embroidery was another of her skills, as was music-making on a variety of instruments. On a more intellectual level, she was familiar with grammar and the standard Latin authors, and could hold attention with her intelligent conversation. It is an idealized picture, certainly, but suggestive of some of the pursuits of a young noblewoman of the time.

In Eleanor's case we would have to add a keen interest in more public matters. Her conversations with her younger sister Petronilla and her strong-minded mother-in-law, the dowager Queen Adelaide, would not have been limited to idle gossip. As for her dealings with her husband, it has been suggested that she exerted a considerable influence over him, and not necessarily for the better, in the affairs of state, forming something of a coterie to this end among the nobles at court.[7] Louis's youth encouraged those around him to pursue their own, sometimes diverging, interests. Suger, the Abbot of Saint-Denis and counsellor to Louis VI, saw himself as principal adviser to the lad but had to face the disapproval of Queen Adelaide, who was herself furthering her own schemes with Count Raoul of Vermandois, Louis's cousin.

The kingdom at this time was far from a cohesive unit, with constant rivalries between the major as well as the minor feudatories, which preoccupied them more than their nominal allegiance to the crown. Although Louis, imbued with the high epic ideal of the king as God's vice-regent, saw it as his duty to exert his authority on these indifferent or even unruly vassals, the looseness of the political structure as well as geographical factors made this difficult. When he did, sporadically, try to impose his will, he tended to act with an impetuosity that contrasted sharply with his natural meekness. This happened when, soon after his accession, the citizens of Poitiers attempted to free themselves from the royal yoke. He marched with an army to quell the insurrection and, having defeated the rebels, had to be restrained by Suger from exacting a savage retribution. What Eleanor's involvement, or attitude, was we can only speculate, as also concerning an expedition to Aquitaine in 1141 that led to Louis's abortive attempt to assert his rights by marriage to the county of Toulouse. But now more serious trouble was brewing for him.

In that same year he tried to have his own candidate installed as Archbishop of Bourges, but was opposed by the cathedral chapter. When another man was elected, Louis withheld his consent, and the matter was referred to the pope. A papal rebuke did not break his resolve, whereupon he was placed under an interdict, which fell short of full excommunication. But worse was to follow.

While this was happening, Raoul of Vermandois had taken it into his head to repudiate his wife, the niece of Thibaut IV of Champagne, and replace her with Eleanor's sister Petronilla. In this, it seems, he had the young queen's support. Bishops were found prepared to perform the annulment on the usual excuse of some degree of consanguinity; but they reckoned without the resource of Thibaut, to whom the discarded wife had retreated. He too appealed to the pope, who, through his legate, suspended the too pliant bishops and excommunicated Raoul. Eleanor, still barely out of her teens, must have felt keenly this indirect snub; and Louis, rankling from the earlier papal intervention, saw fit to take up Raoul's cause. He sent his armies into Champagne on a violent punitive expedition. From 1142 into the following year they ravaged the countryside, burning, pillaging and killing or expelling its inhabitants. Contemporary sources speak with horror of these barbarities, which culminated in the sacking of Vitry-en-Perthois, where the church was set ablaze and reduced to ashes along with those who had taken refuge there – thirteen hundred souls, says one chronicler.[8] For centuries afterwards the town was to be known as Vitry-le-Brûlé.

In reading of these events, one is forcibly reminded of the outrageous behaviour of Raoul of Cambrai in the chanson de geste that bears his name.[9] The surviving text probably dates from the late twelfth century, but is based on historical characters and events of the tenth, though relocated in the reign of Louis the Pious. Here the king is not only weak, but unjust, in that he disposes elsewhere of the infant Raoul's rightful fief of Cambrai.

Having come of age and been knighted, the young man demands its restitution, but is bought off with the promise of the lands of the deceased Count Herbert of Vermandois, if he can wrest them from his four sons. Raoul invades the territory accompanied by his squire Bernier, whose loyalties are divided because of kinship with the Vermandois clan. The town of Origny with its abbey is put to the torch.

> The fierce, proud Count Raoul has the streets set ablaze. Dwellings burn, floors collapse, cellars are awash with spilt wine; hams kindle in the ruins of larders, the fat increasing the intensity of the great fire. It attacks the turrets and main bell tower, bringing down the roofing. So fierce is the furnace within the walls that the nuns burn in that mighty inferno: all hundred are consumed in dire agony. Burnt there was Marcent, Bernier's mother, together with Clamados, Duke Renier's daughter. . . . The bold knights wept for the pity of it. . . . With drawn sword Bernier came to the convent to see the flames leaping through its doors; but to approach closer than a spear-cast from the fire was impossible. Looking towards a precious marble slab, Bernier saw his mother lying beside it, her tender face upturned. On her breast he saw her psalm-book blazing.

There is a public resonance to the poet's voice. Despite the justice of the original cause, our initial sympathy with Raoul drains away as we see him pursuing it with an unrestrained violence known to the French as *desmesure* and condemned as a sin. That, it is made clear, puts Raoul's mortal soul in jeopardy. Can he be saved from damnation? The issue is left in the balance. His determination to gain his ends by the sword had brought down on him even his mother's curse; and the burning of Origny was to hang like a pall over the brief remainder of his life.

The parallels with Louis's own display of *desmesure* are striking. Do they amount to pure coincidence? Or was the poet mindful of the Vitry atrocity as he fleshed out his epic scenes? Is it even possible that the chroniclers of that event added lurid details suggested by some version of the Raoul story circulating in their day? Whatever the truth, this illustrates well the close partnership of history and literature in the Middle Ages, with the one constantly throwing light on the other. In this instance, the public horror evinced by Vitry and by Origny is one and the same. The chanson de geste is a strident cry for ordinary folk to be spared the ravages of internal wars, a sentiment expressed as forcefully in a good deal of the literature of the time as in much Church propaganda.

Louis's own conscience was not immune to such feelings. In one of the chronicles we read of his reaction to Vitry's destruction: 'King Louis, moved with pity, is said to have wept; and some hold that on this account he undertook his pilgrimage to Jerusalem.'[10] It is also claimed that on being admonished by the future Saint Bernard, he fell sick with remorse.

religion

Raised as he had been as a dutiful servant of the Church, his periodic surrender to his more violent impulses was apt to be followed by genuine contrition. He could not have shrugged off the ecclesiastical pressure that was put on him at this period, and which was a force to be reckoned with in matters of state and religion alike. In the latter sphere he had witnessed its operation when, in 1140, he had attended with his court the Council of Sens, where Bernard had levelled the charge of heresy against Abelard, on which he was later condemned.

Eleanor's involvement in all this is largely a matter of speculation. She has been suspected of playing a provocative role, not merely observing but helping to instigate her husband's ill-starred initiatives. It is, however, impossible to say how far her private feelings in these eventful times were in tune with those of Louis. It does, though, appear that Bernard had occasion to give her some cautionary advice. In the saint's *Life*, on the other hand, there is an account of his intercession on her behalf in view of her apparent infertility. His prayers were to be answered by the birth of her first child in 1145; but the royal couple's satisfaction was muted by the fact that it was not a male heir but a girl, named Marie in honour of the Virgin.

By this time Louis was in better odour with the Church and his problems with Champagne had been largely resolved. In 1144 he had attended with Eleanor the rededication of the Abbey of Saint-Denis, which had been largely rebuilt and handsomely adorned by Suger. Yet the grim events of Vitry were still hanging heavy on his conscience when the opportunity arose to make at least partial amends. In December 1144 matters in the Latin territories of the Middle East took a grave turn when the city of Edessa on their north-eastern border was seized by the Turks. The news came as a shock to western Christendom, where the danger

Turkish invasion

to the Kingdom of Jerusalem itself was not underestimated. In November of the following year, Pope Eugenius III received an appeal for help, which he at once addressed to the Christian rulers, including Louis.

*

It seems that Louis had anticipated and may even have prompted the papal call for a new crusade against the infidel. In any case, it was on Christmas Day 1145 at the court he was holding in Bourges that he announced his intention to take the cross himself. Here was his chance not only to expiate some of his recent guilt and to achieve an apparent ambition of making a pilgrimage to the Holy Land, but also to assert his authority as a Christian monarch by being the first Western king to embark on a crusade.[11] Next March, the pope approved his plan and charged Bernard of Clairvaux with preaching the crusade, which he did with dramatic effect. It was on 31 March that Louis himself took the cross at Vézelay together with sundry of his nobility.

Crusade

Bernard

The zeal that fired them and many another is caught by an anonymous crusading song, the first to have survived in Old French.[12] It speaks of the shame and grief suffered at Turkish hands: 'Edessa is taken, as you know well, to the consternation of Christians. The churches are burnt and laid waste: Christ's sacrifice is no more celebrated there. Think deeply on this, you knights renowned in arms, and offer up yourselves to the one who for you was raised on the cross. . . . Follow the example of Louis, who has more possessions than you and is rich and powerful above all other crowned kings. He has abandoned his costly furs, his castles, towns and cities and has turned towards the one who suffered for us on the cross.' So it continues, speaking of the contest joined between Hell and Paradise and calling for victory and the recapture of Edessa; and after each stanza comes the refrain embodying the Crusader's assurance of absolution and salvation:

song of Louis

))

> Who now leaves at Louis's side,
> Hell will ne'er confound him:
> His soul in Heaven shall abide,
> With our Lord's angels round him.

On 11 June 1147 Louis, accompanied by Eleanor, was at Saint-Denis, where he received from Abbot Suger and the pope the oriflamme, the royal banner of France, together with the pilgrim's wallet, and was commended to God's keeping on his enterprise. With his assembled army he took the overland route by way of Bavaria and the Balkans, intending to join up with the Emperor Conrad's German forces at Constantinople, whence they would march east together into Asia to confront the infidel. And with him went his young queen.

Why should Eleanor have accompanied him on this arduous expedition? Some chroniclers suggest that Louis loved her too dearly to leave her behind; others, casting him in the role of the jealous husband of the troubadour lyrics, imply that he did not trust her to stay in France nursing her virtue on her own. Such excuses are hardly necessary; for Eleanor was by nature no stay-at-home, and anyway it was at that time by no means unknown for women of rank to brave the perils of the road in order to make that greatest of Christian pilgrimages to the Holy Places, a journey that was already acquiring the appeal of a medieval version of the grand tour. So it may not have been simply to follow her example that the wives of some of the noblest participants in the crusade, the Countesses of Flanders and Toulouse among them, were in her company. Although they may have added a civilized touch to what was in essence a military enterprise, their presence and that of their necessary household retainers can scarcely have helped its efficient prosecution.[13]

It could, of course, be said that Eleanor had crusading blood in her veins, although her troubadour grandfather's Middle Eastern venture had brought no glory to the house of Aquitaine. Perhaps she felt she owed it to family pride as well as piety to be associated now with a victorious campaign. Her own enthusiasm infected many of the southern nobility, who augmented the force with contingents of her countrymen with whom she would feel well at home: men of culture as well as war, accompanied in all likelihood by a courtly poet or two.[14]

If some poets stayed at home to further the cause with eloquent calls to duty, we know that some did participate in the crusade. One to whom we can put a name is Jaufré Rudel, probably from Blaye, on the Gironde. Jaufré is celebrated as the pining singer of a 'distant love' (*amor de lonh*), which inspired a thirteenth-century

Plate 1 Louis VII and the Emperor Conrad enter Constantinople together, though Conrad in fact arrived before Louis. (15th century: Les Grandes Chroniques de France. *MS fr. 6465, fo. 202.)*

biographer to spin a charming story about the troubadour. Apprised of the virtues of the Countess of Tripoli (in modern Lebanon), Jaufré fell deeply in love with this peerless lady and, in order to see her, took the cross and put to sea; but struck on the voyage by a mortal illness, he arrived in Tripoli only to expire blissfully in her arms. More tangible evidence suggests that he did in fact take part in the crusade, from which he probably never returned. If so, one can assume that he was known to Eleanor; and an intriguing, though unprovable, possibility is that his mysterious, platonic *amor de lonh* was none other than the queen herself.

Another incentive, if one were needed, for her to set forth with her husband was the prospect of making or renewing contact with her uncle Raymond of Poitiers, son of the first troubadour, now Prince of Antioch, patron of letters and still quite a young man.

Threatened by the Turks and coveted by both the Sicilians and the Byzantines, rich Antioch promised to be not just a potential base of operations against the Saracens, but an exceptionally exciting place to break the long journey to Jerusalem. Eleanor had much to look forward to. The crusade, however, was ill-starred almost from the start; and although it was to be for her not without drama, her adventures were not such as she might have anticipated.

The opulence of Constantinople could not have failed to impress her; but the reception of the French, as of the Germans, who had already left, was more cautious than cordial. When, in October, they crossed the Bosphorus and moved on, it was only to find in Nicaea (the modern Iznik) all that remained of the German army after a disastrous savaging by the Turks. Along with the Emperor Conrad and the remnants of his forces, Louis resumed his march by way of Smyrna and Ephesus, where illness forced the emperor to leave his company and return to Constantinople. The army then took to the mountainous hinterland with Attalia (Antalya) as its objective. Plagued by the rigours of midwinter and continually harried by the Turks, it was still struggling through the mountains when an event occurred which almost spelt the end of the crusade. The vanguard was under the command of Geoffrey of Rancon, a Poitevin and one of Eleanor's vassals, who had once given lodging to the royal pair on their wedding journey. Ordered to wait on a hilltop for the arrival of the main army, he went further, leaving it to the mercy of the marauding enemy. In the encounter the French suffered heavy loss of life and equipment; and Louis himself was fortunate to escape from the ambush. Geoffrey was disgraced; and in some quarters the queen herself was unfairly associated with her vassal's blunder. But the army managed to reassemble and painfully make its way down to the coast at Attalia, arriving in early February. There the crusaders lingered in wretched conditions while they waited for ships to take them to Syria. As there were not enough for all, Louis eventually embarked as many men as he could before setting sail with his wife and making port near Antioch on 19 March 1148.

If Eleanor had been guiltless in the matter of the ambush, there was room for graver suspicions concerning her conduct in Antioch. Her uncle Raymond welcomed her with open arms – all too open, some were to hint. And Raymond, if William of Tyre is to be believed, cut a dashing figure fit to stir the heart of any young woman. Handsome and elegant, as polished in conversation as in the practice of chivalry, a patron of letters and a model of liberality, piety and sobriety, yet with a touch of impetuosity, one can imagine Eleanor finding him a refreshing change from Louis, to say the least. Their family ties sealed a relationship that seems to have ripened fast.

Though with the Papal Curia at the time, John of Salisbury gives what is usually taken to be one of the more reliable accounts of the young queen's behaviour at her uncle's court.[15] He speaks of Louis's suspicions being roused by their frequent and lengthy conversations. But matters came to a head when, in the face of the king's wish to continue the expedition, Raymond and Eleanor joined their entreaties for her to be allowed to remain behind in the city. It was finally, says John, on the advice of one of the royal secretaries, a eunuch named Thierry Galeran, that Louis decided to remove her by force from Antioch and its temptations; and this he did, hurriedly quitting Raymond's court by night, with his wife a no doubt protesting captive. Their marriage would never recover from the bruising it received during their brief stay in Antioch.

According to the chronicler, it was at this time that Eleanor mooted the question of its legality in view of the fact that they were related in the fourth and fifth degrees. This problem of canon law had proved no hindrance to the union: distant kinship was a factor often conveniently forgotten or advanced as political or other circumstances required. For Eleanor it was to prove the means of ending a marriage which no longer held any attraction for her despite, says John, Louis's continuing infatuation.

Louis left Antioch on bad terms with not only his wife, but also his host. Raymond had hoped that the French forces, depleted though they were, would join his own in a thrust against Nur ed-Din, the Christians' chief foe, by assaulting his city of Aleppo. Louis, however, demurred, at least partly on the grounds that he felt his primary duty to be the accomplishment of his pledged pilgrimage to Jerusalem. Eleanor, it appears, had supported her uncle's strategy, whether out of good tactical sense or less rational motives we can only guess. In any case, by May they had found their way south to the Holy City, where their pilgrim vows were made good, and the further prosecution of the crusade became a more urgent preoccupation.

Of Eleanor's activities during her remaining months in Palestine we know nothing, though later legend would not respect the silence of history. One must assume that her estrangement from Louis continued and that she played no active role in the final diplomatic and military debacle. Perhaps the arrival of a new contingent of Provençal crusaders helped to reconcile her to her lengthy stay in the Holy Land; but even without them there would still have been much to engage her interest. Not only were there the celebrated sites to be visited, but life in the Latin Kingdom was by no means devoid of culture, secular as well as religious. There was no reason for Eleanor's mind to atrophy.

Louis was once again in the company of the Emperor Conrad, who had completed his own journey after his recuperation. On 24 June the High Court of Jerusalem met at Acre, attended by the two monarchs with sundry vassals and bishops as well as by King Baldwin of Jerusalem and his queen, the Patriarch, the Masters of the Temple and the Hospital and many other dignitaries of Church and state. The intention was to advance the struggle against the infidel, the outcome a disastrous decision to march against an erstwhile ally in Damascus. By the end of July that city had opened its gates to Nur ed-Din; and the besieging Christian army had to turn tail and make its way back to Palestine, having suffered grave losses and final humiliation. Thereupon Conrad left for Constantinople; but Louis, anxious it seems to spend Easter at the Holy Places, dallied there despite urgent letters from Suger begging him to return to France. It was not until the early summer of the following year, 1149, that he and Eleanor set sail from Acre, though in separate ships. A new phase of this calamitous adventure had begun.

The collapse of the crusade was a shock to the Christian world; and although within a few months Bernard, Suger and Peter the Venerable of Cluny were striving to rekindle enthusiasm for another assault on Islam, nothing came of their preaching. Louis's reputation in France was hardly increased by the dismal outcome; and it is tempting to look for some echo of his activities in an entertaining French poem, part epic, part romance, recounting the apocryphal pilgrimage of Charlemagne to Jerusalem and Constantinople. If, as one suspects, Louis lacked a sense of humour, he would hardly have appreciated the story. For Eleanor it might have had more appeal.

The *Pèlerinage de Charlemagne* (*Pilgrimage of Charlemagne*)[16] came down in a single manuscript, now lost, which showed Anglo-Norman features, although the work was probably composed in France, perhaps to entertain the public at the Lendit fair at Saint-Denis. Attempted datings vary greatly; but the middle of the twelfth century is a reasonable assumption. The fact that it was translated into Welsh as well as Old Norse and was used in later French texts suggests a wide dissemination. Its own source was a Latin legend which became attached to Saint-Denis in explanation of the holy relics venerated there, not least by Louis, one imagines.

The poem opens in the abbey itself with Charlemagne, in full regalia, among his barons. He turns to his queen:

> 'My lady, did you ever see any man under heaven so well suited by his sword or the crown upon his head? There are still cities I shall subdue with my lance.' She was unwise, and gave a foolish reply: 'Emperor, you may have too high an opinion of yourself. There's one man I know who cuts a more dashing figure when he wears his crown among his knights: once he has it on his head, it looks better on him.' (ll. 9–16)

Charles, incensed, asks who this king may be. Learning that it is the Emperor of Constantinople, he vows to match himself with this paragon; and woe betide the queen should her words prove false! Like Louis, he receives the pilgrim's scrip at Saint-Denis, then leads a vast army, all mounted on mules, to the east, following much the same route as the later crusaders, but making Jerusalem his first stop. There he is laden with relics by the Patriarch before heading for the opulence of Constantinople. Received by the devious emperor, on whom he and chief lords play, with divine help, various unbecoming tricks, he discovers to his satisfaction that his own crown sits a trifle higher than his host's. With the relics in his baggage and forgiveness in his heart, he returns to France and his queen in Saint-Denis.

The whole story is a burlesque; and I am not the first to see in it possible wry comment on Louis's crusade and a dig at the king's marital insecurity coupled with what might to some have appeared an excess of devoutness. But my real point here is that, whatever its author had in mind, anyone hearing or reading it once the circumstances of that disastrous campaign had become common knowledge could hardly have failed to enjoy a chuckle or two at Louis's expense. Would Eleanor herself have kept a straight face?

To return to the events of 1149, Charlemagne's return from the Holy Land was a good deal more expeditious than that of our royal couple. The Sicilian ships in which they sailed were rounding the coast of the Peloponnese when they ran foul of a flotilla of Byzantine vessels, engaged in operations against King Roger of Sicily in his protracted war with Constantinople. Accounts vary, but according to John of Salisbury Eleanor's ship was captured, and only the arrival of some more of Roger's fleet saved the day, and both Louis and Eleanor were able to proceed with a friendly escort.[17] But somehow their ships became separated; and it was on his own that Louis made port on 29 July in Calabria, where he waited for news of his queen. She, it seems, had fallen sick on the voyage, but eventually arrived safely at Palermo in Sicily.

A week or two later they were reunited and began to make their way north by land, visiting Roger's court at Potenza before meeting Pope Eugenius at Tusculum (modern Frascati, near Rome). There the well-meaning pontiff, making light of the problem of their consanguinity (concerning which tongues had already been wagging for a number of years), lent practical support to their marriage by insisting that for the two days of their stay with him (9 and 10 October) they shared a splendidly appointed bed. Moreover, says John of Salisbury, he tried with friendly words to restore their mutual love. Taking their leave of him, they went on to 'do the sights' of Rome together, then completed their return journey to Paris after an absence of almost two and a half years. On the last stage of their journey, from Auxerre, they were escorted by the faithful Suger, who was no doubt needing reassurance on several counts.

*

So here was Eleanor back in the French court, facing the cheerless winter of 1149-50. Still only in her late twenties, she was a sadder perhaps, but certainly a wiser woman. Her marriage with Louis, despite the pope's blessing, was still in jeopardy. Loveless it may not have been; but the affection was largely one-sided, if William of Newburgh's word is to be trusted.[18] Eleanor, he says, found Louis's ways increasingly hard to live with; and he reports her much-quoted claim to have married not a king but a monk. One can sympathize with young Louis in his perpetual struggle to accommodate his political vision to his Christian conscience; but the cloud under which he now lay must have cast its shadow over his domestic life.

There was another factor that would have preyed on both their minds, especially as regards the future of their partnership. Eleanor (thanks perhaps to the papal encouragement) was now pregnant; and the sex of the child could prove crucial. We do not know when the birth took place; but the couple received the doubtful blessing of a daughter, Alice (Alix), a sister for the five-year-old Marie. This event sealed the fate of the ailing marriage; for dynastic concerns persuaded Louis that his need of a male heir must take precedence over his emotional ties to a disaffected wife. With the death of his mentor Suger the following year (1151), the last persuasions against a divorce were removed. Bernard of Clairvaux, who already in 1143 had raised the question of consanguinity, would smooth the way to the separation. The replacement of unsatisfactory wives was, after all, nothing new to the Capetians; and, as we have seen, the complicated ecclesiastical rules on forbidden relationships were frequently used at this period to justify such manoeuvres.[19] Although a separation along these lines was now a likelihood, it was anticipated by a circumstance that considerably brightened the prospects for Eleanor. In August 1151 the court at Paris received a visit from Geoffrey 'the Fair' of Anjou and his eighteen-year-old son Henry.

Geoffrey Plantagenet – so called, it is said, from the sprig of broom (*planta genista*) he was in the habit of wearing in his cap – cut a gallant figure. When he was still a youth, his marriage had been arranged to the proud Matilda, daughter of Henry I of England, Empress of Germany from the age of nine but recently widowed. Without our going into the intricacies of the English succession, let it be said that Matilda's rights having been irretrievably usurped by Stephen of Blois, grandson of the Conqueror, her claim had devolved on the young Henry, her son. In a ceremony at Carlisle on Whitsunday 1149 the lad had been knighted by his great-uncle, David of Scotland, after which Geoffrey had formally made over to him his own title to the duchy of Normandy. Although this was held in fief from the French king, Louis had

become involved in hostilities with Geoffrey, whose visit to Paris
took place during a truce called to resolve their dispute. The
outcome, ironically enough in view of subsequent events, was the
due performance by Henry of the act of homage to his sovereign
Louis.[20]

It would not have been merely the political power of these
Angevins and their pretensions to the crown of England that
roused Eleanor's interest. Not only were they physically handsome
(the father perhaps more so than the son), but their characters had
a cutting edge that provided a welcome contrast to the monkish
Louis. If she knew the widespread story of a demon ancestress well
back in the Anjou line, she might have sensed a more interesting,
even dangerous, side behind their polished public manner. Gerald
of Wales, followed by Walter Map, was later to claim on dubious
authority that she had found occasion to bestow sexual favours on
Geoffrey, who warned his son against following his own example;
but the Welshman's word is suspect in view of his general
antipathy towards Eleanor.[21] On the other hand, it is beyond
doubt that she was favourably impressed by Henry's personality
and the evident culture of the young knight.

He may have had his earliest lessons in France from Peter of
Saintes, an expert in poetics. Then at the age of nine he went to
England and the Bristol court of his uncle Robert of Gloucester,
frequented by a cultured circle that included Geoffrey of Monmouth, historian of the kings of Britain and promulgator of the
Arthurian legend, and Adelard of Bath, who was versed in
mathematical and astronomical science, gleaned from the Arabs.
Henry's own studies were conducted by a certain Matthew,
perhaps his future chancellor and Bishop of Angers, and completed in France under the celebrated philosopher William of
Conches. However, one should be wary of imagining Henry and
Eleanor, some eleven years his senior, immersed in long conversations about the arts and sciences: there was, after all, vital state
business to be done. On its completion, the two Angevins left
Paris; but they remained in the queen's thoughts.

With the removal of Suger's restraining hand (he had died in
January), the way to the dissolution of the royal marriage lay
open. William of Newburgh asserts that already, finding the
young Duke of Normandy more to her taste than Louis, Eleanor
had resolved to marry him and was putting pressure on the

vacillating king to that end. Others think it more likely that Louis, considering the prospect of a male heir more appealing than the retention of his wife's turbulent patrimony of Aquitaine, readily followed the saintly Bernard's advice to end a union of dubious legality. Whatever the truth, that decision was quickly taken. But before it could be put into effect, fate played another card in the diplomatic game. On the road back to Anjou, Geoffrey rashly took a cold dip in the heat of the day and died of a chill. It remained for Henry, who had left his father to deal with matters in Normandy, to attend his untimely burial at Le Mans.

Louis now set about re-ordering his affairs by making a last journey with his wife to her land of Aquitaine, not this time for any triumphant regal progress, but to dismantle the royal power apparatus, disbanding the garrisons and withdrawing his own administrators. This done, he travelled with Eleanor to a council of the leading French prelates assembled at Beaugency, on the Loire near Orléans. There, despite the known wishes of the pope, the evidence for a relationship within the fourth degree was presented; and on 21 March 1152 the annulment of the marriage was confirmed. The infant princesses were to remain in the care of their father.

Eleanor, still owing the crown allegiance for her fiefs of Aquitaine and Poitou, took leave of Louis for the last time and headed with her retainers for Poitiers. Having reverted to her single state but remaining the richest heiress in Christendom, she took insufficient account of her vulnerable position as a potential bride. Passing by way of Blois, she had to make a nocturnal escape from the clutches of Count Thibaut, son of the late Thibaut of Champagne who had given her such offence a decade earlier. More humiliating still, having reached Tours in safety, she was warned of an ambush laid on the border between Touraine and Poitou by another ambitious wife-hunter. This time it was Geoffrey of Anjou, the younger brother, no less, of the far more desirable Duke Henry. Eluding the spirited adolescent in turn, she eventually reached the security of her own city of Poitiers.

We cannot know the precise tenor of such messages as passed between there and Lisieux in Normandy, where Henry was in conclave with his barons. So whether the initiative was taken by duke or by duchess must remain a point of debate.[22] What is indisputable is that, with fine disdain for the assent of Louis,

whose ward Eleanor remained in feudal law, and also for any
papal dispensation in view of the degree of consanguinity (ironically much the same as for her first union), Eleanor and Henry
celebrated their somewhat furtive marriage, probably at Poitiers,
on 18 May 1152.

QUEEN OF ENGLAND

There was certainly nothing monkish about young Henry. Raised
in an atmosphere of power politics, he was himself already
plunged into them as a leading participant, scheming above all for
possession of the throne of England, to which Stephen's son
Eustace was the rival pretender. Now by this unauthorized
marriage he had offended King Louis, who, as a counter-move,
wed his own sister to Eustace and began leaguing against him with
other nobles, including Geoffrey of Anjou, Henry's thwarted
brother. But, typically, fortune smiled more broadly on Henry
than on Louis; for when the latter advanced on Normandy with
his allies, Henry outmanoeuvred them and had his own position
secure within a few weeks. That done, he joined Eleanor in a
progress through Aquitaine to show the flag, as it were, of the new
partnership. By the turn of the year he was free to pursue his
primary ambition.

His new bride would certainly have taken an alert interest in all
these matters, as well as looking after her own interests in Poitou.
Among her other activities there was her first visit, it seems, to the
abbey of Fontevrault, marking the beginning of a personal association that was to grow ever closer over the years. Her name does
appear in its charters before that, as approving a donation made
by Louis in 1146 just after he had taken the cross. But now in
1152 she went there to confirm her family's benefactions to the
order, and was received by the abbess Matilda, an aunt of her new
husband, whose family had patronized Fontevrault in the past.[23]

One wonders if, during these hectic months, she might have
missed the company of her small daughters, abandoned with Louis
in Paris. That is possible; but the fact is that the relationships of
noble parents to their children, at least during their early years,
were relatively distant at this period. Babies were put in the care of
wet-nurses soon after their birth (it was believed that breast-

*Plate 2 Heads of Eleanor and Henry on a capital from the
church of Notre-Dame-du-Bourg near Bordeaux, possibly
dating from 1152.*

feeding inhibited pregnancy), after which other members of the
household would have charge of them for much of the time, even
before they were ready for any kind of formal instruction; and
that, in the case of boys, often took place at another noble court.
Girls especially, until they became negotiable in the matrimonial
game, tended to remain in the shadows. However, despite clerical
objections, infant betrothals were commonplace; and in fact

Marie and Alice spent only a short while in Paris before being packed off, by 1153, to the courts of selected fiancés. These were, respectively, Henry I of Champagne and Thibaut V of Blois, themselves brothers. Both marriages took place in 1164; and Eleanor's direct contact with her daughters thereafter was at best sporadic, although her cultural ties with Marie are, as will be seen, a rich subject for speculation.[24] By one of those ironies thrown up in this claustrophobic feudal world, the child Marie's hand had been sought by the same Henry as was now her mother's husband, but the match had been disapproved by Bernard of Clairvaux on the grounds of consanguinity; and Thibaut of Blois was that very man who had tried to capture Eleanor for himself on her way from Beaugency.

Separated now from her family of the flesh, she had returned to the lands of the troubadours who might be thought, to some degree at least, her spiritual kin. We do not know exactly how or where she spent the following months, how much time she spent with her indefatigable husband or how she divided her residence between her own domains and his. It is likely, though unprovable, that she became closely acquainted in Rouen with the 'Empress' Matilda, a woman of character like herself, and with the Angevin court at Angers where, it has been suggested, she may have encountered Bernard of Ventadour, perhaps the finest of the troubadours. But thereby hangs a scandal, to which we shall return.

His business in Aquitaine having been duly performed with his wife's help, Henry was eager to press his claims in England, fortified with the knowledge that the pope was inclined to side with him rather than Eustace. So, leaving Eleanor occupied with affairs in France (Matilda doubtless ruled the roost in Normandy), he proceeded north to take ship at Barfleur, just east of Cherbourg and in the Middle Ages one of the main embarkation ports for the Channel crossing. In early January 1153, he landed in England and set about marshalling his forces against Stephen and his obnoxious son. The details of his movements and campaigns do not concern us, though we may be sure that as his messages and dispatches reached Eleanor she followed his fortunes with the close attention of someone whose own future is at stake. A more immediate concern, however, was the birth on 17 August of her first son, William, whose very name was calculated to advertise his

Plate 3 The seal of Henry II.

father's claim to the inheritance of the Conqueror. Sadly, like so many children in these times, the boy was not to survive infancy, dying in 1156. Another landmark in this same year was the death of the great Bernard of Clairvaux, by turns adviser, chastiser and thorn in the flesh of Eleanor. He was to be canonized in 1174.

News from England spoke of Henry's intermittent success in rallying support and reducing the king's position. Then, a week before the birth of his own son, his rival Eustace died, choking it is said on a dish of eels after a violent rampage in East Anglia.

Negotiations with Stephen followed, culminating in a treaty patched up in Winchester in August. Although something of a compromise, it did provide for Henry's eventual succession to the throne, in anticipation of which he was paid homage by the barons at a council held in Oxford in January 1154. By April he felt sufficiently secure to return to France, not having set foot there for about fifteen months. Eleanor was now relieved of some of her responsibilities as Henry resumed the conduct of his continental affairs, satisfying himself that Normandy was fully under control before dealing with a little minor trouble in Aquitaine. With Louis formally renouncing his title to Eleanor's lands, her present and former husbands were now reconciled; and as if to put the past firmly behind him, Louis went on pilgrimage to Santiago de Compostela and returned with a new wife, Constance of Castile.

Now fate made another move to tidy up the vast chessboard by suddenly removing from it the last obstacle to Henry's ambition in the person of Stephen himself, who succumbed to a chill on 25 October. On hearing the news, Henry and Eleanor headed north for Barfleur where, with mounting frustration, they waited for the prevailing gales to abate and the Channel to become navigable. For a month they had to curb their impatience until, on 8 December, they were able to set foot in their new kingdom. At once they made for London; and there, on 19 December, the Sunday before Christmas, they were crowned in the abbey church at Westminster as King and Queen of England.

One has to remind oneself of the relative youth, even by medieval standards, of the royal pair. The hyperactive Henry (Walter Map was to ascribe the exhausting pace he set his household to a fear of growing fat!)[25] was only twenty-one; and although Eleanor was eleven years older, it might seem that she had packed more than a lifetime's experiences into those thirty-two years. Moreover, she was now Queen of England, Duchess of Normandy and Aquitaine, Countess of Poitou, Anjou and Maine, and had a number of lesser titles at her disposal, should she care to use them.

Eleanor's titles

*

I was once asked what Eleanor had taken with her to England; and in the preceding pages I have tried to provide at least a partial answer. Apart from her rich territorial dowry, one could speak with confidence of her strong character and lively southern temperament as well as her evident courage and gift for survival. There can be no doubt either of her efficiency in managing the affairs of her own lands and, as occasion arose, her husband's. Her experience ranged far beyond domestic concerns, involved as she had been as Queen of France with matters of state within and without Louis's own realm: entanglements with the German and Byzantine emperors, the politics and conflicts of the crusade witnessed at the very scene of action, relations with the Norman King of Sicily and the Pope Eugenius. In the course of this activity she had travelled the length and breadth of France, through Germany, the Balkans, to Constantinople and through what is modern Turkey into Asia Minor, Palestine and Jerusalem, returning by way of Sicily and Italy.

A woman possessing at least some modest learning (she could probably read and write Latin), she had come into contact with widely differing cultures ranging from that diffused by some of the leading churchmen and scholars of her day to the more material opulence of Byzantium and at least the outward manifestations of Islamic civilization. Then there was the vernacular literature of France both north and south, which she was more likely to have heard performed or recited than to have read herself; and that, of course, included the verse and music of the troubadours. Now, among the French-speaking aristocracy of England, much of that literary inheritance would have remained within her reach.

England was far from being a barbarian hinterland as far as European culture was concerned. It is remarkable, for instance, that some of the oldest and most significant works in the French vernacular survived in their earliest form in Anglo-Norman manuscripts. *The Song of Roland* is one; another is the chanson de geste describing the heroic deeds of William of Orange, precursor of the house of Aquitaine; a third, as we have seen, is the story of Charlemagne's 'pilgrimage' to Jerusalem and Constantinople. Other important early texts were composed by insular authors. A certain Benedict versified from a Latin original the account of the Irish Saint Brendan's marvellous voyage and dedicated it to Henry I's queen (the manuscripts differ as to whether this was his first wife, Matilda, or his second, Adeliza). At much the same period (about 1120) a rhymester called Philip of Thaon, perhaps of Norman origin, composed a *computus* (ecclesiastical calendar) and then wrote for Queen Adeliza the first bestiary in the French tongue, one copy of which is found with a later dedication to Eleanor. He completed his pseudo-scientific work with a lapidary dealing with precious stones. Of far greater literary interest is the earliest surviving drama, a quite elaborate presentation for a mid-twelfth-century English audience of the story of Adam and the Fall. The elegantly seductive dialogue assigned to the Devil is redolent more of the court and its manners than the cloister.

By this time a very important shift in literary taste was taking place in the northern French courts. The muscular epic was beginning to yield in favour to the new genre of the romance, forerunner of the modern novel. For its origins we have to look to the lettered clerks, who took to turning the legends of Classical Antiquity into French, describing with relish the marvels with which they abounded and also developing with quite unclerical zest such sentimental elements as their plots contained. Three major romances of this kind, all seemingly composed on Plantagenet territory, have survived intact. They constitute the so-called 'classical triad', telling the stories of Oedipus and Thebes, of Aeneas, and of Troy. The dating of these works, as of so much medieval literature, is problematical; but the third, *Le Roman de Troie* (*The Romance of Troy*) by Benoît (Benedict) de Sainte-Maure, contains in an aside a pretty compliment to a 'riche dame de riche rei' commonly taken to be Queen Eleanor. Reto R. Bezzola would go further and detect her inspiration behind all three compositions; but although there is nothing inherently improbable in this, it cannot be proved.[26]

A second, and even richer, fund of stories to be exploited in the new genre was the 'Matter of Britain', material ultimately deriving from Celtic sources. The great vogue for this was really launched by the Oxford clerk Geoffrey of Monmouth in his Latin *History of the Kings of Britain*, part of which tells of the exploits of King Arthur, who is given a biography worthy of Charlemagne. Indeed, Geoffrey may have been consciously providing an insular rival to the Frankish emperor. Completed in 1136, his *History* was translated into French in 1155 by the Jerseyman Wace who, according to his English translator Layamon, presented a copy to Eleanor.[27]

Wace certainly found favour with Henry; for in 1160 he was asked by the king to compile a rhymed history of the Dukes of Normandy, which goes by the title of *Le Roman de Rou* (*The*

Romance of Rollo). This commission reflects Henry's overriding interest in historical writings such as might serve his dynastic preoccupations and ambitions. Of all the works, mostly in Latin, that were dedicated to or are otherwise closely associated with him, the majority fall into this category or treat more general aspects of statecraft. A handful of pious or pseudo-scientific texts form the bulk of the rest.[28] I leave for later discussion the collection of Breton *lais* by the enigmatic Marie de France, of which he was the likely dedicatee.

Geoffrey of Monmouth's History and Wace's version of it, *Le Roman de Brut* (*The Romance of Brutus*, Brutus being the fictitious founder of the British kingdom, from whom its name supposedly derived), had much to interest both Henry and Eleanor. For him there was the especial appeal of Arthur, the neo-Charlemagne, architect of empire, conqueror of Gaul and the Romans and model ruler of his people. There was even the hint, encouraged by popular tradition, that the great monarch was not truly dead but would return to lead his people in their hour of need. It suited Henry well to trace his kingship back to this noble figure, with whom he must have been familiar at least from his boyhood days in Bristol; and although he may have taken his legend with a pinch of salt, he was happy to encourage the identification of the Isle of Avalon, Arthur's last resting place, with Glastonbury, where he had the abbey rebuilt at the end of his reign. It was in 1191, two years after his death, that the monks there exhumed two bodies, which they claimed to be those of Arthur and Guenevere, his queen; but Henry had lived to see the name of Arthur bestowed on his grandson, born in 1187, with whom Eleanor was fated to cross swords at the end of her own life.

A curious indirect indication of Henry's interest in the legendary king is found in a long Latin poem composed by one of his Norman subjects, the monk Stephen of Blois, on the death of the queen mother Matilda in 1167. Entitled *Draco Normannicus* (*The Norman Dragon*), it combines fulsome praise of Henry with some advice to him not to march against Brittany.[29] This is given in a letter written by King Arthur himself from his retreat in Avalon (located in the Antipodes). In his supposed reply, Henry expresses his admiration for Arthur, says he will delay his campaign, and offers to hold Brittany as his vassal.

Eleanor would no doubt have been entertained by these works and the new perspective they opened on her present status as a latter-day Guenevere. A particular attraction would have been the scenes they offered of court life and manners. And raised as she had been amid echoes of her grandfather's amatory exploits and the troubadours' frequent profession of love for married women, she might have embroidered in her imagination Geoffrey's and Wace's fairly reticent descriptions of Guenevere's adultery with Arthur's nephew Mordred while her husband was on campaign beyond the sea. Would she have wondered whether, if faced by Guenevere's final plight, she would like her have turned to repentance and religion as a nun in some remote convent? Perhaps she reflected on Louis's reasons for having taken her away with him on his own less glorious expedition. I shall look more closely in a later chapter at the Eleanor–Guenevere relationship.

Illicit love was a topic in vogue in the new literature, most notably as portrayed in the legend of Tristan and Iseut. A branch of the Matter of Britain, the tragic story was finding significant expression in the romances at this time. Eleanor may even have heard something of it as a child; for a tale of Tristan was credited by one writer to the repertoire of that Welshman Breri or Bleddri who, as we saw, was said to have performed at Poitiers before a Count William, presumably Eleanor's father or grandfather. The legend in its developed form was probably told in a lost romance at about the middle of the century. The earliest surviving though incomplete text seems to be that of Thomas, long designated 'of England'. There is some doubt as to whether he was himself English, but it is commonly believed that he wrote for an insular public, which is most likely to be the court of Henry and Eleanor. The dating is also problematical: certainly after 1155 and probably by the mid-1170s. Sophisticated in the telling, this is another work that would have held Eleanor's attention.

In one of his songs the troubadour Bernard of Ventadour claims he is more sick for love than was Tristan who endured such suffering for the fair Iseut. Which brings us back to the scandal I mentioned earlier. From various allusions in his verse, Bernard's thirteenth-century biographer concocted a story linking him with Eleanor more closely than was proper. The Viscount of Ventadour had given him his marching orders for having an affair with his wife, we are told. And the biographer continues:

He left and went to the Duchess of Normandy, who was young and most worthy, well acquainted with merit, honour and fine flattery. Bernard's verse and songs pleased her greatly, and she received him with a warm welcome. He was at her court for a long time and fell in love with her and she with him; and he composed many excellent songs for her. While he was with her, King Henry of England made her his wife and took her from Normandy to England. Bernard remained behind full of grief and sorrow, then went to the good Count Raymond of Toulouse, with whom he remained until his death. Because of his grief, he entered the order of Dalon, where he ended his days.[30]

Smoke without fire? The historical inaccuracies warn us not to take the story too seriously, though many have. On the other hand, Bernard does, in a lyric full of love and vows of service to his unnamed lady, complain that it is through her that he has left the king, and asks a messenger to go and sing his song to the Queen of the Normans. Moreover, elsewhere in his verse there are indications of his being beyond the Channel at the court of the English and Norman king.[31] So it does appear that at some time the master troubadour was in the royal entourage, paying, perhaps, discreetly amorous compliments to Eleanor herself.

Such tributes would not have been foreign, or unwelcome, to her ears, which, however, may never have caught the strains of passionate longing expressed by one anonymous German poet in his own tongue:

> If all the world were mine
> From sea's shore to the Rhine,
> That price were not too high
> To have England's queen lie
> Close in my arms.[32]

The ardour suggests that its object was still relatively young; but otherwise the doggerel is undatable, like many of the other works I have mentioned; and even the traditional identification of the queen with Eleanor has been questioned.

We have been glancing at writings of various kinds that we know to have been available for Eleanor's edification or entertainment during her years of residence in England. All these have survived; but there is ample evidence for the existence of more ephemeral material now lost, as for instance the repertoire of itinerant minstrels and story-tellers. The Plantagenet court, then, would have been no cultural desert, even without the ever-open lines of communication with the Continent and France in particular, of which Eleanor was frequently to avail herself during the first two decades of her reign. So on the likely assumption that she had retained from her youth and continued to cultivate an interest in the rich literary output of her age, we can be assured that her marriage to Henry would not have removed her from the mainstream of French culture.

*

Her first residence in England was not the by that time dilapidated palace at Westminster, but a more comfortable residence in Bermondsey, across the Thames from the Conqueror's grim Tower and not far from the bustling commercial life of the docks. It was in Bermondsey that, a bare two months after the coronation, her second son, Henry, was born. That was in February 1155; and by the summer of the following year, thanks to the zeal of the king's new chancellor, Westminster Palace had been restored and refurbished for royal occupation.

That chancellor, appointed on the recommendation of Theobald (Thibault), the pious Archbishop of Canterbury and himself a protégé of Bernard of Clairvaux, was Thomas Becket. A Londoner of Norman origin, he had completed his early studies in Paris at the time when Eleanor was reigning there as Louis's queen. After being schooled in law in Bologna and Auxerre, he had been ordained deacon and then, in 1154, archdeacon by Theobald. As Henry's chancellor he was to pursue his great talent for administration, but not to the exclusion of his taste for the good life of the court; for not only did he enjoy its active pleasures such as the hunt, but it was said that he even outshone his monarch in lavish hospitality. Although he was fifteen years older than Henry, the two soon became firm friends and close companions.

In some respects Eleanor's situation at the English court contrasted sharply with that which confronted her as a young queen in Paris. There, as yet little practised in statemanship, she has been supposed nevertheless to have wielded some influence over a monkish consort of about her own age, who ruled under the critical eyes of his venerable advisers Suger and Bernard. Now, matured by experience, she was the wife of a king considerably her junior and dynamic to a fault, who conducted his affairs in collusion with a personable counsellor-companion only a few years older than herself. One imagines her deriving some intellectual satisfaction from her association with the intelligent Thomas Becket, not to mention the archbishop and the latter's gifted secretary, the philosopher John of Salisbury, whom we earlier glimpsed in Paris and Rome. But she may have felt somewhat displaced from the centre of power, at least when Henry was in England. Not that she would have been inactive, since she appears to have often accompanied him on his tireless (though for his company fatiguing) travels round his domains, with visits to such strongholds as Winchester, Wallingford, Oxford, Lincoln and Nottingham or the less austere residences of Clarendon and Woodstock, and on periodic hunting forays in the royal forests.[33]

If we can believe frequenters of the court like the puritanical John of Salisbury or the gossipy Welshman Walter Map, it was a place of scandal as well as statesmanship, frivolity as well as serious culture. John in particular was aware of new fashions of which he scarcely approved: dandified and effeminate clothing, polyphonic music more apt to kindle passion or set the feet jigging than to elevate the soul. Hunting and gaming were taken, he thought, to excess; and he had little time for the host of entertainers in the shape of mimes, jugglers, conjurors, magicians and fortune-tellers, all in brisk demand. In his *Policraticus* he shows especial contempt for the wheedlers and flatterers in the courts of the mighty; and though he speaks in general terms, it is easy to visualize Eleanor at the focus of their attention. So she is unlikely to have found life in her English capital more austere than that in Paris with Louis: probably quite the reverse. We know that she enjoyed substantial revenues of her own; and from records of her expenditures in the pipe rolls it is evident that her lifestyle there was enhanced by imported luxuries. In any case this was, of course, a French-speaking milieu and attracted frequent visitors from France, Italy, Sicily, indeed from all corners of the Continent. That, then, was the stage initially trodden by Eleanor as Queen of England.

William
Henry
Matilda
Richard
Geoffrey
Eleanor
Joanna
John

We can only guess at the state of Eleanor's personal relations with her husband during the early years of their marriage. Certainly they did not prevent her from amply fulfilling her role as provider of potential successors to the throne and daughters whose eventual marriage could extend its sway.[34] Although her first son, William, died a mere infant in 1156, the second, Henry, thrived and, as heir apparent, was placed at a tender age in the care of Thomas Becket. By the summer of 1156 she had presented the king with his first daughter, named Matilda after his formidable mother. She was born in London; and in September 1157 came the birth in Oxford of a third son, Richard. The following year marked the arrival, also in England, of Geoffrey, the future Duke of Brittany. Then three more years passed before the birth at Domfront in Normandy of another daughter, Eleanor, whose advent was followed in 1165 by that of Joanna in Angers. Finally, probably on Christmas Eve 1166, though datings differ,[35] Eleanor produced in Oxford the last of her so-called 'eaglets' in the person of John 'Lackland', the fifth of her sons and her tenth child in all. In the end she had performed her function as mother almost too well, as later events were to suggest.

Meanwhile, Henry had not restricted his fathering activities to the royal bed, from which Eleanor had plainly not expelled him, despite her private feelings concerning her spouse's notorious extra-marital escapades. From one of these, with a common prostitute called Ykenai according to Walter Map, came a son Geoffrey, who was destined to pass by way of the see of Lincoln and the chancellorship of England to become Archbishop of York. Walter's improbable version of events is that Ykenai merely passed the child off as Henry's son at the beginning of his reign and the king unwisely accepted him as such. Modern opinion, though, numbers Geoffrey among Henry's known bastards, albeit admitting that he may have been conceived before his father's marriage.[36] Be that as it may, this was only one of Henry's affairs with assorted ladies of which Eleanor must have been early aware. Perhaps her feelings were less bruised by such disloyalty in view of examples we have seen in her own family history, even if reports of her personal philanderings, most recently with Bernard of Ventadour, are to be discounted.

If Louis had played out the first decade of his reign in more or less close harmony with Eleanor, one might think of the early years of her life with Henry rather in terms of counterpoint. Their separations were frequent and often extended, with Henry after his accession spending more and more of his time occupied with affairs on the Continent. When Eleanor was left behind in England, she acted during the first part of his reign as regent, dealing with matters of state in his name and with his full confidence. She too crossed the Channel for varying periods, but by no means always in his company. Although records of their respective movements are less detailed than we would wish, the following outline will give some idea of the criss-crossing of their paths in the course of the first dozen or so years of Henry's rule.[37]

Henry spent the first part of 1155 consolidating his English domains and, in the early summer, dealing with a recalcitrant baron. The autumn saw him devising schemes for the conquest of Ireland; but in the face of the disapproval of his mother the 'Empress' Matilda these came to naught, and he turned his thoughts to more pressing problems in France. His immediate purpose there was to impose his personal control over Anjou and Maine, though they were also claimed by his brother Geoffrey, who showed little inclination to hand them over. Their particular importance to Henry was that they straddled his communications to his southern territories; so asserting that he had accepted the existing arrangement under duress, and after some skirmishing with Geoffrey, he took them under his wing and bought his brother off.

Eleanor, meanwhile, had remained in England with her infant son Henry, acting as regent after the king's departure. The death of the young prince William in 1156 was partly compensated in June of that year by the birth of Matilda; and shortly after this event, taking with her the baby and the toddler Henry, she herself crossed the Channel to Normandy. By the end of the summer her husband, his business with Geoffrey satisfactorily settled, was reunited with her in Anjou. In October, however, they were on the move again, heading this time for Aquitaine, and once more with the object of securing their fiefs and confirming the allegiance of their vassals. That this was no mere formality is shown by the fact that Henry was forced to take a number of hostages in the course of their progress. But all ended well; and we find them holding

Christmas court at Bordeaux. One can imagine the pleasure Eleanor derived from being back among her countrymen.

Was it, then, with some regret that she left Henry dealing with further matters in France and made her way back with the children to London in February of 1157? A couple of months later the king himself returned to busy himself in various parts of England before leading an incursion into Wales. By early September he seems to have been back in the Oxford area where, on the 8th, Eleanor gave birth to a son, Richard, who had been conceived in her own southern lands. Perhaps that is why she was later to show him particular affection. That year Christmas was celebrated with a ceremonial crowning at Lincoln.

From early in 1158 we find Henry frequently on the move again, though how often in the queen's company we cannot say. It was probably at Easter that the court, assembled at Worcester, attended a ceremony which has puzzled later historians; for a ritual coronation having taken place, the royal pair symbolically laid aside their crowns, never to wear them again. The early summer was marked by some trouble which drew Henry into a brief campaign in south Wales; but this was no more than a tiresome distraction from grander designs connected with his Continental estates. For these he set out in mid-August, leaving behind in Winchester Eleanor, who was once again in an advanced state of pregnancy.

The king's plans required the betrothal of his infant son, the young Henry, to Margaret, the even younger daughter of Louis, who had still not been blessed with a male heir. His strategy was transparent: the eventual gathering of France itself into Plantagenet hands. This dream was to come to naught when, in 1165, Louis belatedly acquired a son, the future Philip Augustus, by his third wife, Adela of Blois and Champagne; but that was more misfortune than miscalculation on Henry's part. The importance he attached now to his son's betrothal was shown by his sending to Paris in advance of his own move his chancellor Thomas Becket. The chroniclers tell us that Thomas arrived for the preliminary negotiations with a pomp quite foreign to the Capetian court and which left the citizens agape with admiration. The outcome was a meeting between the two kings on the Norman border at the end of August. There the agreement was ratified, whereupon Henry paid a less flamboyant visit to Paris to collect the baby princess for safe-keeping in Normandy. He seems to have made a favourable impression on his overlord Louis, who then furthered their relations with a progress through Henry's lands, culminating in a joint pilgrimage to the sea-girt abbey of Mont-Saint-Michel.

While her husband was thus navigating these uncommonly calm waters in his attempt to catch the tide of history, Eleanor remained tactfully in England, acting as regent, nursing their own thoughts about this new Capetian entanglement and, towards the end of September, further populating the Plantagenet house with the prince Geoffrey. Late in November we glimpse her transacting some business in Salisbury. Then in the following month she crossed the Channel to rejoin her husband and spend Christmas with him at Cherbourg. It is likely that they passed the rest of the winter and the early spring of 1159 in Normandy, mainly in Rouen and Argentan, with Eleanor making the acquaintance of her prospective daughter-in-law Margaret, discussing affairs with Matilda the queen mother, and being no doubt privy to, if not instigating, new moves in the south plotted by the restless Henry. For this seemed to him the moment to resurrect Eleanor's claim to Toulouse, seriously compromised by her troubadour grandfather to further his crusading ambitions, but then revived in her name by Louis during their marriage.

It was a quarrel between the counts of Toulouse and of Barcelona that Henry saw as his chance to extend still further the Plantagenet authority. In March he issued throughout his domains a demand for levies and men with the intention of siding with Raymond of Barcelona against his namesake from Toulouse. He proceeded south by way of Poitiers, pausing at Périgueux to knight the Scottish king Malcolm; and by the beginning of July an army of almost crusading proportions had assembled at Agen. It moved against Toulouse; but now Henry's plans began to go awry. Not only did the city fail to capitulate after an extended siege, but by September Louis himself had turned up there in support of the count, his brother-in-law. Reluctant, despite Becket's encouragement, to engage in arms against his overlord, Henry renounced the enterprise, disbanded the army, and returned by way of Limoges to Normandy. There is no record of Eleanor's movements during these events; but it is unlikely that she would have missed the opportunity they provided of breathing again the air of her southern homeland at Poitiers or elsewhere. Christmas finds her keeping the festival with Henry at Falaise. The exceptional severity of that winter would have done nothing to raise her spirits.

At the turn of the year Eleanor made the crossing once more to England, leaving Henry in France, where he was to spend the next three years. Information on her own activities during this period is sparse; and despite a number of more or less extended visits to France, one senses that her role was becoming increasingly peripheral to the major affairs of state. Entries in the pipe rolls for 1160 cover chiefly items of personal expenditure, among which the provision of wine has, one might think, an unduly prominent place. It is possible that in the early part of that year she paid a short visit to Normandy; but it was on more urgent business that she returned there in September, presumably at her husband's summons, taking with her her daughter Matilda and, more significantly, young Prince Henry.

By the spring of 1160 good relations had once again been established with Louis; but King Henry remained on the lookout for any marches he could steal on the Capetians in the power stakes. Now Louis's second wife, Constance, died in giving birth not to the much desired son, but to another daughter, an event that was not in itself to Henry's disadvantage. However when, with somewhat indecent haste, Louis arranged to replace the deceased Constance with spouse number three, Henry heard the alarm bells ringing. It was not merely that Louis might at last achieve a son from this new marriage, but also that his choice had fallen on Adela of Champagne whose brothers, Thibaut and Henry, the Capetian had already marked, as we saw, as the future husbands for Alice and Marie, his daughters by Eleanor. The rival dynasty to the Plantagenets was thus consolidating its position, to Henry's considerable discomfiture. So, never lacking in initiative, he made a swift counter-move. Within a few weeks, having extracted from a pair of conniving cardinals their consent to the theologically objectionable under-age union, he had the marriage celebrated on Norman soil of his five-year-old son to the two-year-old Margaret of France. This was early in November. It had the immediate strategic advantage of securing for him Margaret's dowry, namely the disputed border region of the Vexin, which lay between Paris and Rouen.

under-age union

It is not difficult to grasp on an intellectual level the reasoning behind these manoeuvres; but it is impossible to know (if dangerously easy to imagine) the feelings of the characters involved as their personal fates were determined by political convenience. This is particularly true of the women in that they were more often the manipulated than the manipulators, the concerned spectators of the game rather than the actual players. W. L. Warren's assessment may be over-negative when he says: 'To judge from the chroniclers, the most striking fact about Eleanor is her utter insignificance in Henry II's reign.'[38] It does, though, appear that she never wielded as much influence over the dynamic young Plantagenet as she had over the doting Louis.

One may legitimately wonder how her own forceful temperament adapted to this new situation and how far her feelings as wife and mother coloured her reactions to events and the complex relationships they engendered. Let us recall the facts. She was about thirty-eight, her present husband eleven years younger. She witnessed the precipitate marriage of her small son to the daughter of her estranged first husband, Louis, in the latter's absence. The haste had been due to the death of the girl's mother and Louis's prompt marriage to the prospective sister-in-law of Eleanor's own adolescent daughters by him. The upshot was the consolidation of two rival camps: on the one hand the Plantagenets, including herself, her current husband, their son, and the daughter of her previous husband, and on the other that husband himself and her two daughters by him. One is left to imagine the degrees of affection, warm, cooled or soured, she felt for the individuals in these tangled relationships. Surely she must have suffered some emotional conflicts. If so, might the result not have been at least an element of emotional detachment from the whole political strategy, extending even to Henry, its operator? It would not be surprising if already, after some eight years of marriage and six as queen, she was feeling the need for a new cause or individual apt to engage her personal commitment and give direction to her energies.

Henry's coup had enraged the Capetians, who made a hostile gesture against his territories on the Loire. This, however, he countered with dispatch in time to rejoin Eleanor for Christmas at Le Mans. His first preoccupation in the following year, 1161, was to consolidate his position in the face of Louis's aggressive stance; and his efforts to this end were crowned with a peace settlement in October. A problem which was fraught with more dangerous consequences in the long term was the death in April of Henry's staunch ally and counsellor the Archbishop Theobald of Canterbury. It seemed to him a good tactical move to have him replaced by his intimate the chancellor; and to bring this about he turned his powers of persuasion on the reluctant Becket, whose worldly tastes were not the best qualification for the post. We have no means of knowing Eleanor's inclinations in the matter (the 'Empress' Matilda seems to have disapproved of the step); but her more immediate preoccupation was with the birth of another daughter, Eleanor, at Domfront in September. There is no record of her having made any return journey to England in the course of the year; and that Christmas she spent with Henry at Bayeux.

By the following spring Becket had become reconciled to substituting the function of archbishop for that of chancellor. So in May he was sent back from Normandy to London. He was also given the duty of escorting Prince Henry, to whom the lords spiritual and temporal were to renew at Winchester their homage as to the heir to the throne. Becket was speedily elected, in the prince's presence, to the vacant archbishopric, although he was not yet an ordained priest. That deficiency, however, was remedied shortly afterwards; and on 3 June 1162 he was consecrated archbishop. The royal couple had remained in France while these events were in train; and although they had intended to travel to England for the Christmas festivities, the Channel weather defeated them, and they were forced to celebrate them in Cherbourg instead. It was a month before they were able to cross with the young princesses to Southampton, where they were greeted by the new head of the English Church and his pupil Prince Henry. The lad's child bride is ignored by the chroniclers during this busy year.

In 1163 the king was occupied with various matters of internal and external import, managing to fit in another brief campaign in Wales. It is interesting to find among the royal writs one in favour of the nuns of Fontevrault. But the most memorable feature of this year is that it marks the beginning of the rift between Henry and his erstwhile boon companion Thomas Becket. This is not the place to rehearse the facts and theories concerning perhaps the most celebrated quarrel in English history, especially as Eleanor's part in it, if any, is largely a matter of guesswork. She remains very much in the background during this fateful year which, incidentally, is the last in which we find a writ issued in England in her name.

*

Having been out of his English realm for almost four and a half years, Henry was plainly bent on a period of consolidation and reform. His reviews of such matters as feudal tenure and the country's finances are not likely to have engaged Eleanor's passionate interest; and she may not have felt too concerned when questions of legal jurisdiction were raised and soon became a burning topic in the councils of state. The essential issue was what might now be called the 'interface' between royal and ecclesiastical justice, with the latter traditionally claiming responsibility for the trial and punishment of errant clerics. One can understand the strong-willed Henry's reluctance to surrender more than absolutely necessary to a rival authority; but now he was faced with a new Becket suddenly transformed from being his loyal right-hand man into the wielder of that authority. Having been initially reluctant to accept the primacy and the radically new lifestyle the move involved, Thomas was now understandably determined to exercise the powers pressed upon him to the best of his considerable ability; and that meant championing the Church's cause in any conflict with that of the crown. When now a series of such cases arose, the mounting tension between the two men was almost inevitable. Their previous close friendship seems to have quickly drained away, leaving a bitter sediment behind.

One detects a certain pettiness in Henry's reactions to Thomas's opposition, as when he took back from him the manor of Berkhamsted, which he had been granted when he became chancellor. If that was not unreasonable, the king's choice of it for the holding of his Christmas court in that same year smacks of unregal spite. If we could have observed Eleanor's behaviour at that court, we might have gained valuable insights into her character. Did she connive with her husband's attitudes and actions, or remain as detached as she could from the developing dispute? Or did she secretly despise Henry for his notorious tendency to burst into

Becket

violent and rather petulant rages whenever he was crossed? Becket may have been to some extent her rival in his affections; but he was an honourable man, and we would like to imagine her having some sympathy with his position. Whatever her private feelings, she was at this period of her life playing the part of a queen without any clearly defined role. Did this perhaps draw her closer to her children? It may not be too fanciful to think of her spending nostalgic hours with the six-year-old Richard telling him tales of the sunny lands where he was conceived. But we can never know.

The year 1164 saw Henry's feud with Becket come to a head; and the ageing 'Empress' Matilda, now in her sixties, found her presentiments well founded. In an attempt to outmanoeuvre his archbishop, Henry held in January a council at Clarendon, at

Plate 4 King Henry disputing with Becket. (MS Royal 20, A11, fol. 76.)

which were promulgated the famous Constitutions setting out the king's customary rights over the Church. After initially accepting them, Becket quickly had second thoughts. Henry resumed the offensive. He deployed against Thomas all his powers of diplomacy, persuasion and coercion before finally arraigning him before a council held in Northampton in October. Thomas's reply was to flee the country, seeking sanctuary in Flanders, then France, and finding ultimate haven in the Cistercian abbey of Pontigny, where he was to remain for almost two years.

We know little of Eleanor's activities at this period and none at all of the position she adopted in the continuing controversy. It is likely that she spent Easter in London and much of the summer in the south and south-west of England; she may then have moved with the court to other parts of the country before repairing with it to Marlborough for Christmas festivities that were spent in something less than a general spirit of goodwill. The king would hardly have rejoiced at the news filtering from the Continent of Becket's canvassing support from both Louis and the pope. And if one wonders where Eleanor's sympathies lay, what of those of her son, the nine-year-old Prince Henry? This bitter quarrel between his father and his former respected tutor must have been for him a painful experience, not least because, far from being sheltered from the conflict, he had actually presided with the king at the Council of Clarendon. For as heir presumptive he was already being groomed for the throne and was even provided with his own establishment. To complicate still further the play of conflicting loyalties within the royal household, it was in this year that the marriage of Eleanor's two daughters by Louis had sealed the Capetian alliance with the houses of Blois and Champagne.

In the early days of 1165 Henry pursued his attack on Becket by confiscating the see of Canterbury and exiling members of his family. Some time during Lent he then left for the Continent himself. After a brief meeting with Louis at Gisors, from which nothing of great import emerged, he proceeded to Rouen to negotiate more tactical alliances. This time the pawns in his strategy were the princesses Matilda and Eleanor: the marriage of the first was arranged to Henry the Lion, Duke of Saxony, and actually took place in 1168; but that planned between Eleanor and the youngest son of the Emperor Frederick Barbarossa came to nothing. Hard on the heels of these arrangements, Queen Eleanor, having passed the early months of the year in southern England, crossed to Normandy with Matilda and Prince Richard to rejoin her husband. That was at the beginning of May. The reunion, however, was only to last a couple of weeks; for the restless Henry then took ship again in order to deal with trouble flaring in North Wales. His campaign there proved abortive; and by September we find him leaving Chester for London, then visiting various of his residences in the south of England before spending Christmas in Oxford. His mind would not have been set at ease by the news that on 22 August Louis had at last achieved his ambition of acquiring a son and heir; for on that day to great jubilation in France, if not in England, was born the future Philip Augustus.

Henry had left Eleanor not in Normandy but at Angers, where she was to exercise for the time being the regency over Anjou and Maine. It must have been a delight for her to have again at least limited authority, and in lands adjoining her own native province. There she would have revived old acquaintances, and not least that with her uncle Raoul de Faye. Their relationship seems to have been especially close, if we are to believe an interesting letter of the time from the Bishop of Poitiers. Raoul was known to lack sympathy for Becket's cause; and in his letter to Thomas himself, the bishop advises him not to expect Eleanor's support, since she is under Raoul's strong influence. Indeed, he goes so far as to hint at some scandal in their relations.[39] Unlikely as the rumour is, especially in view of Eleanor's latest pregnancy, it shows that there were still tongues to wag busily at her expense. Anyway, it was in Angers that the queen gave birth to yet another princess, Joanna; and it was there that she appears to have remained for Christmas.

Henry devoted the early weeks of 1166, often at his residence in Woodstock, to a renovation of the traditional legal system. But trouble was brewing on another of the Celtic fringes of his domains. So in mid-March he sailed from Southampton to Falaise and proceeded at once to Maine, where border barons were leaguing with Bretons against Eleanor's authority. Having been joined by the queen, he dealt with the rebellious lords with his usual efficiency before spending Easter in Angers. He planned to follow up this success with a thrust against Brittany, while at the same time pursuing his more insidious campaign against Becket. Thomas himself was by no means inactive and continued to launch long-range spiritual missiles in the form of actual or threatened excommunications against Henry's supporters and even, by implication, against his royal person. Late in June, after an illness that may have been used as as tactical ploy, the king launched his forces against the Bretons and with some difficulty captured Fougères. He then moved on to Rennes, where he secured virtual control of Brittany by means of another strategic betrothal. This time it was the eight-year-old Prince Geoffrey who was affianced to Constance, the child daughter of Conan, claimant to the ducal title. The prince, it seems, was brought over from England for the occasion. The problem of a degree of consanguinity was resolved only later in the year, when Henry managed to elicit papal approval for the match.

Life remained agitated for the king, even after the security of his lands was restored and he had made a confirmatory progress through Brittany. His difficulties with the Church persisted; and he actually quarrelled with his mother over his imprisonment of a papal messenger, though his relations with Rome improved somewhat as the months passed. Becket left his retreat at Pontigny in November as a result of Henry's threats against his Cistercian hosts; but that merely strengthened Thomas's ties with Louis. At the same time Henry was seeking allies where he could; and he may have had brief meetings with both Philip of Flanders and Thibaut of Blois. Frequently on the move, he spent most of his time now in Normandy. However, in order perhaps to show his authority and present his future heir to his southern vassals, he elected to spend that Christmas in Poitiers, where he was joined by Prince Henry, newly arrived from England. Surprisingly enough, unless Eyton's chronology is at fault, Eleanor was not with him.

Her movements throughout the year are largely conjectural; but there is some evidence to justify Eyton's deduction that she returned to England with young Matilda in October or November, that is before her son's departure for Poitiers.[40] And despite the usual dating, logic would seem to demand that it was on 24 December of this year, not 1167, that she gave birth in Oxford to John, the last of her children. Why, then, had she chosen to be in Oxford for the event rather than with her husband in her native Poitiers? Could this be the first sign of a rift developing between them? The explanation, if we could know it, might not be so sinister.

One could invent a scenario showing Eleanor leaving for England with the intention of herself conducting Prince Henry to her own homeland but then, faced by the rigours of winter travel and the approaching term of her pregnancy, taking the wiser course of preparing him for the journey to Poitou and then retiring to Oxford for the imminent birth. A more dramatically appealing, if equally speculative, theory has been advanced.[41] It assumes that the queen had heard rumours of one of her husband's more serious love affairs, this time with Rosamond Clifford, the daughter of one of his knights from the Welsh border, and that the girl had been installed in her own apartments in Woodstock. The enraged Eleanor would have headed for Oxford determined to check the truth of these reports, then remained in the palace there for her lying-in. We shall hear more of the Fair Rosamond.

The paucity of records relating directly to Eleanor at this period is unfortunate and possibly significant. Is it, for instance, purely fortuitous that we have no clear evidence of her personal involvement in the Becket affair? Intense though her interest must have been, did she deliberately avoid any embroilment in the quarrel, or did Henry have her keep her distance? Even if there was at this point no estrangement between them, one is inclined to see their individual interests and commitments now set irrevocably on divergent courses.

For Henry, 1167 was another year of turmoil. His feud with the archbishop and his supporters rumbled on, sometimes to his alarm and often to his exasperation, with the pope, King Louis, and many of the nobility of England and France heavily involved. At the beginning of the year he had felt his presence necessary in his wife's turbulent lands of Aquitaine; and he was even obliged to quell a revolt by one of her uncles, William Taillefer. He did achieve his ambition of gaining the overlordship of Toulouse, but after Easter was confronted by another rebellious vassal, the Count of Auvergne, who was supported by Louis. An abortive conference with Louis in the Vexin gave way to active hostilities there before a truce was patched up in August. But there was still no peace for Henry; and within the month he had marched to suppress an insurrection in Brittany fed by Aquitainian and French support. A further blow came in September with the death of his doughty mother the 'Empress' Matilda, who ended her days committed to works as much pious as political, though one account of her having taken the veil at Fontevrault is unreliable. Henry remained in the north until Christmas, when he held court at Argentan; and there, it seems, Eleanor joined him, having passed the whole year in England.

The main event of her year was the arrival that summer of envoys from the Duke of Saxony, come to bring Princess Matilda (now eleven years old) to the court of her designated husband. No doubt Eleanor supervised the lavish expenditure indicated in the pipe rolls for the proper equipping of the girl, so that she should arrive in her new home in appropriate style. Then in September she escorted her at least to Dover and possibly even across the Channel though without lingering on the other side. After some weeks' residence in Winchester, she left in all probability in December to join Henry in Argentan. Her life now entered a more exciting phase.

A report of more unrest in the south sent Henry post-haste to Poitou to confront the rebels, notably the ambitious Lusignans. He captured their castle and devastated the surrounding territory; but most of the refractory lords remained at liberty. With him he had taken Eleanor, with the intention of leaving her, supported by Patrick Earl of Salisbury, to control her vassals while he went to treat once more with Louis at Pacy, on the Norman border. About Easter, she found herself with Patrick on the road to Poitiers when their unarmed party was ambushed by Guy de Lusignan. Eleanor evaded capture, but the Earl was slain as he covered her escape. In the affray Patrick's nephew, William Marshal, a knight in his mid-twenties, performed one of those gallant feats of arms for which he was to become celebrated. But although, according to his thirteenth-century biographer, he fought like a famished lion or a boar at bay, he was himself taken captive. Attracted as ever by young men of spirit, Eleanor managed to secure his release and rewarded him richly for his heroism.[42] William's exploit truly launched him on an illustrious career: before long he was made tutor and master in chivalry to Prince Henry; and by his death in 1219 he was acting as regent of England.

The king, meanwhile, had negotiated with Louis a complex and somewhat puzzling accord involving the paying of homage to the Capetian by Prince Henry for Anjou and for Brittany (to be held under him by his brother Geoffrey), and by Richard for Aquitaine. An additional stipulation was the betrothal of Richard to Alice

Plate 5 The crowning of Henry the Lion, Duke of Saxony, and Matilda. Probably painted c.1185 when Eleanor was still in disgrace, hence her absence from the family group at King Henry's side. (Herzog August Bibliothek Wolfenbüttel, Codex Guelf. 105 Noviss 2°, fol. 171v.)

(Alais), Louis's daughter by his second wife, Constance, and sister to young Henry's wife Margaret. How far Eleanor was privy to her husband's machinations we cannot say. At this juncture news reached Henry of the Lusignan treachery; but before he was able to return to Poitou, he had word of another conflagration in Brittany. This time Viscount Eudo of Porhoet had been moved to avenge what he claimed was the seduction of his daughter by the lascivious Henry while the girl was being held by the king as a hostage. By July, might if not right had triumphed, and the revolt had been crushed. But now, the uneasy truce with Louis having foundered, Henry found himself engaged for much of the rest of the year in sporadic tactical fighting against the Capetians round his northern borders. At Christmas he was back holding court at Argentan. Eleanor, though, appears to have remained in Poitiers, securing her own position and doubtless nurturing plans of her own, especially as regards the future of Richard, who may have been with her at the time.

Henry, so decisive in his suppression of recalcitrant vassals, was less adept in his confrontations not with physical might and fortifications but with men of peace embattled within the spiritual ramparts of Holy Church. He did not lack negotiating skills and general tactical sense, but found it irksome to have to bide his time in the pursuit of an elusive tactical victory. If this had been illustrated by the events of the past year, those of 1169 followed the same pattern: on the one hand the muscular imposition of his feudal authority within his borders, on the other a frustrating series of shifts of fortune and stalemates in his struggle with Becket.

The year started well enough with an assembly at Montmirail on the Maine border where, on 6 January, the earlier accord with Louis was ratified; and on the following day the princes Henry and Richard did due homage to the French king. So far things had gone to order; but now Becket made his appearance and, while affecting submission to Henry, produced certain cavils over the conditions which sent Henry storming from the gathering. Thereupon Louis himself departed with the archbishop in his train. There is no record of Eleanor having left Poitou for the occasion.

The king himself entered her province in March, but not so much for a family reunion as to effect the submission of a couple of troublesome counts. From there he proceeded into Aquitaine, where he was still attending to his affairs when, in May, the ten-year-old Geoffrey received the homage of his new subjects in Brittany. Not that his travels in the south sheltered him from the Becket storm, which had intensified in April with the excommunication by Thomas of various prominent supporters of the royal cause. Early in August Henry returned to Normandy by way of Angers. Stormy meetings with a party of papal nuncios at Domfront (where he had been hunting with Prince Henry) and afterwards near Bayeux did nothing to remedy matters. He then retired to Rouen, where he spent much of the following months. In November he journeyed to Montmartre for further consultations with Louis, in the course of which it was recognized that Richard, when he became Duke of Aquitaine, would have suzerainty over Toulouse. But this council too was clouded by the presence of Becket, to whom Henry refused the symbolic 'kiss of peace', thus bringing all discussion to an end. Instead, he took steps to isolate Thomas and his party further from their support in England. That Christmas he went to Brittany to hold court with young Geoffrey at Nantes.

Chronicles and records tell us virtually nothing of Eleanor's activities in 1169. It is often assumed that she spent most of her time in Poitiers, restoring the court there to its former glory as a centre of culture and gracious living. We cannot say how much contact she had with her husband; but it is likely that for a good deal of the year she enjoyed the company of their children: Henry and his child-wife Margaret, Richard, Geoffrey and Constance his betrothed, and the princesses Eleanor and Joanna. John, in his third year, was probably at Fontevrault, being cared for by the nuns of the community.[43] There is no trace of any visits by the queen to England at this period. Designedly or not, she appears to have kept a discreet distance from the Becket controversy, though she would certainly have been well informed of developments. There were interested parties in Poitiers and some division of sympathies; for if her uncle Raoul was opposed to Thomas's cause, the Bishop of Poitiers was his staunch ally. One can well imagine Eleanor treading warily in these matters, while doing what she could to assure the stability of her own lands. We may suspect too the slackening of the ties of her partnership with Henry and of her detailed interest in English current affairs, as she thought more and more of the eventual succession and the future roles of her sons.

CVI·FRATER·FVIT·COR·LEONIS·DICTVS
HENRICVS·IVNIOR·SEDEM·IN·NORMANNIA·ARMIS·IVRIQVE·NEGATAM
AN·M·C·LXXXIII·A·MORTE·TANDEM·HIC·AEGRE·TENVIT

Plate 6 Effigy of Henry, the Young King, at Rouen.

The year 1170 was marked by both ceremony and tragedy. It was to end with the final resolution of the Becket affair by which Henry, largely owing to his own obduracy, had continued to be plagued. In January, having tidied things up in Brittany, he returned to Normandy and invited Thomas to Caen for further consultations. However, when the archbishop was on his way to the meeting, he learned of Henry's sudden departure for England on business, as it turned out, that was much closer to his heart, namely to arrange for the coronation of Prince Henry as his designated successor. In April the final plans were laid at a council convened in London.

Eleanor now took steps for a parallel move, the timing presumably fixed with her husband's acquiescence if not on his advice: this was to have Richard installed with due pomp as Duke of Aquitaine. In a preliminary ceremony at Poitiers on 31 May he was enthroned in the church of Saint-Hilaire to receive the lance and standard that were the insignia of the Poitevin counts; and then, in Limoges, the boy took the symbolic ring of the virgin martyr Saint Valerie and was proclaimed Duke. After these festive occasions the queen lost no time in returning to Normandy, where she was cast for a role in support of Henry's current activities.

These involved the coronation of Prince Henry not by the Archbishop of Canterbury, as was his prerogative, but by the Archbishop of York, to the offence not only of Becket and his immediate supporters, but of the pope himself. Anticipating the consequences, Henry moved speedily in order to forestall any counter-moves. On 5 June he had the prince escorted from Caen to England. The Bishop of Worcester, armed with a papal prohibition of the coronation and wishing to make the same journey, was detained in Caen by Eleanor and the constable of Normandy, Richard du Hommet. Henry further managed to slight King Louis by having his daughter Margaret also remain with the queen in Caen instead of joining her young husband for his coronation, though there had been at least half-promises that she would be shipped across the Channel. It must be assumed that Eleanor was happy to play her part in these delaying tactics until Prince Henry was safely crowned as king presumptive. This he was, by the Archbishop of York at Westminster, on Sunday 14 June. Ten days later the king was back in Normandy, prepared to face the threats of an indignant Louis.

The tragic events that ensued must be summarized. Even now Henry's rift with Becket might have been healed; and pressure to this end was applied not least by the pope. In July Henry reached an accommodation with Louis at Fréteval in Touraine, where he then met Becket in a conciliatory mood: Thomas might return to Canterbury and even preside at the crowning of Margaret and re-crowning of the prince. The two had a further meeting, at Amboise, in October and looked forward to another, in Rouen, when Thomas would be on his way to England. That never took place, as Henry was diverted by renewed hostilities on the part of Louis. When he returned to Normandy, the archbishop was already back in Canterbury. By the time the king held his Christmas court near Bayeux, relations had again soured, and he was making provisions for Becket's arrest. Anticipating this event *Murder* and doubtless seeking Henry's approval, four of his knights left *in the* the court on their own initiative and, on 29 December, effected the *Cathedral* notorious murder of Thomas in his cathedral. Henry, it seems, only heard the news after moving to Argentan, where he was said to have remained for forty days, overcome with grief and remorse.

But what were his private thoughts? We have no way of telling. Nor can we judge the reaction of Eleanor, or even be sure that she was with him that Christmas. Of her sons, the Young King was holding court in Winchester, and we know that Geoffrey had been in England for much of the year; but we have no record of her own whereabouts or those of Richard. One senses that her main emotional commitment would have been to her children and her preoccupation with their future in dynastic terms. She would have been as anxious as her husband to see young Henry crowned, and satisfied that Becket's assassination, in which the lad had had no involvement, would leave his position unchanged. She had not been faced with the stark terms of the king's dilemma, for whom matters of state and those of religion had become so inextricably enmeshed. Her former husband would surely have accommodated his secular and spiritual ambitions at an early stage; but Henry, the political manipulator and man of action, could not find it in his character to give best to his opponent; so the final tragedy, if not wanted, was inevitable. Whatever Henry's thoughts, Eleanor had no need to wrestle with her conscience.

The king, however, now lay under threat of excommunication and his realm in danger of the slightly less extreme penalty of interdiction. Reluctant to take these ultimate steps, the pope hesitated for many months while the different parties pressed their cases; and the issue remained in doubt until the May of the following year, 1172, when Henry's supporters finally had their wish, and he was formally absolved of the murder. Before then, on 1 March, Becket had been canonized.

*

Meanwhile, with his spiritual fate in jeopardy, Henry had continued with the practical business of consolidating and, as occasion offered, extending his secular power. During the early part of 1171 he was in Brittany, where Duke Conan's lands had passed, on his death, to Prince Geoffrey. When Henry was satisfied that the lad, who had joined him from England, was secure in their possession, his thoughts turned to another territory on the 'Celtic fringe'. Six years earlier he had harboured plans for the conquest of Ireland, but had then put them in abeyance because of his mother's opposition. Now an outbreak of civil strife in that country re-awakened that ambition. So, after some weeks in Normandy, he crossed the Channel to head this time for Wales and the stormy passage to Ireland, where he arrived in October. That Christmas he held court in Dublin; and by the time he returned to England the following April, he had brought much of the island under his control and, as a bonus that stood him in good credit in Rome, had reformed the Irish Church and aligned it more closely with Western Christendom. In May he returned to Normandy, accompanied by Prince Henry and his still uncrowned wife Margaret; and at Avranches he made his peace with the papal authorities and received his absolution.

The way was now clear for a conciliatory gesture towards Louis in the shape of a new coronation of the Young King, this time with Margaret beside him. It took place in Winchester on 27 August; but Henry himself, having retired to Brittany, was not present. The following month he returned to Normandy, where he was joined briefly in November by the young couple, who were on their way to the French court. On the surface at least, their journey's purpose was a family reunion between Louis and his daughter; but for the Capetian it was an opportunity to propagate if not to sow seeds of discontent in the mind of the seventeen-year-old Henry, whose largely ceremonial powers did not satisfy an ambition inherited from his father. No doubt the latter had his suspicions, as he recalled his son to Normandy for Christmas, whilst he held his own court at Chinon in Anjou. There it appears he was joined by Eleanor and the princes Richard and Geoffrey. But where had the queen been during the past year? It is possible that she was briefly in England in the company of young Henry and his wife; but this cannot be proved.[44]

We often read of her presiding over her flourishing court at Poitiers, surrounded by poet-musicians, convening with her daughter Marie and other noble ladies those so-called courts of love, at which the finer points of amorous conduct were debated and judgements on them given. Marie, now Countess of Champagne, would have forsaken for the time being her residence at Troyes where Chrétien, master of Arthurian fiction, was to compose for her the romance of Lancelot and Guenevere. There too, probably under her influence, Andreas Capellanus (Andrew the Chaplain) wrote his Latin treatise on courtly love, which was largely responsible for the speculation on the ladies' councils.[45] Unfortunately there is no evidence for Marie's presence at Poitiers;[46] and whatever grains of truth there may be in the romantic picture of Eleanor's court as a centre of civilized dalliance, we may be sure she had not lost her devotion to more serious matters.

Now in her fiftieth year, almost elderly in medieval terms, and moved into the political wings while Henry held centre stage, she would have found it prudent to maintain what order she could in her own lands. Since 1170 she was governing these not only on her own behalf, but also for Richard, the adolescent Duke of Aquitaine, whom she kept at her side in Poitiers. It would have been in her interests to side-step her husband's recent embroilments with Louis, now the titular suzerain of her three older sons. One imagines her commenting on the unfolding events to Richard and Geoffrey in particular, who seem to have been in her care, as part of their schooling in statesmanship. Given her political acumen it would have been hard for her, even had she wished, to avoid all criticism of their father. With her own relations with him perceptibly cooling, she may well, almost in self-defence, have ensured that their sympathies remained more firmly with her. It was especially important that Richard should fully appreciate the nature of his patrimony, the dashing chivalric traditions of his

Richard @ 14

ancestors and the rich culture of the south. Was he already, at fourteen or fifteen, showing some of that talent that was to make him, like his great-grandfather, join the ranks of the troubadours? He was in any case to show himself, as an adult, to be very much his mother's son.

That 1172 Christmas court at Chinon is unlikely to have been brimming with seasonal cheer. The fact that it saw the second anniversary of Becket's murder would hardly have lifted Henry's spirits as he brooded over the precocious ambitions of his eldest son, now nursing his grievances in Normandy, and felt the chill that surely marked his relations with Eleanor and the other boys. He may have been aware too of some stirrings of resentment among his barons throughout his dominions, irked by the high-handed way in which he sought to impose his authority. Was his heir apparent, the Young King, being wooed perhaps by some of these malcontents?

His most immediate concern would have been the tension that was building dangerously within his family circle, whether or not it came into the open before the New Year. It can only have sharpened when, in January, Henry summoned the Young King to join them in Anjou. The pretext was that they were all to travel south to negotiate with Humbert, Count of Maurienne (Savoy),

John @ 6

the betrothal of his daughter Alice to the six-year-old Prince John. After some preliminary discussions in Auvergne, a firm agreement was reached in Limoges; and there too Henry managed to resolve a dispute between Count Raymond V of Toulouse and the King of Aragon. Raymond moreover undertook to do homage for his fief to Henry and the Young King and also to Richard as Count of Poitou. To all appearances Henry had made some more adroit moves in his never-ending power game. In fact, in the course of his negotiations he had lit the fuse that was to lead to his family being blown apart. One condition in the settlement with Humbert was that John would eventually be given the three strongholds of Chinon, Mirebeau and Loudun – a reasonable provision on the face of it, but to the Young King a final provocation.

Shown by the example of his dear master Becket how to be his own man, long groomed for kingship, and primed for chivalric action by the dashing William Marshal, young Henry was determined to be more than his father's shadow. Already conspicuously lavish, even profligate, in his life-style, he wished now not just to live like a king, but to rule like one; and for that he needed his own domain – England, Normandy or Anjou at the least. Now at Limoges his father was not merely continuing to ignore his demands: he was even making over fortresses in the territory he coveted to his infant brother John. It is said that Raymond of Toulouse privately warned Henry of sedition brewing in his family; and that was perhaps why he banished a number of potential trouble-makers from among the young knights in his son's household before, in early March, the Plantagenets headed back north.

The royal party now divided. While Eleanor, whether or not of her own free will, returned to Poitiers with Richard and Geoffrey, the Young King was forced, under strict surveillance, to accompany his father on the road to Normandy. Their route took them by way of Chinon, where they arrived on 5 March. That night young Henry made his dramatic move. Under cover of darkness, he bribed or somehow evaded the castle guards; and in the morning his father found him gone. Wasting no time, he set off in pursuit. But though he trailed him to Alençon, then on to Argentan, he was unable to prevent him from heading east to cross the frontier and find haven in the Capetian court. Henry's demand that Louis send his son back was met with a firm snub. What part, if any, Eleanor played in these and subsequent events was a matter for rumour. William of Newburgh had no doubt: he reports that, with Louis's connivance in his evil plots against his father, the Young King went secretly to his mother's court and with her approval lured Richard and Geoffrey back with him to Paris. Eleanor herself had ignored her husband's appeal to return to him with their sons: the rift was final.[47]

Again we may pause to take stock of Eleanor's position. Now well into middle age, she was back on her home territory with a life full of event to look back on. As a girl she had been swept off to share the throne of France with the young Capetian, whose idealism was tempered by fluctuating moods and a certain impracticality. Her fourteen years with him had their frustrations; but she was never far from the seat of power and had ample opportunity to observe political scheming at work and even to play some part in it herself. She had partaken too of the high adventure of the abortive crusade and its aftermath. Then began a quite different, though equally important phase of her life. By 1173, she had for twenty-one years been the wife of an excitingly energetic man more than a decade her junior; yet paradoxically her own participation in public events had been curtailed. More observer now than direct actor, she still had a vital role to play. For what might have been for her a figuratively sterile period was literally quite the opposite, as it saw the birth of her five sons, four of whom survived, and three further daughters. Whereas she had spent little time with the two princesses she had presented to Louis, circumstances now made motherhood a much more significant part of her life, as she laid with Henry a solid base for his dynastic ambitions.

If she now enjoyed a new kind of fulfilment, she found new opportunities for personal initiatives as a great heiress in her own right or as a woman with a taste for adventure (her brush with the Lusignans in 1168 may briefly have rekindled old flames). Some noble ladies in her position might have resigned themselves to a life of seclusion dwelling on their memories or even, faced with a husband's notorious infidelities, have made the common gesture of taking the veil. But not Eleanor. Although she maintained close links with Fontevrault (her first recorded personal donation to the abbey dates from about this time), she had no wish to douse her undiminished energies in the cloister. If her husband could dispense with her now, she felt that her sons (with the exception of young John, whom Henry kept with him) stood in particular need of her. Equally, she needed them; so she committed herself fully to their cause.

What, then, was she to do? The Young King had escaped his father's clutches in March. By Easter the banners of rebellion were being unfurled in many parts of Henry's domains. Should Eleanor remain in Poitiers, hoping to hold it for her sons, or at least for Richard, as a base for future operations? It would be safer to join the boys, all now at the French court, however painful the memories or embarrassing a flight to her former husband. Her uncle, Raoul de Faye, was perhaps already there. Whatever her reasoning, she at some point decided to quit Poitiers and head secretly for Paris. Of the chroniclers only Gervase of Canterbury, writing at about the end of the century, mentions what followed. Though giving no date or place for the event, he situates it between his accounts of the princes' departure for Paris and the start of open rebellion. The queen, he tells us, had left to follow her sons and was being pursued, by whom is not stated. She then, 'having changed from her woman's clothes, was apprehended and detained in strict custody. For it was said that all these happenings were prepared through her scheming and advice. For she was an extremely astute woman, of noble descent but inconstant [*instabilis*]'.[48] She was soon returned, a prisoner, to her estranged husband. This time, her venturesome spirit had proved her undoing.

Eleanor was to remain in close custody until well after her sixtieth birthday; and one can imagine her frustration as matters of family and state ran their tumultuous course without her being personally able to participate in them by word or deed. But if for many of her subjects she must eventually have faded to a distant memory, she would have remained present in the thoughts and consciences of her immediate kin, like a hidden ember not yet extinguished and capable of being stirred into new life, should the occasion arise. Let us, then, leave her for the moment as a captive of her husband in that summer of 1173, perhaps in Rouen or other of his temporary headquarters. In whatever fortress she was held, she was doubtless kept informed of events in the outside world. These must now be briefly reviewed.

*

On Louis's advice, the Young King secured with lavish promises the allegiance of a large number of barons in England and on the Continent before opening hostilities against his father just after Easter. There were revolts in Aquitaine, Anjou and Brittany. Unrest spread north of the Channel; and the King of Scotland was poised to join young Henry's cause. After a spell of inaction unusual for him, the elder Henry proceeded to wrest the initiative from his rebellious sons who, with Louis and their allies, had achieved some military successes in the Normandy frontier region. A peace conference in September at Gisors having proved abortive, the main action switched to England and its northern borders.

Henry remained in Normandy until July 1174, when he decided to deal personally with the trouble being fomented by the Young King, who was himself planning to cross to England. His father, however, anticipated his move by landing at Southampton, whence he proceeded to do penance at Becket's tomb in Canterbury. This act coincided, some said through divine intervention, with the capture in Northumberland, by loyal barons, of the Scottish king; and before long the remaining rebels in England had been dealt with. Abandoning his own schemes, the Young King joined Louis, who was now besieging Rouen. In August Henry crossed to France and relieved his city, while Louis and the Young King retreated to Capetian territory. By the end of the following month he had contrived a meeting with his three errant sons; and they, however reluctantly, accepted his not ungenerous terms for peace. Their rebellion had run its course. Richard was sent back to Poitou and Geoffrey confirmed in his Breton inheritance, whilst the Young King consented to the provision for his brother John, still in Henry's wardship, of certain estates in England and Normandy.

The young Henry remained in Normandy under his father's wary surveillance until, in May 1175, they crossed the Channel together and made a joint prilgrimage to Saint Thomas's shrine. August saw them both in York, ratifying the harsh terms imposed on William of Scotland by the Treaty of Falaise, whither he had initially been hauled as a captive. That Christmas they spent in Windsor, and the following Easter were joined in Winchester by Richard and Geoffrey. The year 1177 found young Henry and Richard campaigning together in Poitou, while their father, who had earlier announced his intention of crusading in the Holy Land, occupied himself instead in England for most of the year, one item of business being to establish John, with the pope's assent, as 'Lord of Ireland'. That August Henry returned to Normandy, remaining on the Continent until the following July. His sons meanwhile went about their affairs without causing him undue anxiety, although the Young King's increasing preoccupation with tournaments and the more frivolous side of chivalric practice was not to his liking. (Following Church disapproval, Henry maintained throughout his reign a ban on the mounting of tournaments in England.)

In 1179 dramatic events at the Capetian court served as a warning to young Henry of the frailty of the flesh. King Louis had decided that the time was ripe to have his son Philip 'Dieu-Donné', now approaching his fourteenth birthday, crowned as his successor. The ceremony was to take place in Reims on 15 August; and young Henry left England in order to attend. The French party travelled by way of Compiègne; and Prince Philip, with his father's consent, went to hunt in the nearby forest with a few companions, from whom he somehow became separated. Lost and benighted in the vast wilderness, the terrified prince is said by the chroniclers to have wandered for many hours before coming across a peasant, who guided him back to his distraught father. So traumatic was the experience for Philip that he fell seriously ill. Louis, in his anxiety, proceeded not to Reims but to Canterbury, where he was joined by the elder Henry in a vigil at Becket's tomb. Philip's coronation was rearranged for 1 November, when it did indeed take place, although by then the pious Louis had been gravely incapacitated by a stroke. In fact he never recovered but, with his son now governing the kingdom as Philip Augustus, died in the September of the following year.[49]

His accession to the monarchy encouraged the adolescent Philip to flex his political muscles, much to the discomfort of some of his subjects and allies and to the passing concern of the Plantagenets. In 1180 young Henry arrived in England to consult with his father, whereupon both left for Normandy. The elder king returned just over a year later, leaving young Henry, Richard and Geoffrey to campaign successfully on Philip's behalf against the unruly Count of Flanders. Reminded perhaps by Louis's death of his own mortality, the English king solemnly made his will in 1182 before travelling back to the Continent to keep a watchful eye on the situation there. That Christmas he held sumptuous court at Caen with his three older sons.

Early in 1183 trouble erupted between the Young King and Richard, who stormed off to his lands in Poitou. Young Henry, with his father's connivance, aggressively followed his brother south and established himself in Limoges. Alarmed by the ensuing feuding, the elder king himself marched to the Limousin and encamped before Limoges, hoping to lay a restraining hand on young Henry. But the latter, now joined by Geoffrey, prevaricated; and though at one point he vowed to take the cross, he in reality launched a campaign of plunder further south, in the course of which he pillaged the shrine of Rocamadour, even, it is said, filching from it the great sword of the hero Roland. Then suddenly he succumbed to a violent attack of dysentery. Attempting to return to Limoges, he could go no further than the village of Martel. There, realizing that his end was near, he prostrated himself on a bed of ashes and called for the crusader's cloak to be laid upon him, having earlier sent a message to his father. In it he asked that provision be made for his followers and for Margaret his wife; and he begged Henry's forgiveness for his mother Queen Eleanor. William Marshal, who was by his side, took his cross to have it carried to the Holy Land. The date was 11 June 1183. Eleanor, on hearing the news, was reported to have replied that she already knew, having seen in a dream her son wearing not only his earthly crown, but also the bright circlet of immortality.[50]

When Eleanor learned of the premature death of her oldest son (though he was only 28), she was still in captivity, unable to attend his burial in Rouen. What, then, had been her fate since we left her, made over as a prisoner to her husband a decade earlier? For some months she had been held on the Continent, though exactly where has not been divulged by the chroniclers. She reappears for us as she is transported from Normandy by Henry when he crosses to Southampton one stormy July day in 1174. A fellow-captive was the Young King's wife Margaret; but in England they were parted, Eleanor being taken to Wiltshire, probably to the fortress of Old Sarum, now Salisbury, whilst Margaret was sent elsewhere, perhaps together with Alice and Constance, the betrothed of Richard and Geoffrey respectively.

A fellow-countryman, Richard le Poitevin, was to apply his rhetoric to an anguished lament for Eleanor. Where now is the rich living she once enjoyed to the music of flute and drum? Where is her court, where her family? Captive of the king of the North Wind, she languishes, consumed with sorrow. But let her not despair: one day her cries for deliverance will be heard by her sons, and they will free her to return to her native land.[51] Though we know nothing of the conditions of her imprisonment, we may suspect this picture of her sunk deep in despair as being too negative for a woman of her resolve. Her spirit was far from broken.

Evidence for this, if contemporary rumours were well founded, comes late in 1175. The rumours were occasioned by the visit to Henry in Winchester of the papal legate. It was said that the king consulted him there about the possibility of divorce, on condition that Eleanor would retire to spend her declining years harmlessly at Fontevrault. But she would have none of it; so the plan, if plan there was, came to nothing. Even in Salisbury Tower she was not ready to renounce the world, in which her heart still lay, for the cold comfort of the cloister. The 'king of the North Wind' might have her for the moment in his grasp; but her 'eaglets' were still flying on unclipped wings.

Eleanor's confinement in Salisbury may not have been completely unbroken. In 1176 Joanna, the last-born of her daughters, was living in Winchester when she was promised in marriage to King William of Sicily; and later in the year she was escorted from England on the first stage of her journey to her new home. Eleanor, it seems, was herself at Winchester that Michaelmas, having perhaps been allowed to spend some time with the eleven-year-old princess before her nuptial journey. A slight easing of her circumstances at this time may be indicated by an entry in the pipe rolls covering the expense of cloaks and capes of rich material as well as furs and an embroidered coverlet for herself and her servant girl. It would be wrong in any case to think of her as grimly immured in comfortless quarters. Held by one or other of the king's barons, she would, one assumes, have enjoyed some social life in her captivity and not have been entirely excluded from the flourishing secular culture of the 'Twelfth-Century Renaissance'.

It was in 1176 that Rosamond Clifford, 'Fair Rosamond', died, having taken the veil at Godstow. The later legend ascribing her death to foul play by Eleanor can, of course, be discounted. A more likely development is that by now Henry's roving eye had lit on his son Richard's fiancée, Alice of France, who was still living in England. Rumours to this effect circulated widely, to be eagerly seized upon by scandal-mongers such as Gerald of Wales, and even reached the ears of the girl's father King Louis. When in 1191, following Henry's death, Richard after years of prevarication finally refused to marry her, it was on the grounds, supported by witnesses, that she had once provided his father with a son. True or false, Richard's assertion was accepted by Alice's brother, now King Philip, and he was released from his original pledge.[52] Surely Eleanor would not have remained any less aware of such gossip than of her husband's more public enterprises.

So the years of captivity dragged on, with news from the outside world filtering through to her as she waited, probably for the most part at Salisbury, until the tide of events might turn in her favour. Before then, as we saw, there occurred two deaths which could not

[handwritten margin note: mistress Rosamond died]

have left her indifferent. The first, in 1180, was that of her first
doting, though not equally appreciated, husband Louis. The
second was of young Henry, not maybe her favourite son, but dear
to her nevertheless, and endowed with something of her own
spirit. When in 1183 the grave closed over him, for her the gates of
liberty began to open.

*

The Young King's death had led Philip Augustus to put forward a
claim on behalf of the widowed Margaret to certain lands in
England and on the Norman border. Henry rebutted this, asserting that they had come to his son through Eleanor. It was probably
that dispute rather than the Young King's death-bed entreaty that
turned his attention at last to his captive wife. He was in
Normandy at the time; and it was perhaps in the late summer of
1183 that he summoned her from England, his plan being to have
her rights to those dower lands conspicuously asserted by her
visiting them in person.[53] She must have complied with his wishes,
happy no doubt to breathe again the air south of the Channel.
There is no record of her return to England, but her absence is
unlikely to have been prolonged.

By Easter 1184 she was in the care of Ralph Fitz-Stephen, who
received an allowance of £32 14s for her maintenance until
midsummer. Other pipe-roll entries suggest that her household
was now being enlarged and her life-style enhanced. Her movements too seem less constricted. Easter was spent at Thomas
Becket's former residence at Berkhamsted, and she later paid a
visit to Woodstock. June saw her joining in Winchester the exiled
Duke of Saxony and his wife, her daughter Matilda, who was
shortly to give birth; and with them she moved again to Berkhamsted.[54] In November Henry recalled the princes Richard,
Geoffrey and John to England; and, at a court convened for the
election of a new archbishop of Canterbury, Eleanor was able to
meet them at Westminster. It must have been a moving and
fascinating reunion. That Christmas the royal court was held at
Windsor; and although Geoffrey had by then left for Normandy,
Eleanor there enjoyed the company of her children Richard, John
and Matilda as well as the latter's sons and daughters, her own
grandchildren.

Early in 1185 we find her for a while in Winchester. In March John, now eighteen, was knighted by Henry in Windsor before he left to assume his Irish throne. Whether Eleanor was present is uncertain; but a week or so later formal restrictions on her movements were removed at the instigation, it is said, of Baldwin the new archbishop. Not that this made her at all a free agent. She may have recently behaved herself well enough in Henry's eyes to earn her notional freedom; but past experience would not allow him to place in her his complete trust. However, while keeping her on a tight rein, he would soon find a more positive role for her in his political schemes; so her twelve-year enforced isolation from the affairs of state was virtually over, and at the age of sixty-three she was on the threshold of another exciting phase of her life.

In April that year Henry crossed to Normandy. His unruly son Richard, having quarrelled with his brother Geoffrey, was now causing considerable trouble in Poitou, and Henry judged that some restraint was called for. First he summoned Eleanor from England; and she duly arrived, accompanied by her daughter Matilda. Henry then sent word to Richard that he was to join him in Normandy and also surrender to his mother the authority over Aquitaine with which he had been invested in 1170. Grudgingly Richard complied. But the measure turned out to be only temporary; for the duchy was returned to his control some time within the next two years. Early in 1186 Henry confirmed once more to Philip Augustus his intention to see Philip's half-sister Alice eventually married to Richard. Then, having strengthened the garrisons in Aquitaine, he left his son to deal with the troublesome count of Toulouse and in April returned with Eleanor to England.

By August there came news that brought the king fresh worries, for it appeared that Geoffrey was now with Philip in Paris, hatching new plots against him. Whatever agreements Henry reached from time to time with the Capetian, it was clear that the latter's long-term aim was to undermine Plantagenet power on the Continent; and for this purpose he could count on Henry's frequent quarrels with his sons. The old king was well aware of the dangers. Had he not, according to Gerald of Wales, once had his fears expressed in a fresco that had been painted for him in one of the rooms in his palace at Winchester? It depicted a great eagle with wings spread being attacked by its four offspring, three of them wounding it in wings and belly, the fourth tearing at its eyes.[55] Though one of the eaglets was now dead, three still remained to torment him.

However, any moves being planned by Philip and Geoffrey were fated to come to nothing. For on 19 August, while showing his prowess on the tournament field, the young Count of Brittany (he was barely 28) was unhorsed in a mêlée and trampled to death. Eleanor had lost the second of her eaglets. Though her regrets may have been more heartfelt than her husband's there was no chance for her to go to Paris to mourn at his tomb in Notre-Dame. He had left a daughter christened with her own name, and of whom, as the presumed heiress of Brittany, Philip was prompt to demand the wardship. In fact, his claim lost its point when, in the following March, Geoffrey's widow Constance gave birth to his posthumous son, Eleanor's grandson. The infant was fittingly given the name of Arthur, the legendary king so beloved by the Plantagenets.

Eleanor was herself in Winchester for at least part of this time, as was Henry when, in October, his messengers came to Paris, seeking to buy time from Philip. On hearing of Geoffrey's death, he had sent for his beloved John, with whom he spent Christmas at Guildford. His rivalry with Philip continued to smoulder; and in February 1187 he crossed back to Normandy to continue fruitless negotiatons as, together with Richard and John, he prepared for war with the Capetian. Hostilities opened in May, with parts of his armies under the command of his two sons; but these were inconclusive and were followed by an uneasy truce. That was the moment Richard chose to leave his father and head for Paris where, in view of later allegations concerning his sexual proclivities, he opened a suspiciously warm camaraderie with Philip Augustus.

Late that summer the troubles in Europe were overshadowed by news which devastated the whole of Christendom: the Christian armies in the Holy Land had been routed on the plain of Hattin by the Muslim forces of Saladin. By October Jerusalem itself had fallen. Richard's reaction was prompt. Fired perhaps by recollections of his mother's tales of her own experiences on the Second Crusade, he followed her example and took the cross without hesitation or his father's leave. Henry himself, having already been pledged to the struggle for some ten years, was now stirred to action and, together with Philip, donned the crusader's surcoat with its cross. A truce between them was agreed until their return from the expedition, and preparations for its financing went ahead. Meanwhile, Eleanor remained with her memories and reflections in England. Records suggest that she spent a good deal, though not the whole, of her time in Winchester, with all her needs properly provided for. Her role this time was to be that of spectator, not participant. Events, however, were to run an unexpected course.

By early 1188 Henry's relations with Philip had soured once more, with Richard being again at the centre of the brewing storm. Not only had the question of his marriage to Alice remained unresolved, but he also found himself offending the French king by his treatment of the rebellious Raymond, count of Toulouse. When this particular difficulty was smoothed over, Henry suspected complicity between Richard and Philip in the affair. Then to bring matters to a head, Philip in mid-June broke the truce by seizing certain border fortresses. Within a month Henry had left England and, supported now by Richard, engaged the French with some success. A lengthy parley between the two kings ensued. It took place in the now traditional spot, by a great elm tree at Gisors. But this time, when the talks broke down, Philip ordered the symbolic destruction of the famous tree. Hostilities were resumed, punctuated by truces and devious attempts by Richard to use the situation to his own advantage: he at one stage even demanded his immediate marriage to Alice. By the end of the year he had once more deserted his father, done homage to Philip as heir to Henry's lands, and gone off with the Capetian, a further truce having been arranged until January. It is likely that during this troubled year Eleanor had again been placed under strict surveillance in England. Her husband spent a worried Christmas at Saumur in Anjou.

That winter Henry was a sick man. A final bid for peace between the two great houses was made by the papal legate in the name of the Church, but in vain. The following June the French attacked, with Richard in support. Henry was forced to leave his birthplace, Le Mans, with his enemies in hot pursuit. As the loyal William Marshal was covering his retreat, or so we read in his *Life*, he found himself confronted by Richard, helmeted but with no other protection. William spurred towards him. 'By God's legs, marshal!' called Richard, 'Don't kill me – that would be wrong, completely unarmed as I am!' The marshal's reply was terse: 'Oh no. Let the devil kill you, because I won't!' With that he plunged his lance into Richard's horse, bringing him with it to the ground.[56]

Suffering from an old ulcerated wound, Henry passed south by way of Chinon then, with defeat staring him in the face, agreed to meet Philip at Colombières (now Villandry) near Tours. So sick that he had to be supported on his horse, he heard his enemy's terms: he must do homage to Philip Augustus, surrender Alice, have his barons swear fealty to Richard, undertake the crusade with the Capetian, and make various other reparations. To this he agreed; but as he gave Richard the kiss of peace, says Gerald of Wales, he growled: 'God grant that I may not die until I have had my revenge on you!' His prayer was not to be answered. Returning to Chinon, his only personal demand having been that the two sides should exchange lists of their own adherents, the fevered king retired to his room. The roll of his enemies was brought to him; and on it the first name was that of his beloved son John.

John's betrayal

Plate 7 The castle of Chinon, where Henry II died.

When he heard it, runs Gerald's account, he turned his face from the messenger to the wall. 'Now let everything go as it will', he said. 'I care no longer for myself or for anything else in this world.' Next day, 6 July 1189, he died, having uttered his last, anguished words: 'Shame, shame upon a conquered king!' William Marshal had his body carried the few miles to the abbey of Fontevrault for burial. That night Richard came to kneel briefly before his father's bier.[57]

Henry dies

QUEEN MOTHER

On Richard's orders, the marshal made his way to England to report to the queen, perhaps to release her. But on arriving at Winchester he found Eleanor at liberty, 'more at ease than was her wont':[58] the news had travelled faster than the gallant marshal. As the events of that fateful summer were pieced together for her, her emotions must have been strangely mixed. The husband she had once admired and surely loved, but who latterly had been her gaoler, was no more. He had been betrayed at the end by her two surviving sons: Richard her favourite, and John, on whom Henry's own hopes had rested. But she had no time to brood: there was work to be done.

Nor was there time for mourning, even for Eleanor's daughter Matilda who, having left England for the Continent two years earlier, died only a week after her father. With Richard now in Normandy, being invested as its duke and, among other urgent business, settling his outstanding differences with Philip Augustus, England had to be prepared to receive its new king. This Eleanor accomplished with all her old energy and despatch, touring the regions, ensuring the loyalty of the leading barons, and ordering the release of many of her late husband's prisoners in the process. Hardly to be described at the age of sixty-seven as a new broom, she was nevertheless determined that the kingdom should be swept clean for the arrival of her dear son. Richard himself, having assured Philip yet again of his intention of marrying the long-suffering Alice and pledged that he would leave with him on crusade the following Lent, finally landed in England at Portsmouth on 13 August amid great rejoicing. On the same day, his

Plate 8 The seal of Richard Coeur-de-Lion.

brother John disembarked at Dover. There followed a royal
progress by way of Winchester, Salisbury, Marlborough and
Windsor to Westminster, where with great pomp the coronation
took place on 3 September. Of the lords spiritual and temporal
taking part in the ceremony we find the familiar name of William
Marshal, who bore the sceptre with the cross. For Eleanor, queen
mother, it must have been a day of triumph.

Richard
coronation (margin note)

The ensuing weeks saw a flurry of activity from Richard, more
used to dealing with affairs in Aquitaine than in England, where he
had never spent a great deal of time in the past. His main efforts
now were not designed to win the hearts of his leading subjects, as
they were devoted to squeezing as much money as he could from
his already impoverished kingdom for the financing of the coming
crusade. He confirmed with Philip that he would join him at
Vézelay next 1 April in order to leave for Jerusalem, then crossed
to Calais on 12 December, spent Christmas near the Norman
border, and at the end of the year met the French king at
Nonancourt. Eleanor, meanwhile, had not been idle; and at
various times that autumn and winter she turns up in Winchester,
Salisbury, Windsor, Hampshire and Canterbury. She was evidently once more immersing herself wholeheartedly in public
affairs, although she was not to act officially as regent during
Richard's absence.

Early in 1190 Richard visited Poitiers and other of his more
southern lands. Then in mid-March he summoned a council at
Nonancourt, at which Eleanor, recently arrived from England,
and John were present as well as his bride-in-waiting. A record of
the family discussions there and Eleanor's contribution to them
would have made interesting reading. One known result was that
Richard, wary of his throne being usurped in his absence, stipu-
lated that neither John nor his half-brother the bastard Geoffrey,
now prospective archbishop of York and Henry's staunch companion during his last days, was to set foot again in England for three
years. The prohibition of John's return in fact proved to be
short-lived.

A few days later the two kings had a further meeting in Dreux,
where it was decided that their departure for the crusade would
have to be deferred until the beginning of July. Other of the
participants had already left; and the growing impatience in some
quarters is reflected by the fire-breathing troubadour Bertran de

Born, lord of Hautefort in the Dordogne, a fervent admirer of the young king Henry and now a supporter of his new lord Richard. In a poem addressed to Conrad of Montferrat, an early arrival in Palestine, he expresses the frustration of many: 'Lord Conrad, I know two kings who withhold their help from you. Now hear who they are: King Philip is one, for he is suspicious of King Richard, who is suspicious of him in turn. Would that both of them were in Sir Saladin's fetters, for they talk light-heartedly about God, having taken the cross but without doing a thing about going!'[59] Eventually, after spending some time in Chinon, Richard received his pilgrim's scrip and staff in late June, then met Philip in Vézelay on 2 July. By stages they made their way independently south through Italy and on to Sicily, where Richard arrived at Messina on 14 September and Philip two days later.

Meanwhile, Eleanor had not been wasting her time, but had typically been giving thought to the future of her now depleted family. Should the worst happen and Richard fail to return from the Holy Land, the crown of England would be likely to fall into the hands of either John or the bastard Geoffrey; and she viewed neither prospect with any pleasure. Richard himself had young Arthur of Brittany in mind as his successor. To Eleanor, though, it seemed far better that Richard should have a son of his own as incontestable heir to his lands. But if this was to happen, neither he nor she favoured poor fading Alice as the prospective mother: that had long been apparent.

How far she had consulted Richard in the matter is a source of speculation; she had, though, by now decided that Berengaria, the daughter of King Sanchez of Navarre, would make a good wife for her son. She therefore sent for (or some say travelled south to fetch) the princess who, according to contemporaries, was more sensible than she was physically attractive. Too much credence should not be attached to the romantic story that Richard had once paid her homage in his verse while tourneying in her kingdom. What is certain is that by mid-winter the indomitable queen had taken the road to Italy with Berengaria in her company. They travelled by way of the inhospitable Alpine passes, then proceeded steadily down the whole length of the peninsula. For part of the journey they were joined by Philip, the count of Flanders to whom Chrétien de Troyes had dedicated his unfinished *Perceval*, the first Grail story. It may be recalled that

Chrétien's earlier romance which launched the Lancelot and
Guenevere legend had been composed for Eleanor's first-born,
Marie of Champagne. One likes to think of these fellow-travellers
enlivening their wintry journey with conversations that found
room for their mutual literary interests. Philip took ship at Naples;
but Eleanor preferred to continue south as far as Reggio, where
her party was met by Richard and escorted across the straits to
Messina.

It was now the end of March, and the crusade was still not
properly under way. There had been problems in Sicily, mostly
occasioned by the death in 1189 of its king, William, the husband
of Eleanor's daughter Joanna. The couple had remained childless;
and the throne had been usurped by Count Tancred, William's
illegitimate nephew, despite the prior claim of his aunt Constance,
wife of the future German emperor. Richard's first act on his
arrival in Sicily had been to have Joanna released from her
confinement by Tancred, who then attempted to play the two
crusading monarchs off against each other. He finally sided with
the Plantagenet, their alliance being sealed when Richard mooted
the betrothal of his nephew Arthur of Brittany to Tancred's infant
daughter and, a more flamboyant gesture, presented him with no
less a gift than the legendary King Arthur's supposed sword
Excalibur. That trophy, it was claimed, had been discovered at
Glastonbury during excavations initiated by the late King Henry.
The pact infuriated Philip Augustus, who yet again demanded that
Richard marry his half-sister Alice forthwith. It was then that
Richard alleged Alice's seduction by his father as an insuperable
obstacle to the union. With that, Philip conceded defeat, but on
condition that after their return from the Holy Land Richard
would hand over his rejected bride plus an indemnity of ten
thousand marks. With a tact bred of his indignation, the Capetian
then set sail for Palestine from Messina only hours before the
arrival there of Eleanor and Berengaria.

Eleanor was able to enjoy the company of Richard and Joanna,
with whom Berengaria appeared to form a close friendship, for
only three days. During that brief space she would have discussed
affairs in Britain and on the Continent, no doubt expressing her
worries over John's presumptuous behaviour in England in collusion with his half-brother Geoffrey the bastard archbishop elect.
She would surely, too, have nostalgically recalled her other visit to

Sicily forty-two years earlier when she was still a young woman, and in reminiscence travelled again the routes taken by the crusaders whom she followed in those days before they were forbidden the company of women. An exception to that more recent prohibition was now to be made for Berengaria in view of the fact that it was not proper for her marriage to be celebrated during Lent or for Richard to linger further in Sicily. So she was allowed to sail with his fleet in the company of Joanna; and it was actually in Cyprus that on 12 May the wedding took place and she was crowned Queen of England. As for Joanna, five months later Richard, as part of a peace initiative, was to offend her deeply by offering her in marriage to the brother of the arch-infidel Saladin. Her refusal prevented a situation stranger than a common fictional theme of the time, which showed a Christian hero taking a Saracen bride, subject of course to her conversion.

On 2 April, eight days before Richard's own departure, Eleanor bade her farewells to her children and left Messina for Salerno. From there she headed for Rome, where she probably arrived in time for the consecration of the new pope, Celestine III, on Easter Sunday. While in Rome, she took the opportunity of discussing with him certain English arrangements. But she had no wish or reason to prolong her stay. Once she had drawn the funds to meet the expenses of her journey, as the pipe rolls confirm, she made her way back over the Alps and on to Rouen. In Normandy she was well placed to keep her eyes on the English as well as the Continental scene; but what she saw was not greatly to her liking.

*

It is usually claimed that it was at Eleanor's request that Richard, before his departure, reversed his decision to ban John from England. If so, it was an error of judgement on her part. Suffice it to say that John, with the Plantagenet propensity for intrigue and family rift, was soon scheming as though his brother were already as good as dead. Geoffrey too had not been slow to tread English soil again, turning the tables on William Longchamp, the chancellor acting as regent, who had briefly detained him only to be ignominiously banished by John. Such were the events that Eleanor viewed with a wary eye from the other side of the Channel. That Christmas of 1191 she spent at Bonneville-sur-

Touques near the modern Deauville. Her thoughts must often have been with the crusaders in 'Outremer', as the European territories in the east were called. Richard himself was at that time with his army at Latrun to the west of Jerusalem, accompanied by Berengaria, Joanna, and Guy de Lusignan the titular king of Jerusalem.

By then Richard, having made Cyprus secure for the crusaders, had followed Philip to the siege of Acre, which had eventually fallen to the Christians in July. For Philip, who had fallen ill, that was to mark the end of his participation in the entire enterprise: early in August he sailed for home, in bad odour with Richard and fully reciprocating his fellow-king's feelings. Once in France, he demanded the return to his care of the spurned Alice, only to be met with the forthright refusal of Eleanor, who mistrusted his intentions, and not without reason. That was in January 1192; and word soon reached her that John had assembled a fleet and was about to cross the Channel to contrive some mischief with the Capetian. This move too she thwarted by taking ship to England to consult her barons and discreetly undo her son's preparations.

In Palestine Richard had continued to campaign with a mixture of gallantry and savagery, triumph and failure, being in the end unable to wrest Jerusalem from Saladin. In October 1191 he had tried to engineer that pact with his chivalrous foe which was to be sealed by the marriage of Joanna to Safadin, Saladin's brother. Nothing, however, came of it; and by the following September Richard, after himself falling sick, decided to leave the Holy Land. And this he did on 9 October, having arranged a three-year truce and packed Berengaria and Joanna off ahead of him. That was the end of the Third Crusade; and Richard's subsequent misfortunes are well known. A shipwreck followed by an attempt to return incognito to his kingdom by the overland route were his undoing; for he fell into the clutches of the Austrian duke Leopold, cousin of that Henry, no friend of Richard's, who had acceded to the German throne when his father Frederick Barbarossa had drowned on the crusade.

The news of the celebrated Coeur-de-Lion's captivity reached Philip Augustus in Paris at the end of 1192 and was passed to Eleanor a few days later. The English king's value as a hostage escaped nobody's attention. Philip was quick to urge that he be held in close confinement; but though he was moved from stronghold to stronghold, he was not kept incommunicado. It was nevertheless some time before, by dint of sending emissaries to the German lands, his anxious mother was able to discover his whereabouts. In the meantime, emperor and duke had been devising terms for his ransom.

For John, his brother's imprisonment was a chance too good to miss. In the middle of January 1193 he crossed to Normandy to present himself as heir to the duchy before hurrying to his ally in Paris. There he paid homage to Philip Augustus for the Plantagenets' Continental possessions, and even offered to marry poor Alice, still held in Rouen, into the bargain. Then in March he returned to England and apparently set about raising funds on the pretence that they were for Richard's ransom. The next month saw Philip occupying the much-disputed fortress of Gisors and moving against Rouen to secure the equally disputed princess; but finding the gates shut against him, he withdrew to his capital. In England, Eleanor was putting her statecraft to the test by defusing for the time being John's treasonable plans, while securing the coast against any possible invasion.

The emperor had by that time taken over the custody of Richard and obtained his grudging consent to a massive ransom, which included the payment of 100,000 marks and the delivery of two hundred noblemen as a surety. Richard was now in correspondence with his mother; and, as well as expressing his gratitude for her devoted care of the realm and advising on the election of a new archbishop of Canterbury, he begged her to meet the terms of the ransom. Eleanor complied with his wishes by supervising, at a court convened at St Albans in the first week of June 1193, arrangements for milking the required money from an already impoverished kingdom.

Sadly, there is no truth in the story of the discovery of Coeur-de-Lion's place of imprisonment by his faithful troubadour Blondel de Nesle, though a poet of that name did exist. But it does accord with Richard's interest in the art, which he himself practised. Indeed, one of his two surviving songs was composed during his captivity and addressed to his half-sister Marie of Champagne. From the pride heavily overlaid with bitterness one senses that this is no mere poetic exercise:

No captive will ever speak his mind honestly other than with grief; but to console himself he can compose a song. I have many friends, but their gifts are paltry, for which they will feel shame, should I be a prisoner these two winters for lack of my ransom.

My vassals and my barons, English, Normans, Poitevins and Gascons, are well aware that I had no companion so poor that I would leave him in prison for lack of money. I say this not as a rebuke; but I myself am still a prisoner.

Now I know it to be a certain fact that no dead man or captive has friends or relations, when I am abandoned for lack of gold or silver. I feel great concern for myself, but still more for my people, since after my death they will be heaped with reproach, should I remain a prisoner for long.

It is no wonder I am heart-broken, when my overlord keeps my land in torment. Should he now remember the joint oath we both took, I am quite sure I should not long be a prisoner in here.

Those young knights of Anjou and Touraine who now enjoy both wealth and health know well of my plight far from them in a stranger's hands. They used to love me dearly, but now not a jot. The plains stand empty of splendid arms now that I am a prisoner.

Those companions of mine whom I used to love and still do, those from Caen and the Perche – say, my song, that they are fickle, though I was never false or half-hearted towards them. If they turn against me, they are despicable, so long as I am a prisoner.

Countess, my sister, may He to whom I cry and for whose sake I am a prisoner save and preserve your matchless worth.

I do not refer to the lady of Chartres, Louis's mother.[60]

There exist three eloquent letters said to have been addressed by Eleanor to the pope, pleading with him for his help in securing Richard's release and styling herself 'Eleanor, by the wrath of God Queen of England'. Although the attribution is probably false and we may suspect the plaintive style to be untypical of her, one is struck by this pithy assessment of her position presumably by one of her contemporaries. In reality, she not only busied herself with collecting the ransom, but late in December sailed with the ships bearing it to Germany: the mother had come not to lament her son's fate, but to reclaim him. On 6 January 1194 she is found celebrating the Epiphany at Cologne; and by the 17th, the date set for Richard's release, she had arrived at Speyer with the funds for the ransom.

Her worries, though, were still not at an end. On learning the terms for the release, Philip had written to John bidding him beware, for now 'the devil is loose'. Eleanor's miscreant son heeded the message, and by about the end of July he was back in France framing with the Capetian a counter-bid for the person of his brother. To the emperor Henry they proposed either that he accept their more lucrative offer or that he hold Richard in detention for a further nine months. But the captive had himself got wind of their schemings; and furthermore he had involved himself in certain of Henry's own affairs and thus earned himself some gratitude in imperial circles. The upshot was that on 2 February Henry summoned his chief lords to a council at Mainz, at which Richard and Eleanor were present as well as representatives of Philip and John. Its purpose was finally to determine the captive's fate; and now such services as Richard had rendered the Germans stood him in good stead, for the solution sought by the two machinators was rejected. There was, however, a price demanded beyond the ransom money, namely that Richard was to do homage to Henry for all his lands. This requirement was then limited, apparently through Eleanor's intervention, to his holding just the kingdom of England as the emperor's vassal. So the homage was duly paid; and two days later Richard was released 'into the hands of his mother', as a chronicler put it, after a captivity of some thirteen and a half months.

At long last Coeur-de-Lion was able to complete his eventful return from the crusade. With Eleanor he travelled by way of Cologne, Louvain, Brussels and Antwerp, finally crossing to Sandwich and thence, having paid a devotional visit to Becket's shrine at Canterbury, to London and a joyous welcome from his subjects. It was now mid-March; and at once they set off on a tour of the Midlands, where John's supporters held some fortresses, notably Nottingham. These soon surrendered; and the royal party headed south again for Winchester where, on 17 April, Richard was ceremonially crowned for the second time. A week later the king and his mother moved on to Portsmouth, from where they dealt with sundry affairs of state. Then, in mid-May, they embarked for Barfleur with the purpose of countering the activities of Philip and John in Normandy and bringing the whole duchy back under their rightful control. Neither of them was to see England again.

Their immediate task proved easier than they might have anticipated since, having visited Bayeux and Caen and come thence to Lisieux, they were there confronted one evening by John, now full of contrition and good intentions. Perhaps Eleanor had smoothed the path to reconciliation. In any case, the chroniclers assure us that Richard was prompt to pardon his younger brother (who was then an immature 27) with all the leniency normally shown to a child who has fallen in with bad company. So now the queen mother had the last of her eaglets back under her wing.

Richard's accommodation with his brother did not spell the end of his troubles with Philip, against whom he was soon actively campaigning. For Eleanor, though, it restored the semblance of family harmony; and, finding perhaps her reserves of energy diminishing with the years, she took the opportunity to seek at least a semi-retirement from the hurly-burly of public affairs. She must always have thought of Fontevrault as a sanctuary to which she could retreat, not necessarily for good, at a time of her own choosing. Built on her ancestral lands, it had been the refuge of both wives of her reprobate grandfather, the place where John her last-born had been schooled, and the final resting-place of her second husband, whose aunt Matilda had been its third abbess, and whose mother may possibly have taken the veil there. Her family had liberally endowed the abbey, and we have records of personal donations by Eleanor over the previous decade and a half. It is not surprising, then, that she should choose to withdraw there, not to hide behind a veil, but to keep an eye on Plantagenet fortunes with the support of a modest household. For such alert inactivity she was well placed in Fontevrault, on the border of Poitou and Anjou and close to the royal stronghold and treasury of Chinon.

By late July 1194 Richard had thwarted Philip Augustus' intrusions into Normandy, dealt with his supporters in Poitou and the south and agreed with him a truce to last until 1 November

Plate 9 Effigy of Henry II at Fontevrault.

1195. Under no illusions, however, about the durability of such a settlement, he pursued diplomatic manoeuvrings to strengthen his own position. Moreover, with an eye to future campaigns, he encouraged the practice of arms among his nobility and lifted his father's prohibition on the holding of tournaments in England. His precautions were fully justified, because for the rest of his life the story of his relations with the Capetian was to be one of bouts of open warfare punctuated by hopeful truces and abortive treaties: neither king's ambitions could be reconciled with those of his rival.

Little is heard of Eleanor during this period. There is, for instance, no record of her having joined her son at his Christmas courts, held successively at Rouen, Poitiers, Bur-le-Roi (unidentified), Rouen again and Domfront. We can, though, assume that she maintained contact with Richard as well as with John, now found acting in his support, and remained as committed as ever to the broad Plantagenet cause as she viewed its fortunes from the sideline. Certain family matters would have roused her particular interest. In 1195 the question of the long-neglected Queen Berengaria came to the fore. Whatever the truth of the report that Richard's reconciliation with her followed a hermit's warning to him to abstain from homosexual practices and a sudden illness that ensued, it does seem that the royal couple resumed cohabitation, at least for a time, that April. But if the aim was to produce an heir, Berengaria might just as well have stayed in her dower lands in Maine; and any hopes Eleanor may have entertained for a grandson to be schooled for succession to the throne remained unfulfilled.

By August, on the occasion of one of the ultimately fruitless parleys between Richard and Philip, other matrimonial schemes of potential interest to Eleanor were aired. One of them concerned her son's one-time betrothed, the languishing Alice, now in her mid-thirties, whose value even as a bargaining chip was fast eroding. Richard decided to hand her back at last to her brother, so that she might finally be disposed of in marriage to one of his vassals. One imagines Eleanor treating this news with an amused shrug while being more concerned at the further proposal that her namesake and granddaughter, the sister of Arthur of Brittany, should be wed to Philip's son and heir Louis. Nothing, however, was to come of that. On the other hand. Eleanor would surely have derived satisfaction from the marriage the next year, 1196, of her daughter Joanna, the widowed Queen of Sicily, to Raymond VI of Toulouse; for that long-disputed inheritance of hers was brought back into the family by the union, consecrated at Rouen, which was blessed the following summer by the birth of a son and heir. So here was another grandchild for the ageing queen. But if that gave her pleasure, it was countered by the pain occasioned in 1198 by the death of her other well-loved daughter Marie of Champagne, who had in the past matched her in the eager patronage of poets.

Another family misfortune, a harbinger of later disaster, involved her grandson Arthur, the child count of Brittany and Richard's designated successor. In April 1196 Richard had demanded the wardship of the boy, then in his tenth year, from the Bretons. When they proved recalcitrant, he marched against them, but only to find that Arthur had been spirited away by his tutor and delivered to the Capetian court in Paris, there to be brought up with Philip's son Louis: another pawn had been captured by the Frenchman in his ruthless game.

A greater grief, however, was in store for Eleanor. In March 1199, while the possibility of a more enduring treaty with Philip hung in the balance, Richard left his fortress of Chinon to besiege the small castle of Châlus south-west of Limoges in the context of a squabble with the count of Poitiers. While inspecting its fortifications with Mercadier, the leader of his mercenaries, he was struck in the shoulder by a bolt from a crossbow. The wound did not heal, but after a few days turned gangrenous. Realizing the mortal nature of his injury, the king sent a messenger not to his wife, but to his dear mother in Fontevrault. On the evening of 6 April, having named John as his heir and successor, he died at Châlus with Eleanor at his side. Heading back north with her favourite son's remains, she attended five days later on Palm Sunday his solemn burial within the walls of Fontevrault. His heart, it is said, was taken for interment in Rouen cathedral. At the age of 77, the dowager queen was left with a sole surviving son, the headstrong, unreliable John, whose succession had still to be assured.

*

There was no question of her dwelling long on the past and turning her back on this new crisis in the Plantagenet fortunes. For

Plate 10 Effigies of Eleanor and Richard at Fontevrault.

some time there had been in legal as well as political circles a debate as to who should assume the crown on Richard's death; and this is mirrored in an exchange which took place, according to William Marshal's biographer, when, late on the eve of the burial, the news reached Rouen where the marshal was staying. He rushed to consult the Archbishop of Canterbury, who happened to be lodged nearby. The latter, despairing at the passing of true prowess, feared that the kingdom would quickly fall prey to the French unless they were prompt to choose a successor. He was sure it should be Arthur. But the marshal disagreed: not only was Arthur under bad influence and of a stubborn, arrogant character – he was also anti-English. So his vote was for John, on the grounds that his claim as the deceased's younger brother was stronger than that of a dead brother's son. 'So be it!' replied the archbishop. 'But I warrant that you will never repent any deed of yours so much.'[61] A similar debate may well have taken place in Eleanor's private thoughts. If so, she evidently came to the same conclusion as the marshal.

Ironically, John was in Brittany visiting Arthur at the time of his brother's death, possibly up to no good. Recalled to Chinon and Fontevrault, he arrived too late for the obsequies, but spent some days there with Eleanor, savouring the prospect of kingship, plans for his accession being now in train. At this time Arthur, a spirited twelve-year-old, was living under the tutelage of his re-married mother Constance and harbouring ambitions that had been nurtured at the Capetian court. Mother and son wasted no time in pressing his claim; and they left Brittany with an army to occupy Angers and then Le Mans where Philip, who had also made his move, accepted the boy's homage for Anjou, Maine and Touraine. John, meanwhile, finding himself outmanoeuvred, had withdrawn to Rouen, there to be proclaimed Duke of Normandy on 25 April. It was left to his venerable mother to take more positive steps with the help of Richard's stalwart captain Mercadier, whose troops were summoned from Châlus. Captain and queen together marched against Angers, which they seized with many prisoners. Though John now took Le Mans, the young pretender had by then rejoined Philip in Tours and was soon safely in Paris once again. John promptly sailed for England and a hurried coronation at Westminster on 25 May before returning to Norman soil.

Arthur of ...

Eleanor, understandably enough, was not present at the ceremony; but she was by no means idle. There remained the unfinished business of the unrest in the south on which Richard had been engaged when he met his end at Châlus. Avoiding that particular trouble-spot, she was determined to make one further tour of her domains as Duchess of Aquitaine; for she had no intention during her lifetime of seeing her personal lands fall prey to Arthur or be prematurely claimed by her last-born. So from late April until mid-July she made her stately progress, apparently amid popular enthusiasm, by way of Poitiers and Bordeaux throughout the whole length of her territories, covering, it has been estimated, over a thousand miles. Visiting one monastery near Bordeaux, she renewed its privileges in a document tinged with nostalgia:

Eleanor, by the grace of God, Queen of England, Duchess of Normandy and Guienne [Aquitaine], Countess of Anjou, to the archbishops, bishops, abbés, salutation. The late King Henry, our very dear husband of gracious memory, and we ourselves long ago took the monastery of the Grande-Sauve under our special protection. But that Henry, as well as our son Richard, who succeeded him, having both died, and God having left us still in the world, we have been obliged, in order to provide for the needs of our people and the welfare of our lands, to visit Gascony. We have been brought in the course of our journey to this monastery.[62]

And she proceeded to confirm the earlier privileges.

One unfortunate necessity required by feudal custom was the act of homage by which she would be maintained in her own titles; and that had to be performed to the French crown in the person of Philip Augustus, the man she had so much cause to detest and mistrust, despite their family relationship. We are left to imagine with what icy dignity she would have gone through the ritual at Philip's court in Tours. Then, in September, she formally acknowledged John as heir to her own duchy.

During that month she visited John in Rouen, feeling as in former days that she could contribute from her own experience to the strategies of state. Perhaps it would be possible after all to achieve an alliance with the house of Capet such as would limit the damage done by their conflicting interests. Then fortune dealt her another harsh blow. Her daughter Joanna had met her on her recent tour of her lands with tales of the indifference of her husband Raymond and of treacherous behaviour towards her of his knights. Now here she was on her mother's doorstep, pregnant once more as well as sick, and seeking not merely comfort and refuge but also, quite irregularly in her condition, entry into the order at Fontevrault. Arrangements were hastily made, but none too soon, because a day or two after taking her vows she died, shortly before the delivery of a son who himself survived only long enough to be baptized. Eleanor's second daughter Alice of Blois having died earlier and, more recently, Marie the first of her brood, she had now lost all but two of her children: her namesake the Queen of Castile, and John last of the 'eaglets'.

The ebb and flow of Plantagenet-Capetian relations continued and, in January 1200, produced an arrangement which was to lead in May to the treaty of Le Goulet. Among its terms were the acceptance of John as Richard's heir by Philip, to whom he then did homage for his Continental lands, and the consequent recognition of Arthur as John's vassal. The marriage was also agreed between Blanche of Castile, Eleanor's granddaughter and John's niece, and Philip's son Louis, although both were still young children. So in anticipation of the treaty's ratification, Blanche was to be fetched from Castile. And who should perform this quite arduous mid-winter mission? Despite the frailty of her years, the indomitable Eleanor was her son's choice; and soon she was heading once more for Poitiers and Bordeaux on her road to Spain.

She had reckoned without the volatile Lusignans, whose domains lay on her route. Despite their improved relations with Richard at the time of the crusade, they had never accepted Plantagenet lordship over the county of La Marche to the east of their chief stronghold. The present lord of Lusignan, Hugh 'le Brun', now sought, according to some accounts, to bring the issue to a head by intercepting Eleanor, taking her to his castle, and then allowing her to proceed only after she had surrendered the county to him. Having extricated herself, and not for the first time, from Lusignan hands, she was able to complete her journey to Castile.

Once more she had passed through the lands of her youth and no doubt heard again the voices of the troubadours who were still charming the southern lords and ladies: poet-musicians like Peire Vidal who in his verse had mentioned her own daughter keeping her husband the king elegant company in his Castilian court, who had sung the praises of this gracious Spanish society and had elsewhere poured scorn on Philip for having quit the crusade, whereas Richard languished in captivity.[63] What memories must have enlivened this journey, for her almost a pilgrimage; and what tales she must have poured into the ears of her young charge on their more leisurely way north! Almost a lifetime ago she too had travelled these roads as bride for a Capetian prince, though her marriage enjoyed less success than that of Blanche, who was to mother a future saint: King Louis IX.

They broke their journey to spend the Easter celebrations at Bordeaux, where an unfortunate incident occurred, as is reported by Roger of Hoveden. The reliable Mercadier having joined them there, he was killed in the city by some Gascon underling. Roger goes on to say that 'wearied by her age and the exertions of the long journey, Queen Eleanor betook herself to the abbey of Fontevrault and there remained'. The archbishop of Bordeaux took charge of Blanche and proceeded with her to Normandy. There she was handed over to her uncle and, on 23 May, married to Louis on the French border, Philip's own kingdom being at the time under a papal interdict because of some marital transgression of his own. No sooner had Philip escorted the bridal pair into France than Arthur of Brittany arrived to do homage to John, before himself rejoining the Capetian as his ward.[64] Not long afterwards a chronicler speaks of a severe depression which had afflicted young Blanche: presumably a bout of home-sickness. In the absence of her grandmother's sympathetic attention, it was left to a visiting bishop to put her in better spirits.[65]

In Fontevrault Eleanor found a new preoccupation, namely with John's personal conjugal problems and their consequences. In 1176 he had been betrothed to his second cousin Isabelle of Gloucester, whom he had married in 1189 despite a degree of consanguinity which would normally have called for a papal dispensation. In the event, the marriage seems virtually to have lapsed, with Isabelle taking no part in his coronation; and John now had it declared void, with an eye to finding some more advantageous replacement. In the course of a progress through his southern lands during the summer of 1200, his eye lit on the twelve-year-old daughter of Count Aymer of Angoulême, another Isabelle or Isabella as she is generally known. Unfortunately, though, she was already betrothed to Hugh le Brun, that Lusignan with whom Eleanor had been forced to do a deal over La Marche. In a confusion of passion and politics and with her father's connivance, John married the girl on his road home, whisked her off to England, and on 8 October had her crowned as his queen in Westminster Abbey.

We can only guess at Eleanor's reaction to this marital coup and wonder whether she was consulted at any stage. The couple may well have called on her at Fontevrault as they headed by way of Chinon for the Channel ports. The fact that she dowered Isabella with the cities of Niort and Saintes shows at least her acceptance of the situation;[66] but she still had wit enough to appreciate the dangers of the snub to her troublesome Lusignan vassals. The following spring, with John still travelling about his English lands, she got wind of trouble in Poitou and sought to defuse it by enlisting the support of a kinsman who had earlier been alienated by her son. She wrote to John of her move: 'I want to tell you, my very dear son, that I summoned our cousin Amaury of Thouars to visit me during my illness and the pleasure of his visit did me good, for he alone of your Poitevin barons has wrought us no injury nor seized unjustly any of your lands.' She goes on to say that Amaury has pledged John his support.[67] We have no other information about the illness she mentions.

Despite Eleanor's warnings, it was June 1201 before John thought fit to return from England. Finding Philip on this occasion well disposed and prepared to mediate with the Lusignans, he adopted a policy of prevarication that won him no friends. Then Philip, once he had sorted out with the pope his own matrimonial problems, decided the time was ripe to bring the Plantagenets to heel once and for all. On the pretext that John, as his vassal, had failed to obey a summons to his judicial court, in late April 1202 he declared his fiefs of Aquitaine, Poitou and Anjou to be forfeit. Further, he proceeded to knight the fifteen-year-old Arthur, to whom he betrothed his infant daughter; and he followed this by receiving Arthur's homage not only for Brittany but also for all John's Continental lands except Normandy. Against that duchy he now threw his army.

Eleanor's worst fears had been realized. By being more of an opportunistic adventurer than a statesman, the last of her sons had brought the whole Plantagenet empire into jeopardy. Even at the age of eighty she could not watch passively from what she must have thought of as her final retreat. Late in July she left the seclusion of Fontevrault with a small escort and headed cautiously for her ancestral home of Poitiers. One of her halts was at Mirebeau, a stronghold near the border of Anjou and Poitou. Her presence there was discovered by Arthur with his French force operating with the Lusignans and their rebel Poitevins. Doubtless seeing in her person a hostage of rare value, they were soon in possession of the walled town, while Eleanor was compelled to find refuge with her armed guards in the castle itself. This was not immediately stormed. Accounts vary over the details of what followed; but it seems that the attackers then bivouacked in the town, blocking up all but one of its gates. The outer defences of the castle may have been breached, so that Eleanor found herself trapped in the keep. If one anonymous chronicler is to be believed, her spirit remained unbroken:

> Arthur managed to speak to his grandmother, demanding that she evacuate the castle with all her possessions and then go peaceably wherever she wished; for he wanted to show nothing but honour to her person. The queen replied that she would not leave it; but if he behaved as a courtly gentleman, he would quit this place; for he would find plenty of castles to attack other than the one she was in. She was, moreover, amazed that he and the Poitevins, who should be her liegemen, would besiege a castle knowing her to be in it.[68]

Some eighty miles away in the vicinity of Le Mans, John received from his mother an appeal for help which had been smuggled out of Mirebeau. A forced march with part of his army brought him there surprisingly quickly by the night of 31 July; and in the early morning they attacked. Our chronicler continues:

> When those on watch saw them coming they raised the alarm: 'To arms, to arms!' Then the Poitevins ran to arm themselves. Geoffrey of Lusignan was sitting down to eat. This excellent knight, who had many times shown his prowess on this side of the sea and beyond, was waiting for a dish of pigeons. On being informed that a large force had been sighted approaching, probably John's men it was thought, and that he had better leave his meal and arm, he swore by

God's head that he would never get up before he had eaten his pigeons.[69]

His delay allowed John's troops to burst into the town before the remaining gate could be closed. There was a sharp encounter during which Hugh le Brun was unhorsed and John himself maimed another knight; but soon the rebels were overcome and all their leaders, including Arthur, were captured. Now Eleanor could leave her refuge; and John was able to send a triumphant dispatch to his English barons, whilst his mother completed her journey to Poitiers. Philip eventually withdrew to Paris to lick his wounds. As for Arthur, he was led off as a captive and shut away in a dungeon at Falaise.

Arthur's subsequent fate is one of history's darker mysteries. John had promised the noble who led his assault on Mirebeau that he would not take any vengeance on the youth. According to one chronicler he indeed offered him peace and prosperity should he abandon his Capetian alliance; but Arthur treated these overtures with scorn. Others give grimmer reports: that his uncle ordered his mutilation or ultimately, after Arthur had been transferred in the spring of 1203 to John's tower in Rouen, that the king in a drunken fit and 'possessed by the devil' killed him with his own hands and disposed of the body in the Seine.[70] On 16 April John sent from Falaise to Poitou a letter bearing greetings to his mother, the archbishop of Bordeaux, the seneschals of Poitou, Gascony and Anjou, and other nobles presumably also at the court. It contains the following cryptic message:

We send to you brother John of Valernt, who has seen what is going forward with us, and who will be able to apprise you of our situation. Put faith in him respecting those things whereof he will inform you. Nevertheless, the grace of God is even more with us than he can tell you; and concerning the mission which we have made to you, rely upon what the same John shall tell you thereof.[71]

It has been conjectured that the information fit only for oral transmission was the news of Arthur's liquidation. Be that as it may, the Count of Brittany had vanished from the face of the earth.

John's triumph at Mirebeau did not point to the shape of things to come. Retiring to Normandy, he let the French and their allies regroup their forces and again take the initiative. By the end of 1203 he was back in England with his Continental possessions crumbling. Was it mere coincidence that the Plantagenet fortunes and the old queen's life were ebbing away together? A decade earlier Eleanor might have brought her experience and wisdom into play to instil a little more statecraft into her son. But in her retreat in Poitiers her physical and mental energies alike were failing fast. Communication with John in Rouen was by no means secure at this time; and we have no means of knowing how closely she was kept in touch with the general situation or whether she had expressed any views or tried to bring influence to bear regarding John's treatment of Arthur. Did she even care any more?

Plate 11 Effigy of John in Worcester Cathedral.

Her favourite son, Richard, had built the greatest of Plantagenet castles on his Norman border, Château Gaillard, which he boasted would prove impregnable to any Capetian assault. Early in March 1204 it fell to Philip's siege. It was as if fate was speaking in symbols. Within the month, on 1 April, Queen Eleanor's seemingly unconquerable spirit submitted to death. One chronicler says that she ended her days in Poitiers, another that she was back in Fontevrault, having finally joined the community there. That is the impression given by her glowing entry in the necrology of that abbey, her final resting-place. There at least she was remembered as a paragon among women 'who illuminated the world with the brilliance of her royal progeny. She graced the nobility of her birth with the honesty of her life, enriched it with her moral excellence, adorned it with the flowers of her virtues and, by her renown for unmatched goodness, surpassed almost all the queens of this world.'[72]

One takes with a grain of salt so shining a tribute by the abbey to its benefactress. Posterity has been more equivocal. Even in her lifetime Richard of Devizes followed a passage of fulsome praise with a hint that she had not always been above blame. He speaks first of 'Queen Eleanor, an incomparable woman, beautiful yet virtuous, powerful yet gentle, humble yet keen-witted, qualities which are most rarely found in a woman . . . still tireless in all labours, at whose ability her age might marvel'. But then he slipped in a word of caution behind his hand: 'Many know what I would that none of us knew. This same queen, during the time of her first husband, was at Jerusalem. Let no one say any more about it; I too know it well. Keep silent!'[73] Discretion or sly innuendo? Others have been less tight-lipped with their gossip.

3

Legend

Historical truth in the Middle Ages was a perishable commodity, apt to degenerate with time. Its recording was largely in the hands of churchmen, who were not above adapting it to their own code of values, slanting it perhaps to the advantage of their own community or to the detriment of a rival cause, and often with the intention of courting the favour of a patron. Such considerations apart, the facts of Eleanor's multifarious activities, wide-ranging in space as well as time, readily lent themselves to honest misinterpretation if not malicious distortion. Not only had she spent her long life caught in countless currents of political intrigue which the best informed of chroniclers would find it hard to chart; but she was also a woman and therefore, in clerical eyes and almost by definition, unreliable, fickle, deceitful and in some degree tainted with Eve's first sin. Her very nature made her motives, for them, open to suspicion. In any case, the chroniclers were only exceptionally witnesses to the events they set down, even when they happened in their own day and their own land. They gleaned most of their information from reliable eye-witnesses at best, but more often filtered through a series of intermediaries. They had no reference libraries to check their facts, but were often content to pillage from each other, introducing such variations into their accounts as style or purpose suggested. So they frequently relied on hearsay; and the more colourful the story the better for their own glossing or elaboration. Fictions, then, were blended with facts by a natural process; and legends grew as readily as an oak from an acorn. So it was with Eleanor; and in her case the process is well illustrated by that episode in the Holy Land to which Richard of Devizes made his guarded reference.[1]

ELEANOR AT ANTIOCH

We may start with John of Salisbury who, from his post at the Papal Curia as the events unfolded, was in a good position to hear some authentic details, although he did not set them down in his *Historia Pontificalis* until the 1160s. He tells how Louis arrived in Antioch and was nobly entertained by Prince Raymond.

> He was as it happened the queen's uncle, and owed the king loyalty, affection and respect for many reasons. But whilst they remained there to console, heal and revive the survivors from the wreck of the army, the attentions paid by the prince to the queen, and his constant, indeed almost continuous, conversation with her, aroused the king's suspicions. These were greatly strengthened when the queen wished to remain behind, although the king was preparing to leave, and the prince made every effort to keep her, if the king would give his consent. And when the king made haste to tear her away, she mentioned their kinship, saying it was not lawful for them to remain together as man and wife, since they were related in the fourth and fifth degrees. Even before their departure a rumour to that effect had been heard in France, where the late Bartholomew bishop of Laon had calculated the degree of kinship; but it was not certain whether the reckoning was true or false. At this the king was deeply moved; and although he loved the queen almost beyond reason he consented to divorce her if his counsellors and the French nobility would allow it. There was one knight among the king's secretaries, called Terricus Gualerancius [Thierry Galeran], a eunuch whom the queen had always hated and mocked, but who was faithful and had the king's ear like his father's before him. He boldly persuaded the king not to suffer her to dally longer at Antioch, both because 'guilt under friendship's guise could lie concealed' [Ovid, Heroides, iv.138], and because it would be a lasting shame to the kingdom of the Franks if in addition to all the other disasters it was reported that the king had been deserted by his wife, or robbed of her. So he argued, either because he hated the queen or because he really believed it, moved perchance by widespread rumour. In consequence, she was torn away and forced to leave for Jerusalem with the king; and, their mutual anger growing greater, the wound remained, hide it as best they might.[2]

The chronicler, then, seems to have kept an open mind. Someone who may have shared Thierry Galeran's suspicions was the Gascon troubadour Cercamon. Little is known of his life, though he wrote a lament on the death of Eleanor's father and refers elsewhere to her marriage to Louis. It has been suggested that in one of his songs, possibly composed in the Holy Land, he alludes to her supposed adultery in Antioch when he inveighs against the woman who lies with more than one man: 'Better for her never to have been born than to have committed the fault that will be talked about from here to Poitou.'[3]

William, archbishop of Tyre, who himself lived in the East until his death in 1185, had no doubts as to Eleanor's guilt. He tells of Raymond's hope of expanding his principality and says that he counted greatly 'on the interest of the queen with the lord king'. In the face of Louis's determination to continue on to Jerusalem, he felt frustrated and openly plotted against him.

> He resolved also to deprive him of his wife, either by force or by secret intrigue. The queen readily assented to this design, for she was a foolish woman. Her conduct before and after this time showed her to be, as we have said, far from circumspect. Contrary to her royal dignity, she disregarded her marriage vows and was unfaithful to her husband.[4]

A little later Gervase of Canterbury, who mentions matters best left unspoken, and Gerald of Wales echo the presumed scandal;[5] and we have noted Richard of Devizes' provocative discretion.

It was left to an anonymous minstrel from Reims, writing in about 1260, to throw all caution to the winds in his collection of historical anecdotes. Louis's barons, he says, agreed that he should be married; 'and they gave him the duchess Eleanor, a very wicked woman, who held Maine, Anjou, Poitou, Limoges and Touraine: fully three times as much land as the king'. Having decided to go crusading, Louis put to sea with a great company; and after a month's voyage he arrived at Tyre.

> Seeing his weakness and ignorance, Saladin challenged him to battle several times, but without the king being willing to engage. When Queen Eleanor observed how negative the king was and heard of the goodness, prowess, intelligence and generosity of Saladin, she fell madly in love with him. Then, through an interpreter of hers, she sent him greetings and the assurance that, if he could manage to abduct her, she would take him as her husband

and renounce her faith. When Saladin learned this from the letter passed to him by the interpreter, he was delighted, for he was well aware that this was the noblest and richest lady in Christendom. So he had a galley equipped and set out from Ascalon, where he was, to go to Tyre with the interpreter; and they arrived at Tyre shortly before midnight.

Then the interpreter went up by a small concealed entrance into the room of the queen, who was expecting him. 'What news?' she asked when she saw him. 'My lady,' he said, 'the galley is here all ready and waiting for you. Hurry now so we're not spotted!' – 'Well done, by my faith!' said the queen. Then she fetched two maidens and two chests crammed with gold and silver, which she wanted to have taken into the galley. One of the girls then realized what was happening. Leaving the room as quietly as she could, she came to the bed of the sleeping king and wakened him with the words: 'There's trouble brewing, sire! My lady's wanting to go to Saladin in Ascalon, and the galley's waiting for her in the harbour. Make haste, sire, in God's name!' On hearing her, the king jumped up, dressed and got ready, then had his household arm and went to the harbour. There he found the queen with one foot already in the galley. Seizing her by the hand, he led her back to her room. And the king's company captured the galley and those in it; for they were so taken by surprise that they were unable to defend themselves.

The king asked the queen why she wanted to do that. 'On account of your cowardice, in God's name,' replied the queen, 'for you're not worth a rotten apple! And I've heard such good reports of Saladin that I love him better than you; so you can be quite sure that you'll never get any satisfaction from holding on to me.' At that the king left her and had her well guarded. Then he decided to return to France, as he was running short of money and achieving nothing but shame where he was.

So he put to sea again with the queen and returned to France. Then he took all his barons' advice on what he should do with the queen, telling them how she had behaved. 'Truly,' said the barons, 'the best advice we could give you is to let her go; for she's a devil, and if you keep her much longer we're afraid she'll have you murdered. Above all, you've had no child by her.' The king acted like a fool and took this advice: he would have done better to have her walled up, so he would have had her great land all his life, and the disasters of which you are about to hear would not have happened.

So the king sent Queen Eleanor back to her country. Then she immediately sent for King Henry of England (the man who had Saint Thomas of Canterbury killed). And he gladly came and married her, paying the king homage for the land he was acquiring, which was vast and rich. He then took the queen off to England and kept her until he had had three sons by her. The first of them was Henry Curtmantle, a worthy man and fine knight; and the second was called Richard, who was valiant, bold, generous and chivalrous; and the third was named John, who was wicked, disloyal, and did not believe in God.[6]

In Eleanor's progressive vilification regarding her relationship with her uncle, we have seen her possibly tactless behaviour the subject perhaps of general rumour followed by spiteful hints, then accepted as a guilty liaison, and finally turned into a poisonous brew of half-remembered history laced with lust and treason. Poor Eleanor! Within the lifetime of some of her erstwhile subjects, she was portrayed as a faithless harlot and an apostate to boot. Let us hope that the minstrel's tale never reached the ears of the good nuns of Fontevrault!

THE QUEEN AND THE CHRONICLERS

In the Holy Land scandal, then, we have a clear illustration of the way in which Eleanor attracted legend to herself like a magnet: some possibly innocent activity giving rise to whispered rumours which would soon congeal into hard certainty, itself prompting fictional embellishment until any truth remained only as a distant echo. And such disfigurement of historical fact was inevitably accompanied by the misinterpretation of motives and hence by general character distortion. As a result, we cannot turn with any confidence to Eleanor's contemporaries for a reliable picture of her psychological make-up any more than for a physical portrait.

For this we should not heap too much blame on the chroniclers. We have seen some of the constraints under which they laboured in ascertaining the facts of Eleanor's activities, quite apart from the motivation behind them. It would therefore be vain to turn to them for any coherent insight into her personality. For one thing she was not at the focus of their attention to the same extent as were her husbands, or sons, or even an illustrious subject like Becket. She was not favoured with a dedicated biographer, some familiar clerk whose regular contact with her would have allowed close observation over a long period. The twelfth-century chroniclers mainly caught her only out of the corner of their eyes as they tracked down their bigger game. For them too she possessed a degree of remoteness. No stay-at-home, she would for any relatively static observer often have been 'elsewhere' for long periods rather than readily accessible for his scrutiny: in fact her lengthiest unbroken stay in any one country, her childhood excepted, was during her captivity in England; but then she was by necessity largely out of the public eye. An additional source of Eleanor's remoteness for contemporary chroniclers was the fact that she was a foreigner to all those who hailed from the north, whether from England or even the French or Norman domains; and along with her southern tongue, her native temperament and cultural background would not have made her character any easier for them to read. Their assessments, then, even without any ulterior motive, must be subject to caution. From men wary of giving offence we may expect conventional praise; from those with some axe to grind or with a taste for scandal uninformed blame should come as no surprise.

Richard of Devizes may be an exception to the general rule. We found him at first sight somewhat ambivalent in his attitude. His lavish praise of Eleanor's public image smacks of the conventional: her beauty, virtue, humility and unusual intelligence are the stuff of the court panegyrist, and only that cautionary footnote gave us pause for thought. As a monk at Winchester, Richard would have had some personal knowledge of Eleanor; and being a loyal supporter of her son Richard, he is likely to have held her too in some regard. This would seem to be confirmed by a sympathetic description he gives of her dealings with the people of Ely in 1192, at a time when they were suffering under an interdict imposed by their bishop:

> That matron, worthy of being mentioned so many times, Queen Eleanor, was visiting some cottages that were part of her dower, in the diocese of Ely. There came before her from all the villages and hamlets, wherever she went, men with women and children, not all

of the lowest orders, a people weeping and pitiful, with bare feet,
unwashed clothes, and unkempt hair. They spoke by their tears, for
their grief was so great that they could not speak. . . . Human
bodies lay unburied here and there in the fields, because their
bishop had deprived them of burial. When she learned the cause of
such suffering, the queen took pity on the misery of the living
because of their dead, for she was very merciful. Immediately
dropping her own affairs and looking after the concerns of others,
she went to London.

She proceeded to intervene successfully on their behalf. 'And who,'
asks Richard, 'would be so savage or cruel that this woman could
not bend him to her wishes.'[7]

The good monk probably wrote his chronicle after Eleanor had
left England; and although he could not know she would never
return, we may assume that his flattering words were not framed
in order to curry favour. In his work, which is largely original and
covers the period from Richard's coronation to 1192, he airs
certain strong prejudices including his contempt for the French,
but not, it seems, in pursuit of any personal advancement. So one
is inclined to accept his praise of the queen mother as sincere, and
consequently to read into his allusion to unfortunate events in
Antioch no malice, but a reluctant acknowledgement of certain
youthful indiscretions that were common knowledge in his day.

In the 1160s the Norman poet Wace had been more conventional in his praise, not unexpectedly in view of his likely
dedication to Eleanor of his translation of Geoffrey of Monmouth.
He composed his *Roman de Rou* for her husband Henry; and in it
he gives a thumb-nail biography of the queen:

Noble Eleanor is wise and of great virtue. In her youth she was
queen of France, joined to Louis in a distinguished marriage. They
went on a lengthy crusade to Jerusalem, both suffering much stress
and tribulation. After their return, the high-born queen parted from
Louis on the advice of the barons; and she came to no harm from
that separation. She left for Poitiers, her native home, to which she
was the sole heir in her family. King Henry made with her a rich
marriage, holding the maritime lands between Spain and Scotland,
from shore to shore.[8]

We notice that whatever Wace may have heard of the cause of
Eleanor's rift with Louis, he keeps his own counsel on the subject.

Another Norman, William Marshal's biographer, did not spare his compliments in his verse when mentioning the lady before whom William had demonstrated his early prowess. Afterwards, of course, the marshal became a staunch servant of the English crown and eventually acted as regent on the death of her son John. When the poet reaches the year 1189, he speaks of William coming to Winchester and finding at liberty Queen Eleanor, whose name contains the elements 'd'ali et d'or', connoting a coin minted from gold. Two years later he depicts her giving good and wise counsel on the government of the country.[9] His use of poetic licence in extolling her precious quality is such as might have been used by Bernard of Ventadour or many another of her troubadour admirers.

Eleanor did not, then, lack admirers during her lifetime. Legend, however, feeds more greedily on vice than on virtue, as we have seen exemplified by the Antioch affair. Regarding that, we found John of Salisbury, who was writing at about the same time as Wace, non-committal. This is in keeping with his characteristic prudence. Something of an ideologue, he was well versed in statecraft, being successively secretary to Archbishop Theobald of Canterbury and to Becket, whom he admired and supported, yet without entirely sacrificing his relations with Henry. He ended his life as Bishop of Chartres in 1170.

William of Tyre, who began his history at about that date, had less need to be circumspect from his distant bishopric in Palestine, where he had been born and spent much of his life. He was not a man of violent prejudices and has the reputation of a careful sifter of facts. It is possible that he had had some contact with the crusaders. But he would have been a teenager at the time; and by the time they passed south on their way to Jerusalem, Eleanor was already in strict custody and disgraced. So it is no wonder that he should have taken her guilt for granted, especially if, as is supposed, he was writing his chronicle for a French audience.

The monk Gervase of Canterbury wrote his history about 1188, four decades after the crusade. But despite his distance from the events in question, and although at that time his queen was still kept on the periphery of public life, it would hardly have been wise for him to give gratuitous offence. His main interest was in any case in inter-monastic disputes. Yet he did go so far as to say that on Louis's return from Jerusalem there arose discord between him and Eleanor concerning certain things which happened on the crusade and which are probably best passed over in silence.

Discretion was foreign to the nature of Walter Map, who was clerk to the royal household during Henry's reign and subsequently chancellor of Lincoln and archdeacon of Oxford. A Welshman from the borders, he was a friend of Gerald of Wales, to whom we shall return; and he obtained a reputation more as a witty raconteur than a sober historian. His *De Nugis Curialium* (*Courtiers' Trifles*) is largely anecdotal and full of tall stories such as we can imagine him exchanging with Gerald to their mutual relish. Neither seems to have approved of Eleanor; and Walter may have taken advantage of her fall from favour (his book was written in the 1180s) to mention another supposed scandal from her past. He speaks of the death of Stephen:

> To him Henry, son of Matilda, succeeded, and upon him Eleanor, queen of the French, cast her unchaste eyes, and contrived an unrighteous annulment, and married him, though she was secretly reputed to have shared the couch of Louis with his father Geoffrey. That is why, it is presumed, their offspring, tainted at the source, came to nought.[10]

Some years later, Helinand of Froidmont, pious chronicler and poet at the court of Philip Augustus, used even stronger terms in his characterization of Eleanor:

> The abandoned wife of Louis king of the French was carried off by Henry, count of Anjou and duke of the Normans, thereafter king of England. That brought about a war between them. It was on account of her lasciviousness that Louis gave up his wife, who behaved not like a queen but more like a harlot.[11]

For the French in particular her reputation was now in tatters; and time was no mender, for late in the eighteenth century a monk from the abbey of Barbeau, in the course of a sympathetic biography of Louis VII, dismissed her as a veritable man-eater, a 'fille incontinente et corrompue', who 'ne pouvait vivre sans hommes'.[12]

For certain writers who took a grander view of history she was more than a simple erring woman who happened to be a queen. They saw her as playing out her shadowy role on the cosmic stage.

Gerald of Wales was one of these. Son of a Norman knight from Pembrokeshire, he was a man of wide, but sometimes thwarted, ambitions as well as a full share of self-importance and reforming zeal. He was well into his seventies when he died in 1223 after a life spent in playing Church politics and seeking with varying success his own advancement. He had mixed feelings towards the Plantagenets, with admiration and criticism both finding their place in his numerous writings; but for Eleanor he found little to approve. Taking the broader view, he saw the vengeful hand of God resting on the whole family.

Gerald devotes a whole chapter of his *De Principis Instructione* (*On the Instruction of a Prince*) to an exposition of the corrupt stock from which both Henry and Eleanor sprang and in which he saw the root of all their misfortunes.[13] He begins by recalling Eleanor's grandfather's scandalous affair (wrongly attributed to her father) with the Viscountess of Châtellerault ('la Maubergeonne') and tells of a hermit's prediction that no happy progeny would come from that liaison. Eleanor's mother, of course, was the wanton lady's legitimate daughter; but Gerald makes no fine distinctions: the queen bore the taint of a profligate line, as reflected in her conduct in Palestine.

As for Henry, his race was vitiated by the bigamy of his mother, we are told. But worse than that, his father Geoffrey had had carnal relations with his present wife:

> Geoffrey, count of Anjou had seduced Queen Eleanor when he was seneschal of France, concerning which, it is said, he frequently put his son Henry on his guard, warning and commanding him not on any account to touch her, both because she was the wife of his lord and because she had already been known by his father.[14]

How, asks Gerald in righteous horror, could one expect a happy family to stem from such a union? Now in full flow, he goes on to tell of the demon countess of Anjou, who always left church before the Mass: then, when an attempt was made to restrain her, she flew out of the church window to the amazement of the onlookers. Gerald adds that Richard, when king, would jest that his family, having come from the Devil, would surely return to him. He concludes that Henry's sons became the instruments of divine vengeance, an opinion he had earlier passed in his *Expugnatio Hibernica* (*The Conquest of Ireland, c.*1186).

We can see how with this loquacious Welshman history was already becoming liberally seasoned with legend. In our own day he would have made a first-rate reporter for the popular press, so avidly did he augment his facts with racy anecdotes, portents and sweeping judgements. Like so many of his contemporaries, he must have been all too ready to suspend disbelief when he read Geoffrey of Monmouth's *History of the Kings of Britain*, perhaps even in Wace's translation as presented to Eleanor. He actually claims to have visited the newly discovered tomb at Glastonbury of King Arthur and shows no scepticism in his lengthy description. On several occasions too he refers to Merlin the seer and the fulfilment of some of his prophecies.[15]

In his lament for the captive Eleanor, Richard le Poitevin had drawn much of his inspiration from the prophecies of Merlin as retailed by Geoffrey of Monmouth. That is where he found his figure of the king of the North Wind, whom he equated with Henry. They are also the source of the representation, common among the chroniclers, of Eleanor as an eagle with her brood. Richard himself spoke of the insurrection of Henry's sons against him, and added: 'Their mother, Queen Eleanor, described by Merlin Ambrosius by the figure of "the Eagle of the Broken Covenant", had rebelled against him.' In Geoffrey the relevent prophecy is followed by another, often taken to refer to the turbulent princes:

'The Eagle of the Broken Covenant . . . will rejoice in her third nesting.

The cubs shall roar as they keep watch; they will forsake the forest groves and come hunting inside the walls of cities. They will cause great slaughter among any who oppose them, and the tongues of bulls shall they slice off. They shall load with chains the necks of the roaring ones and live again the days of their fore-fathers.'[16]

The chroniclers understood by the eagle's 'third nesting' the birth of Prince Richard, Eleanor's third and favourite son (her daughters being conveniently ignored).

Merlin also appears in the chronicle originally ascribed to Benedict of Peterborough but now more usually to Roger of Hoveden (or Howden). There is a reference to the revolt of 1173:

Prominent, moreover, among the instigators of this heinous treason were Louis the king of France and, as is said in some quarters, Eleanor queen of England herself and Raoul de Faye. The afore-mentioned queen had in her custody at that time her sons Richard duke of Aquitaine and Geoffrey count of Brittany; and she sent them to the Young King their brother in France in order to join with him against their father the king.

Then, says the chronicler, Merlin's prophecy was fulfilled; and, after quoting Geoffrey's account of the vicious cubs, he continues:

That was Merlin's prediction regarding the sons of King Henry, the empress Matilda's son; and in calling them roaring cubs, he meant that they would rise against their father and his dominion and wage war against his person.[17]

We have seen Eleanor being accused on the one hand of a variety of discreditable actions, for few of which (her collusion with her sons being an exception) is there a sound basis in known facts; and on the other hand her life story was woven into a tapestry of legends and seen in part as fulfilling the dire vaticina-tions of King Arthur's familiar sorcerer. To say she had become a legend in her own lifetime is no empty rhetoric; and for future centuries she was a ready subject for the spinners of historical fictions, sensationalizers and romantics alike. In the rest of this chapter I shall not attempt a survey of these fictions as they proliferated in Britain and on the Continent, but will confine myself to a few examples of her legend in its different aspects.

FAIR ROSAMOND

The infidelities of Henry, eleven years younger than his wife, made public gossip in his day. The most notorious was his affair with Rosamond Clifford.[18] Born perhaps before 1140, she was the daughter of Walter de Clifford, a Norman knight whose castle on the Welsh borders Henry may have visited in the course of his campaign of 1165. Nine years later a document speaks of a manor given to her father by Henry 'for the love of Rosamond, his daughter'. Under the year 1174, Gerald of Wales inveighs against

the king's lapse into vice and the manner in which, having
imprisoned Eleanor, he brought his adulterous ways into the open
by publicly taking advantage not of a rose of the world (*mundi
rosa*) but of a false or impure rose (*immundi rosa*): a bad example
indeed for a king to set.[19] We have no reason to doubt the bare
facts as given by Gerald or his claim that they were public
knowledge. If so, it is unthinkable that Eleanor remained ignorant
of the situation; but whether this knowledge perturbed her unduly
is another matter. The early chroniclers pass no opinion on that.

Benedict of Peterborough (if it is not Hoveden) tells of a visit by
Bishop, later Saint, Hugh of Lincoln to the nunnery at Godstow
near Oxford, where Rosamond had been buried after her early
death in 1176 or 1177. He went into the church.

There, as he prayed at length before the high altar, he saw in front
of the altar a particular tomb draped with a silk cloth and
surrounded by the illumination from burning candles, for it was
held in great reverence by the aforementioned nuns. Then he asked
those standing about him who lay in that tomb which they revered
so highly. They told him it was the tomb of Rosamond, whom
Henry king of England had so favoured that for love of her he had
enriched that house, which had earlier been poor and indigent, with
many handsome gifts. And he had embellished it with noble
buildings and had also made large payments to the church for the
provision of permanent illumination round the tomb.

To them the bishop replied: 'Remove her from here, for she was a
harlot, and that love between her and the king was unlawful and
adulterous! And bury her with the other dead outside the church,
lest the Christian faith come into disrepute, and for that to be an
example for other women outside to guard against illicit and
adulterous intercourse.' Then they did as the bishop told them and
took her for burial outside the church.[20]

It seems, then, that in Eleanor's lifetime the conduct of both
Henry and Rosamond was seen as open to censure, whereas
Eleanor's only association with the affair was as the wronged wife
and presumably distant observer. That was the view of Ranulf
Higden, the monk of Chester, when early in the fourteenth century
he composed his *Polychronicon*, a universal history which was
only as reliable as its sources, Gerald of Wales among them. The
work was translated in 1387 by John Trevisa, who deals with the
now expanded account of Henry's adultery in this fashion:

He that hadde prisoned his wif Eleanore the queene, and was
priveliche a spouse brekere, leveth now openliche in spousebreche,
and in nought aschamed to mysuse the wenche Rosamond. To this
faire wenche the kyng made at Wodestoke a chambre of wonder
craft, wonderliche i-made by Dedalus werke, lest the queene
schulde fynde and take Rosamounde: but the wenche deide sone,
and is i-buried in the chapitre hous at Godestowe besides Oxen-
forde with sich a writynge on her tombe:

'Hic jacet in tumba rosa mundi, non rosa munda,
Non redolet, sed olet, quae redolere solet.'

That is, Here lieth in tombe the rose of the world, nought a clene
rose; it smelleth nought swete, but it stinketh, that was wont to
smelle ful swete. This wenche hadde a litel cofre scarsliche of two
foot long, i-made by a wonder craft, that is yit i-seyn there.
Therynne it semeth that geantes fighten, bestes stertelleth, foules
fleeth and fisches meoven with oute manis hond meovynge.[21]

Here we have our earliest mention of Henry's construction of
the 'maze' at Woodstock, later to become a central feature of the
Rosamond legend. His palace there was for him a favourite retreat
and hunting-lodge and was quite often frequented by Eleanor
before her captivity; but the maze is pure myth, clearly patterned
on the Cretan labyrinth of the Theseus story. Its introduction here
is a little clumsy, since the provision of a secret trysting-place
clashes with the charge of open adultery brought against Henry.
By explaining its purpose as a means of stopping Eleanor from
catching Rosamond, Higden may have opened the way for the
queen, hitherto merely glimpsed in the wings of the drama, to
move centre stage.

In the middle of the fourteenth century an anonymous clerk
compiled his *Croniques de London*, a series of annals for the years
1259–1342. In it he gives a grisly account of Rosamond's fate.
However, wrongly identifying the king and queen as Henry III and
his wife Eleanor of Provence, he dates it to 1262. My translation
begins with the queen incurring the wrath of the populace of
London:

In that year the queen was savagely booed and jeered on London
Bridge on her way from the Tower to Westminster because she had
had a noble young lady, the most beautiful known to man, put to
death, accusing her of being the king's concubine. For that the

queen had her seized and stripped naked, then made her sit between two great fires in a tightly closed room, to the terror of the lovely damsel. She, feeling sure she was going to be burnt, broke into bitter laments. Meanwhile, the queen had had a bath prepared, into which she had the beautiful girl climb, whereupon she had a wicked old woman strike her with a lance on both arms. Then as soon as her blood spurted forth, another abominable sorceress arrived carrying two hideous toads on a shovel[?]. She placed them on the lovely girl's breasts, which they immediately seized and began to suckle. Then two more old crones held her arms outstretched to prevent her from sinking into the water before all the blood had left her body. The whole time those foul toads sucked at the beautiful damsel's breasts, while the queen laughed and mocked at her, jubilant at being thus avenged on Rosamond. Then, when she was dead, she had her body taken and buried in a filthy ditch, and the toads with it.

But when the king heard the news of how the queen had dealt with the lovely damsel he so loved and cherished, he was grief-stricken and lamented bitterly: 'Alas, wretch that I am! What shall I do for the fair Rosamond? For she never had her equal in beauty, nobility of character and courtliness.' Having thus vented his grief at length, he wished to know what had become of the beautiful girl's body. The king then had one of the wicked witches seized and put to great torture, to make her tell the whole truth concerning their treatment of the noble damsel; and he swore by almighty God that should she tell one word of a lie, she would suffer a punishment as vicious as man could devise. Then the old woman began to talk and to tell the king the complete truth: what the queen had done with the lovely body of the noble girl, and whereabouts it was to be found.

In the meantime the queen had the beautiful damsel's body exhumed and ordered it to be taken to a religious house called Godstow, two leagues from Oxford, so that Rosamond's remains should be interred there. This was to cover up her wicked deeds, so that nobody would get to know the foul, hideous things the queen had done, and to avoid blame for the death of the most noble damsel. Then the king set out to ride to Woodstock, where Rosamond, who was so dear to his heart, had been so treacherously murdered by the queen. And as he approached Woodstock, he met with Rosamond's corpse tightly sealed in a casket strongly banded with iron. The king asked at once about the corpse and the name of the body that was being borne away, to be told that it was the body of fair Rosamond. On hearing that, King Henry immediately ordered the casket to be opened, so that he might see the cruelly martyred body. The king's command was at once obeyed, and he was shown the corpse of Rosamond, who had so foully been put to death. On having the whole truth revealed, King Henry swooned for grief and lay on the ground for a long time in a trance before anyone could draw a word from him.

When the king came round from his swoon, he swore a mighty oath that he would be well avenged for the vile crime committed out of pure envy against the noble damsel. Then he began to lament and express his deep grief for the very lovely Rosamond whom he loved so much with all his heart. 'Alas, wretched girl!' he said. 'Sweet Rosamond, you never had your equal: so gentle and fair a being was never found. Now may merciful God, the Three-in-One, have pity on the soul of sweet Rosamond and forgive her all her sins. True God omnipotent, beginning and end, never suffer her soul to perish in dire torment but, in thy great mercy, grant her full remission for all her sins!' Then, having uttered this prayer, he at once gave the command to ride straight on to Godstow with the girl's body. There he had her tomb constructed in the nuns' holy house, and ordered that thirteen chaplains should sing mass for the soul of the said Rosamond so long as the earth should endure. I tell you certainly that in this religious house of Godstow fair Rosamond lies buried. May the true, almighty God have mercy on her soul. Amen.[22]

We do not know where the rather workaday and sensationalist chronicler came across this grim account, if he did not elaborate it himself. In any case, this, as far as we can tell, is the first appearance in the Rosamond story of a vengeful and jealous Eleanor bringing about her death. It could, as we saw, have been Higden who dropped the initial hint of her possible intervention; but if so, his maze has left no trace in the London chronicle. What we do find is a surprisingly vicious portrait of the queen set in sharp contrast to that of her love-sick husband, whilst praise of Rosamond and her beauty is laid on with a heavy brush: even her adultery is mentioned only as an unsupported charge by Eleanor, whereas her place in heaven seems assured.

Although it bypassed the London chronicle, the fiction of the Woodstock maze must have continued to develop in English lore. The Thesean element of the clew (ball) of thread is first found in the chronicle of another Londoner, Robert Fabyan, at the end of the Middle Ages (he died in 1513). After describing the 'howse of wonder workyng or Dædalus' werke which is to mean, after moost exposytours, an house wrought lyke unto a knot in a garden called a *maze*', he adds: 'the common fame tellyth that lastly the quene wane to her [Rosamond] by a clewe of threde or sylke and delte with her in such maner that she lyved not long after. Of the maner of her deth spekyth not myne auctor.'[23]

The notion of a private love-bower or apartment was a commonplace of medieval romance, figuring for instance in the Tristan legend and in a form reminiscent of the Woodstock fabrication in Chrétien de Troyes's *Cligés*, which was composed, possibly for Eleanor's daughter Marie of Champagne, at about the time of Rosamond's death. In the romance Cligés, in collusion with Fénice the reluctant wife of the Greek emperor, smuggles her into such a retreat, which had been cunningly constructed by John, a serf of his. Cligés is first taken to view the premises, which are reached through a secret door in an isolated tower. John opens that door;

> and, one behind the other, they go down a spiral stair to a vaulted apartment where John worked at his craft when he chose to make something. 'My lord,' he says, 'of all the men God has created none but us two have ever been where we are now; and yet the place is well fitted out, as you'll see very shortly. I suggest this as your retreat and that your sweetheart be hidden here. A lodging such as this is suitable for such a guest, for it contains bedrooms and bathrooms with hot water for the baths piped in under the ground. If anyone wanted to find a comfortable place to hide his sweetheart away, he would have to go far to find anywhere so delightful. When you've been all over it, you'll find it very suitable.'
>
> John then showed him everything, the fine rooms and painted vaulting, and pointed out many of his works, which pleased him greatly. Then, when they had seen the entire tower, Cligés said: 'John, my friend, I free you and all your descendants and am entirely in your hands. I want my beloved to be quite alone in here, with no one knowing of it except only for myself and you and her.'[24]

Through another hidden door lies a secret garden, where the lovers are eventually discovered, not by the agency of a clew of thread, but when a young knight scales its wall in pursuit of his hawk. One cannot prove the direct influence of this tale of discovered adultery on the Rosamond legend; and its ending is very different, with the betrayed emperor dying of grief and the lovers being united in a blissful and legitimized union. But at the least it has a prominent place in the background of romantic fiction against which the story of Rosamond continued to evolve.

The later medieval chroniclers and early antiquarians hand that story down in its more or less elaborated form. By the sixteenth century an implausible attempt was made to give it more historical substance by claiming that Rosamond was the mother of Henry's known bastards Geoffrey, the future archbishop of York, and William Longsword, who became Earl of Salisbury; but it is a claim that does not stand the test of chronological investigation. It was in any case the manner of Rosamond's death that most fascinated these writers. Bishop Thomas Percy in his *Reliques* (1765) introduces a ballad on the subject with a brief sketch of the material's history, in the course of which he refers to John Stow (d. 1605), Raphael Holinshed (d. 1580?), John Speed (d. 1629), and John Leland (d. 1552) as well as Higden:

> Most of our English annalists seem to have followed Higden, the monk of Chester, whose account, with some enlargements, is thus given by Stow: 'Rosamond, the fayre daughter of Walter Lord Clifford, concubine to Henry II (poisoned by Queen Elianor, as some thought) dyed at Woodstocke [AD 1177], where king Henry had made for her a house of wonderfulle working; so that no man or woman might come to her, but he that was instructed by the king, or such as were right secret with him touching the matter. This house after some was named Labyrinthus, or Dedalus worke, which was wrought like unto a knot in a garden, called a Maze; but it was commonly said, that lastly the queene came to her by a clue of thridde, or silke, and so dealt with her, that she lived not long after: but when she was dead she was buried at Godstow, in an house of nunnes beside Oxford, with these verses upon her tombe:
> Hic jacet in tumbâ Rosa mundi, non Rosa munda:
> Non redolet, sed olet, quæ redolere solet.'
> How the queen gained admittance into Rosamond's bower is differently related. Holinshed speaks of it, as 'the common report of the people, that the queene . . . founde hir out by a silken thread, which the king had drawne after him out of hir chamber with his foot, and dealt with hir in such sharpe and cruell wise, that she lived not long after.' On the other hand, in Speed's Hist, we are told that the jealous queen found her out 'by a clew of silke, fallen from Rosamund's lappe, as shee sate to take ayre, and fastened to her

foot, and the clew still unwinding, remained behinde: which the queene followed, till shee had found what she sought, and upon Rosamund so vented her spleene, as the lady lived not long after.' Our ballad-maker, with more ingenuity and probably as much truth, tells us that the clue was gained by surprise from the knight who was left to guard her bower.

It is observable, that none of the old writers attribute Rosamond's death to poison (Stow mentions it merely as a slight conjecture).

Percy adds Leland's reference to the discovery of Rosamond's remains at the dissolution of the nunnery: 'Rosamunde's tumbe at Godstowe nunnery was taken up [of] late; it is a stone with this inscription, "Tumba Rosamundæ". Her bones were closid in lede, and withyn that bones were closyd yn lether. When it was opened a very swete smell came owt of it.'[25]

The blend of history and legend is now ready to be taken over into the domain of literature. Only the feature of the poison remains to be fully exploited. It has been conjectured that the supposed finding on Rosamond's tomb of the engraving of a cup inspired the notion that it was by taking a poisoned drink that she died at the hand of Eleanor. Be that as it may, the Elizabethans found in the tragedy a fit subject for poetry, in which flights of fancy are not merely condoned but required. From their day a body of literature has built up which has eclipsed the historical facts and largely conditioned the perception of Eleanor's character among educated circles as well as in popular lore. Let us, then, turn to some of the treatments of the Rosamond story in the literature of the next three centuries.

The ballad 'Fair Rosamond' published by Percy was written near the end of the sixteenth century by Thomas Deloney, a silk-weaver by trade, but poet and pamphleteer by inclination. He takes us into his story with all the gusto of popular verse:

> When as king Henry rulde this land,
> The second of that name,
> Besides the queene, he dearly lovde
> A fair and comely dame.

Most peerlesse was her beautye founde,
Her favour and her face;
A sweeter creature in this worlde
Could never prince embrace.

Her crisped lockes like threads of gold
Appeard to each man's sight;
Her sparkling eyes, like Orient pearles,
Did cast a heavenlye light.

The blood within her crystal cheekes
Did such a colour drive,
As though the lillye and the rose
For mastership did strive.

Yea Rosamonde, fair Rosamonde,
Her name was called so,
To whom our queene, dame Ellinor,
Was known a deadlye foe.

The king therefore, for her defence
Against the furious queene,
At Woodstocke builded such a bower,
The like was never seene.

Most curiously that bower was built
Of stone and timber strong,
An hundred and fifty doors
Did to this bower belong:

And they so cunninglye contriv'd,
With turnings round about,
That none but with a clue of thread
Could enter in or out.

And for his love and ladye's sake,
That was so faire and brighte,
The keeping of this bower he gave
Unto a valiant knighte.

Their idyll was short-lived because, owing to the revolt of Henry's 'ungracious' son, he had to leave for France. His lingering farewell was punctuated by Rosamond's tearful requests to be allowed to go with him, serving as a page or squire or even chambermaid. But her pleas were in vain; and the king left, never to see her again.

> For when his grace had past the seas
> And into France had gone,
> With envious heart, queene Ellinor
> To Woodstocke came anone.
>
> And forth she calls this trustye knighte,
> In an unhappy houre;
> Who with his clue of twined thread
> Came from this famous bower.
>
> And when that they had wounded him,
> The queene this thread did gette,
> And went where ladye Rosamonde
> Was like an angell sette.
>
> But when the queene with stedfast eye
> Beheld her beauteous face,
> She was amazed in her minde
> At her exceeding grace.

queer coded?

> 'Cast off from thee those robes,' she said,
> 'That riche and costyle bee;
> And drinke thou up this deadlye draught,
> Which I have brought to thee.'
>
> Then presentlye upon her knees
> Sweet Rosamonde did falle;
> And pardon of the queene she crav'd
> For her offences all.
>
> 'Take pitty on my youthfull yeares,'
> Faire Rosamonde did crye;
> 'And lett mee not with poison stronge
> Enforced bee to dye.
>
> I will renounce my sinfull life,
> And in some cloyster bide;
> Or else be banisht, if you please,
> To range the world soe wide.

And for the fault which I have done,
Though I was forc'd thereto,
Preserve my life, and punish mee
As you thinke meet to do.'

And with these words, her lillie handes
She wrunge full often there;
And downe along her lovely face
Did trickle many a teare.

But nothing could this furious queene
Therewith appeased bee;
The cup of deadlye poyson stronge,
As she knelt on her knee,

Shee gave this comelye dame to drinke,
Who tooke it in her hande,
And from her bended knee arose,
And on her feet did stand;

And casting up her eyes to heaven,
Shee did for mercye calle;
And drinking up the poison stronge,
Her life she lost withalle.

And when that death through everye limbe
Had showde its greatest spite,
Her chiefest foes did plaine confesse
Shee was a glorious wight.

Her body then they did entomb,
When life was fled away,
At Godstowe, neare to Oxford towne,
As may be seene this day.[26]

Here we see Rosamond as a paragon of beauty and even virtue: her 'youthfull years' may excuse her offence, and in any case she was 'forc'd thereto'. Eleanor, though, appears as a woman pitiless in her jealousy, furiously bent on vengeance. We note that this was wreaked, with some rearrangement of history, during Henry's absence in France, where he was seeking to scotch his son's rebellion.

The timing is different in Samuel Daniel's more sophisticated poem, 'The Complaint of Rosamond', which was printed with a collection of sonnets in 1592.[27] Daniel was an Oxford-educated son of a music master. He died in 1619, having risen to a post at court and composed various masques for festivities there. In his later years he also, appropriately enough, acted as tutor to Anne Clifford, daughter of the Countess of Cumberland. Steeped in Renaissance conceits, his 'Complaint' views the affair in retrospect through the guilt-ridden words of Rosamond's shade:

> Out from the horror of infernall deepes,
> My poore afflicted ghost comes here to plain it,
> Attended with my shame that never sleepes,
> The spot wherewith my kind, and youth did staine it.
> My body found a grave where to containe it:
> A sheete could hide my face, but not my sin,
> For Fame findes never Tombe t'inclose it in.
>
> And which is worse, my soule is now denied
> Her transport to the sweet Elisian rest,
> The ioyfull blisse for Ghosts repurified,
> The ever-springing Gardens of the blest:
> Caron denies me waftage with the rest,
> And saies my soule can never passe the River,
> Till Lovers' sighs on earth shall it deliver.

As Rosamond proceeds with her story, we find a very Christian moral displayed within the Classical frame. Her innocent upbringing by fond parents in their country home was left behind when she came to court and the notice of King Henry.

> For after all his victories in France,
> And all the triumphs of his honour wonne,
> Unmatcht by sword, was vanquisht by a glance,
> And hotter warres within his breast begunne.
> Warres, whom whole legions of desires drew on:
> Against all which, my chastitie contends,
> With force of honour, which my shame defends.

Even Henry's 'feeble age' did not quell his desire; and after a lengthy struggle, Rosamond's resistance was overcome by a go-between who urged the case for public honour against private virtue. So she was swept off by the king to a 'sollitarie Grange', where she was pampered with jewels and a rich casket carved with lusty mythological scenes. Prompted by 'iealousie increas'd with age's coldnesse', Henry built there a palace in the form of a maze:

> None but the King might come into the place,
> With certaine Maides that did attend my neede,
> And he himselfe came guided by a threed.

Plagued, like the jealous husband of troubadour lyric and courtly romance, by the fear of prying eyes, he turned Rosamond's freedom into a resented captivity. If only, she laments, she had not come to court, 'But liv'd at home a happy Countrey Maide' instead of becoming a 'maide misled'. Even in what has now become for her a prison Justice could not keep rumour at bay:

> And this our stealth she could not long conceale
> From her whom such a forfeit most concerned:
> The wronged Queene, who could so closely deale,
> That she the whole of all our practise learned,
> And watcht a time when least it was discerned,
> In absence of the King to wreake her wrong
> With such revenge as she desired long.

> The Labyrinth she entered by that Threed,
> That serv'd a conduct to my absent Lord,
> Left there by chance, reserv'd for such a deed,
> Where she surpriz'd me whom she so abhor'd.
> Enrag'd with madnesse, scarce she speakes a word,
> But flies with eager furie to my face,
> Offring me most unwomanly disgrace.

> Looke how a Tygresse that hath lost her Whelpe,
> Runnes fiercely ranging through the Woods astray:
> And seeing her selfe depriv'd of hope or helpe,
> Furiously assaults what's in her way,
> To satisfie her wrath (not for a pray),
> So fell she on me in outragious wise,
> As could Disdaine and Iealousie devise.

> And after all her vile reproches usde,
> She forc'd me take the Poyson she had brought,

To end the life that had her so abusde,
And free her feares, and ease her iealous thought.
No cruelty her wrath could leave unwrought,
No spitefull act that to Revenge is common;
(No beast being fiercer than a iealous woman.)

Here take (saith she) thou impudent uncleane,
Base gracelesse Strumpet, take this next your heart;
Your Love-sick heart, that over-charg'd hath beene
With Pleasure's surfeit, must be purg'd with Art.
This potion hath a power that will convart
To naught those humors that oppresse you so.
And (Gerle) Ile see you take it ere I go.

What, stand you now amaz'd, retire you back?
Tremble you (Minion)? Come, dispatch with speed;
There is no helpe, your Champion now you lacke,
And all these teares you shed will nothing steed;
Those dainty fingers needes must doe the deed.
Take it, or I will drench you else by force,
And trifle not, lest that I use you worse.

Having this bloody doome from hellish breath,
My wofull eyes on every side I cast:
Rigor about me, in my hand my death,
Presenting me the horror of my last:
All hope of pitty and of comfort past.
No meanes, no power; no forces to contend,
My trembling hands must give my selfe my end.

Those hands that beautie's ministers had bin,
They must give death, that me adorn'd of late,
That mouth that newly gave consent to sin,
Must now receive destruction in thereat,
That body, which my lust did violate,
Must sacrifice it selfe t'appease the wrong.
(So short is pleasure, glory lasts not long.)

And she no sooner saw I had it taken,
But forth she rushes (proud with victorie)
And leaves m'alone, of all the world forsaken,
Except of Death, which she had left with me
(Death and my selfe alone together be),
To whom she did her full revenge refer.
Oh poore weake conquest both for him and her.

Having learnt her lesson too late, Rosamond expatiates upon it with her long-dying breath. One should defend one's chastity against lust:

> The spot is foule, though by a Monarch made,
> Kings cannot priviledge what God forbade.

Scarcely has her soul left her body than the king arrives 'to see his dearest ioy'. Finding only her corpse, he collapses in sighs and lamentations before embracing it and wishing for his own death.

> Yet ere I die, thus much my soule doth vow,
> Revenge shall sweeten death with ease of minde.

That revenge is not, however, reported by the ghost of Rosamond, who simply adds that her body was interred with due ceremony at Godstow.

With all its pious moralizing (the only relief being the courtly thought that lovers' sighs may work the soul's redemption), Daniel's poem serves less as a celebration, like the ballad, than as a warning. The liaison of king and courtesan is presented not as a thwarted idyll, but as an affair steeped in sin. Yet here too Eleanor, though 'the wronged Queene', is depicted more as a she-devil than as a righteous avenger. Legend seems to have cast her irrevocably in the villain's role. However, if we move on a century we have a surprise in store.

In 1707 Joseph Addison tried his hand at an opera, *Rosamond*, on the subject.[28] It was a flop, as even his devotee Thomas Tickell concedes in a preface to his works. The blame, though, he lays on the music, not sufficiently to the Italian taste; but 'the Poetry of this piece has given as much pleasure in the closet, as others have afforded from the stage, with all the assistance of voices and instruments'. In some fulsome introductory lines he asserts:

> . . . the charm'd reader with thy thought complies,
> Feels corresponding joys or sorrows rise,
> And views thy Rosamond with Henry's eyes.

Addison ingeniously leavens the rhetoric, pomp and circumstance of the main action with an amusing subsidiary plot, in

which Sir Trusty, 'Keeper of the Bower', is suspected by his wife
Grideline of himself casting lecherous eyes on Rosamond. The
piece opens with a page showing the bower to Eleanor and
prompting from her a series of passionate outbursts:

> Curse on the name! I faint, I die,
> With secret pangs of jealousie.
>
> . . . .
>
> My wrath, like that of heavn'n, shall rise,
> And blast her in her Paradise.
>
> . . . .
>
> In such an endless maze I rove,
> Lost in the labyrinths of love.
> My breast with hoarded vengeance burns,
> While fear and rage
> With hope engage,
> And rule my wav'ring soul by turns.
>
> . . . .
>
> Eleanora, think betimes,
> What are thy hated rival's crimes!
> Whither, ah whither dost thou go!
> What has she done to move thee so!
> – Does she not warm with guilty fires
> The faithless Lord of my desires?
> Have not her fatal arts remov'd
> My Henry from my arms?
> 'Tis her crime to be lov'd
> 'Tis her crime to have charms.
> Let us fly, let us fly,
> She shall die, she shall die.

So this is the furious Eleanor established by the earlier texts. But
suddenly she seems to hesitate:

> I feel, I feel my heart relent,
> How could the Fair be innocent!
> To a monarch like mine,
> Who would not resign!
> One so great and so brave
> All hearts must enslave.

Her qualms are short-lived; for at that moment Henry returns
from his wars to the sound of trumpet, fife and drum. It is too
much for the queen:

Henry returns, from danger free!
Henry returns – but not to me.
He comes his Rosamond to greet,
And lay his laurels at her feet,
His vows impatient to renew;
His vows to Eleanora due.
Here shall the happy nymph detain
(While of his absence I complain),
Hid in her mazy, wanton bower,
My lord, my life, my conqueror.
No, no, 'tis decreed
The Traitress shall bleed;
No fear shall alarm,
No pity disarm;
In my rage shall be seen
The revenge of a Queen.

There follows a lively, comic tiff between Sir Trusty and
Grideline, which causes him to lament:

How hard is our fate,
Who serve in the state,
And should lay out our cares,
On publick affairs;
When conjugal toils,
And family-broils
Make all our great labours miscarry!
Yet this is the lot
Of him that has got
Fair Rosamond's bower,
With the clew in his power,
And is courted by all,
Both the great and the small,
As principal pimp to King Harry.

Seeing Rosamond draw near, he eavesdrops on her heart-rending
lament regretting Henry's tardiness in coming to her; but the high
tone is deflated by his down-to-earth aside:

How much more bless'd would lovers be,
Did all the whining fools agree
To live like Grideline and me!

In the following scenes Harry arrives with another flourish of trumpets and is escorted by Trusty into Rosamond's presence, rhapsodizing as he goes. Yet after only a brief reunion, he retires to rest in a nearby grotto.

At this juncture the page, sent by Grideline to spy on Trusty, in fact points out the bower to Eleanor; and she reacts with characteristic fury:

> I see, I see my hands embru'd
> In purple streams of reeking blood:
> I see the victim gasp for breath,
> And start in agonies of death:
> I see my raging dying Lord,
> And O, I see my self abhorr'd!

She shortly appears before Rosamond with a bowl in one hand and a dagger in the other. She gives her fair rival the choice:

> Or quickly drain the fatal Bowl,
> Or this right hand performs its part,
> And plants a Dagger in thy heart.

Rosamond's pleas for pity or to be shut away in some deep dungeon seem to evoke a passing scruple in Eleanor's mind:

> Moving language, shining tears,
> Glowing guilt, and graceful fears,
> Kindling pity, kindling rage,
> At once provoke me, and asswage.

But no:

> Thou shalt die.
> . . . .
> Prepare to welter in a flood
> Of streaming gore.

And faced with the dagger-wielding queen, Rosamond finally takes the bowl and drinks, though not without a desperate threat:

> At dead of night,
> A glaring spright,
> With hideous screams
> I'll haunt thy dreams
> And when the painful night withdraws,
> My Henry shall revenge my cause.
> O whither doe my frenzy drive!
> Forgive my rage, your wrongs forgive.
> My veins are froze; my blood grows chill;
> The weary springs of life stand still;
> The sleep of death benumbs all o'er
> My fainting limbs, and I'm no more.

At once Eleanor calls for attendants and bids them bear the corpse for burial to a convent beside the Isis.

So Addison has taken the by now familiar legend, padded it out a little with a few comic scenes, and brought in the choice of death by dagger or by poison. He has, however, a final trick up his sleeve. Sir Trusty comes upon the corpse and tell-tale bowl. In a paroxysm of grief, he drains the rest of its contents before penning a brief note to the king:

> 'Great Sir,
> Your Rosamond is dead
> As I am at this present writing.'
> The bower turns round, my brain's abus'd,
> The Labyrinth grows more confused,
> The thickets dance – I stretch, I yawn.
> Death has tripp'd up my heels – I'm gone.

In a soliloquy, Eleanor declares that 'Rosamond shall charm no more' and 'My Henry shall be mine alone'.

But the opera has still a few minutes to run, the first of which are taken up by the presentation to the slumbering Henry of an angelic vision predicting the nation's glorious future. This so fires the royal blood with patriotic zeal that he solemnly vows, if with some regret, to abandon love for duty. Enter the queen at the side of a stage garnished with bowl, dagger, body of Sir Trusty, and the latter's note now being read by Henry. Still hoping to regain her husband's love, she is noticed by the distracted Henry:

> But see! the cause of all my fears,
> The source of all my grief appears!
> No unexpected guest is here;
> The fatal bowl
> Inform'd my soul
> Eleonora was too near.

There follows a bout of mutual recriminations; but then Eleanor's heart is softened:

> My Lord, I cannot see you mourn;
> The Living you lament: while I,
> To be lamented so, cou'd Die.

Faced by Henry's incredulity, she asks whether, should Rosamond be alive, he would not renew the wrongs she has suffered.

> Oh no; by Visions from above
> Prepar'd for grief, and free'd from love,
> I came to take my last adieu.

His queen, overjoyed, explains that the supposed poison was in reality a sleep-inducing drug;

> But soon the waking nymph shall rise,
> And, in a convent plac'd, admire
> The cloister'd walls and virgin choire:
> With them in songs and hymns divine
> The beauteous penitent shall join,
> And bid the guilty world adieu.

Mutual forgiveness follows immediately: there shall be no more disloyalty or grief between them, for they will 'ever more united live'. After Sir Trusty has staggered in, not knowing whether he is alive or dead, king and queen proclaim together 'the sweets of virtuous love'.

With his happy ending, Addison has finally thumbed his nose at history, though his confinement of the living Rosamond to the convent at Godstow is not wholly implausible. As for Eleanor's unexpected streak of tenderness, this is pure melodrama, not informed character portrayal.

Eleanor's fame, or notoriety, in England seems by this time to have rested largely on her apocryphal dealings with fair Rosamond. The story is taken up again in the 1820s by a curious book entitled *The Unfortunate Royal Mistresses, Rosamond Clifford, and Jane Shore, Concubines to King Henry the Second and Edward the Fourth, with Historical and Metrical Memoirs of those Celebrated Persons.*[29] The Preface contains a half-hearted attempt to accommodate history to legend, accepting for instance that Rosamond's death by poison had been ably refuted by Carte (in his *History of England*, 1747–55), 'who states, that through grief at the defection of her royal admirer on his marriage with Eleanor, she retired from the world, and became a nun at Godstow, where she died, and had a tomb erected to her memory'. The author adds: 'It is very improbable, that if Queen Eleanor had been placed in captivity, on account of the part she had in the death of Rosamond Clifford, that her youngest son, King John, who was greatly attached to his mother, should repair Godstow nunnery, and endow it with yearly revenues, that the holy virgins there might relieve with their prayers the souls of his father King Henry, and of Lady Rosamond, there interred.' As for the real cause of the latter's death, the suggestion is that Eleanor 'treated her harshly; with furious menaces, we may suppose, and sharp expostulations, which had such an effect on her spirits, that she did not long survive it'.

The first of the 'metrical memoirs' is Deloney's ballad. Then, after a long antiquarian excursus on Godstow, there follows 'The Unfortunate Concubine; or, Rosamond's Overthrow'.[30] As the following extracts show, some attempt has been made in it to relocate the legend in its historical context:

> As three young Knights of Sal'sbury
> Were riding on their way,
> One boasted of a fair lady,
> Within her bow'r so gay.
> I have a sister, Clifford swears,
> But few men do her know;
> Upon her face the skin appears
> Like drops of blood on snow;

My sister's locks of curled hair
Outshine the golden ore,
Her skin for whiteness may compare
With the fine lilly flow'r:
Her breasts are lovely to behold,
Like to the driven snow:
I would not, for her weight in gold,
King Henry should her know.

King Henry had a bower near
Where they were riding by,
And he did Clifford over-hear:
Thought he immediately,
Tho' I her brother should offend
For that fair white and red,
For her I am resolv'd to send
To grace my royal bed.

Matching deed to thought, Henry sends the girl three letters by her brother.

Then with her fingers, long and small,
She broke the seals of gold;
And as she did to reading fall
At first you might behold
The smiles of pleasant sweet delight,
As if well satisfy'd;
But e're she had concluded quite,
She wrung her hands, and cry'd;

Why did you boast beyond your bounds,
When Oxford you did see?
You might have talk'd of hawkes and hounds,
And never bragg'd of me.
When by the King I am defil'd,
My father's griefs begin;
He'll have no comfort of his child,
Nor come to my wedding.

Go, fetch me down my planet-book
Straight from my private room;

For in the same I mean to look,
What is decreed my doom.
The planet-book to her they brought,
And laid it on her knee;
And found that all would come to nought,
For poison'd she should be.

I curse you brother, then she cry'd,
Who caused my destiny;
I might have been some Lord's fair bride,
But you have ruin'd me.

Summoned to the court, she blushes with embarrassment at the king's demand that she grace his royal bed. However,

The gifts and presents of a King
Soon caused her to comply;
Thinking there was not any thing
Like royal dignity.
But as her bright and golden scene
In Court began to shine,
The news was carry'd to the Queen
Of this new Concubine.

At which she was enraged so
With malice in her breast,
That till she wrought her overthrow
She could not be at rest.
She felt the fury of the Queen,
E're she had flourish'd long;
And dy'd just as she had foreseen
By force of poison strong.

The angry Queen with malice fraught,
Could not herself contain,
Till she fair Rosamond had brought
To her sad fatal bane.
The sweet and charming precious rose,
King Henry's chief delight!
The Queen she to the bower goes,
And wrought her hateful spight:

But when she to the bower came,
Where lady Clifford lay,
Enraged Elinor by name
She could not find the way,
Until the silken clue of thread
Became a fatal guide
Unto the Queen, who laid her dead,
E're she was satisfy'd.

Alas! it was no small surprize
To Rosamond the fair:
When death appear'd before her eyes,
No faithful friend was there,
Who could stand up in her defence,
To put the potion by;
So, by the hands of violence,
Compell'd she was to die.

O most renowned, gracious Queen,
Compassion take of me;
I wish that I had never seen
Such royal dignity.
Betray'd I was, and by degrees
A sad consent I gave;
And now upon my bended knees,
I do your pardon crave.

I will not pardon you, she cry'd;
So take this fatal cup:
And you may well be satisfy'd
I'll see you drink it up.
Then with her fair and milk-white hand,
The fatal cup she took;
Which being drank, she could not stand,
But soon the world forsook.

Now when the King was well inform'd
What Elinor had done,
His breast he smote, in wrath he storm'd
As if he would have run
Besides his senses; and he swore,

For this inhuman deed,
He never would bed with her more;
His royal heart did bleed.

The King did not stand pausing long,
How to reward her spleen;
But straight in a close prison strong
He cast his cruel queen:
Where she lay six and twenty years
A long captivity,
Bathed in floods of weeping tears,
Till his death set her free.

Now when her son he did succeed
His father, great Henry,
His royal mother soon he freed
From her captivity:
And she set many more at large,
Who long for debt had lain;
Her royal pity did discharge
Thousands in Richard's reign.

So perhaps this rhymester had a sneaking regard for Eleanor after all, which he contrived to show by adding his footnote about her attested release of many of Henry's prisoners: an odd historical touch in this welter of poetic licence. There is a note of sympathy too in a further poem, 'The Epistle of Rosamond to King Henry the Second'.[31] Here we find Rosamond bemoaning her guilt from the labyrinth at Woodstock while Henry lingers abroad, fighting his sons. She imagines herself an object of universal loathing:

The married women curse my hateful life,
Wronging a faire Queen, and a vertuous wife;
The maidens wish, I buried quick may die,
Well knew'st thou what a Monster I would be
When thou did'st build this Labyrinth for me.

To this the king replies in 'Henry to Rosamond':[32]

Long since (thou know'st) my care provided for
To lodge thee safe from jealous Ellinor;

The labyrinth's conveyance guides thee so,
(Which only Vaughan, thou, and I doe know)
If shee do guard thee with an hundred eyes,
I have an hundred subtill Mercuries,
To watch that Argus which my love doth keepe,
Untill eye, after eye, fall all to sleepe.

One may think the mythological decoration overstrained not only with the unoriginal equation of Eleanor with Argus, but especially when Rosamond is seen as the Minotaur!

The section of the book on Rosamond concludes with a 'brief history of this "Unfortunate Concubine", from the pen of a celebrated modern writer'. We are told in lyrical vein of how Rosamond's 'beauty, wit, and extreme good humour' captivated her monarch, who built for her a proud palace at Woodstock and then enclosed it with a labyrinth 'to baffle the prying curiosity of the queen'.

Months rolled on, and every day seemed but to dawn on the increasing fervour of his affection. Never were such a fond couple yet seen. Their felicity was too pure for earth; and cruel fate, as if indignant at their early anticipations of heaven, seemed resolved to mar their happiness, for the jealous queen, alarmed at the growing indifference of her royal consort, persuaded his confidential servant to hint the cause of his alienated affections. Profuse bribery was resorted to, and the ungrateful domestic was not proof against the splendid temptations that were held out to him. He consented one evening to betray the abode of poor Rosamond, and lead the infuriated queen into the very apartment that contained her enemy.

It was a fine evening, and Fair Rosamond was seated at her woodbine bower, singing the song that had so often charmed her lover. It was a strain of delicious nature, and was heard by the distant nightingale, who prolonged by her sweet voice the melancholy plaint of her rival. Tears stole down her cheek; she wept she knew not why – her Henry was indeed away, but had he not promised to return by the change of the waning moon? On a sudden the sound of approaching footsteps was heard in the silence of twilight. 'It is my Harry,' exclaimed the delighted girl, and sprung in ecstacy to meet him. A form did indeed advance, but it was not the form that she had been accustomed to hail so fondly. A female of haughty mien approached the affrighted Rosamond, and in a voice of passion, desired her to drink the contents of a bowl she held in her hand. The poor girl requested permission to retire, the tears stood in her lovely eyes; but the queen seemed bent on her destruction. Weary with supplication, she at last faulteringly besought permission to write one last letter to her lover, a request which was granted with a sneer. Rosamond then swallowed the envenomed contents of the bowl, and while the hues of death passed over her sweet face, inscribed this simple letter to her monarch.

'Henry, my own dear Henry, we must part for ever; a poisonous reptile has stung your poor Rosamond to death, and she will never again behold you. But do not forget me, love; sometimes visit the grave where she who was once your's now reposes, and her spirit will yet be happy; for if souls are ever permitted to re-visit earth, I will come to you, and talk of the happiness of our re-union. Henry, I can write to you no more, I am already dying; but the last fond name that trembles on my lips, shall be the dear, dear name of Henry.'

On concluding this letter, the poor girl sank back in a swoon on her couch: she held out her hand as if imploring forgiveness on the head of her murderer, and in a few minutes her pure spirit had passed away.

It was now the change of the moon, the period promised for Henry's return. He was punctual to his appointment, and arrived in a state of ecstacy at the beautiful bowers he had so long left. He hastened to the favourite alcove of his mistress; and the woods and the grottos echoed back his fond exclamation; 'Rosamond, dear Rosamond, why do you not come to meet me?' No voice of greeting replied, but all was desolate and forlorn. He reached the bower, and beheld the letter of his love. He wept not — but a deep sigh escaped him, as he requested to see the spot where she was buried. There he spent days and nights in a state of the deepest gloom; and for months and months afterwards, a soft tender voice was heard at the hour of twilight, echoing through the groves of Woodstock — 'Rosamond, dear Rosamond, why do you not come to meet me?' This could not last; he died of a broken heart, and at the hour of his dissolution, consoled himself by reflecting that he should at least meet his mistress in heaven.[33]

It is plain that Romanticism has passed this way. Who is this Henry, whose soft tender voice was heard cooing through the groves of Woodstock until, poor love-lorn swain, he died of a broken heart? As for Eleanor, despite her haughty mien, she is still damned by her victim as a poisonous reptile, at least until that possibly redemptive gesture. One cannot wonder that would-be historians, familiar with such literary or sub-literary fancies along with the unreliable accounts of their predecessors, but lacking sound editions of much of the basic source material, should find it hard to strip away legend from fact. This was the case with Agnes Strickland, whose biography of 'Eleanora of Aquitaine' appeared in the first volume of her *Lives of the Queens of England*, dedicated to the young Queen Victoria.[34] Regarded as a standard work, this must have consolidated the picture of Eleanor in the minds of countless young (and older) Victorians.

Strickland admits that 'It is not a very easy task to reduce to any thing like perspicuity the various traditions which float through the chronicles regarding queen Eleanora's unfortunate rival, the celebrated Rosamond Clifford.' Pinning too much faith on 'the learned and accurate Carte' (Thomas Carte, who wrote his *History of England* in 1747–55), she asserts:

> It appears that the acquaintance between Rosamond and Henry commenced in early youth, about the time of his knighthood by his uncle the king of Scotland; that it was renewed at the time of his successful invasion of England, when he entered privately into marriage contract with the unsuspecting girl; and before he left England, to return to his wife, his noble boy William, surnamed Long-éspée, was born.

Strickland wonders how queen and mistress were kept in ignorance of his perfidy. She soon resorts to an even less reliable source, John Brompton, who passed as a chronicler in the first half of the fifteenth century.

> As Rosamond was retained by him as a prisoner, though not an unwilling one, it was easy to conceal from her the facts, that he had wedded a queen and brought her to England; but his chief difficulty was to conceal Rosamond's existence from Eleanora, and yet to indulge himself with frequent visits to the real object of his love.
>
> Brompton says, 'That one day queen Eleanora saw the king walking in the pleasance of Woodstock, with the end of a ball of floss silk attached to his spur; coming near him unperceived, she took up the ball, and the king walking on, the silk unwound, and thus the queen traced him to a thicket in the labyrinth or maze of the park, where he disappeared. She kept the matter secret, often

revolving in her own mind in what company he could meet with balls of silk. Soon after, the king left Woodstock for a distant journey; then queen Eleanora, bearing her discovery in mind, searched the thicket in the park, and discovered a low door cunningly concealed; this door she had forced, and found it was the entrance to a winding subterranean path, which led out at a distance to a sylvan lodge in the most retired part of the adjacent forest.' Here the queen found, in a bower, a young lady of incomparable beauty, busily engaged in embroidery. Queen Eleanora then easily guessed how balls of silk attached themselves to king Henry's spurs. Whatever was the result of the interview between Eleanora and Rosamond, it is certain that the queen did not destroy her rival either by sword or poison, though in her rage it is possible that she might threaten both. That Rosamond was not killed may be ascertained by the charters before named, which plainly show that she lived twenty years, in great penitence, after her retirement from the king. It is extremely probable that her interview with Eleanora led to her first knowledge that Henry was a married man, and consequently to her profession at Godstow, which took place the second year of Henry's reign.

Strickland reasons that Rosamond's death twenty years later happened to coincide with Henry's imprisonment of his wife; and this gave rise to the report of Eleanor's complicity. Brompton's 'chronology of the incidents is decidedly wrong, but the actual events are confirmed by the most ancient authorities'.

The story of Fair Rosamond was thus sanctioned by 'history' and indeed has remained the stuff of guide-books to this day. For later nineteenth-century writers it was available as one of the collection of popular narrative themes such as the Tristan or Faust stories and had the particular advantage of its similarity with the Garden of Eden myth, with Eleanor readily cast as the serpent. A medley of history and legend, it was there to be treated with as free a hand as the writer chose, historical truth entirely at the mercy of the individual imagination. A glance at two plays by leading Victorian poets will show Eleanor adapted to her new environment, while retaining her unsavoury reputation.

The first is an immature drama by Swinburne, published in 1860 and ignored thereafter, although not devoid of psychological and poetic interest.[35] A short piece, drenched in Pre-Raphaelite sentiment and verbiage, it reduces history to the dramatic setting

for Eleanor's revenge. Rosamond fears the loss of Henry's love,
should he be reconciled to his dark-haired, sun-dried queen, whom
'men call . . . an adder underfoot'. Jealous of her fair rival, Eleanor
schemes to be taken to her, promising to do her no harm, to wear
men's clothes, even to kiss the dust from her guide's feet if need be.
Yet she does not mask her hatred: 'Hell's heat burn through that
whorish mouth of hers!' And in a scene with Henry her 'French
blood, south blood' rises against him too. We are shown the king
in the bower, trying to reassure the weeping Rosamond:

> O sweet, what sting is this she makes in you?
> A Frenchwoman, black-haired and with grey lips
> And fingers like a hawk's cut claw that nips
> One's wrist to carry – is this so great a thing
> As should wring wet out of your lids?

In their final confrontation neither rival wants for words.
Rosamond claims there was no malice in her sin:

> If you could see the pained poor heart in me
> You would find nothing hateful toward you
> In all the soft red record its blood makes.

But Eleanor is implacable. Seizing Rosamond by the throat, she
offers her in convoluted terms the choice of death by sword or by
poison. She has no wish to break her oath by harming her directly.
But when the drink is taken, she makes it clear that this was no
potion like that dreamed up by Addison:

> It is done indeed.
> Perchance now it should please you to be sure
> This were no poison? as it is, it is.
> Ha, the lips tighten so across the teeth
> They should bite in, show blood; how white she is,
> Yea, white! dead green now like a fingered leaf.

Henry arrives and turns to the gloating queen:

> Thou art worse caught than anything in hell –
> To put thy hands upon this body – God,
> Curse her for me! I will not slay thee yet,
> But damn thee some fine quiet way.

With a final kiss he seals the death of Rosamond; and his lament ends the play.

Tennyson had been attracted to the theme in his youth and treated it in an unfinished lyric. When he took it up again in his five-act drama *Becket*, he wove it into a fully researched historical tragedy.[36] This was written in 1884 and successfully staged in 1891. Although he seems well versed in the facts as set forth in his day in works like Agnes Strickland's, as a dramatist he had enough belief in his art to make them dance to its tune. The result is a complex but powerful play, in which Eleanor is given a substantial role and her character allowed some development.

Time and place are straddled by the play's action; or rather actions, since the Rosmond theme is interwoven with the political, as we follow Henry's souring relations with Becket in the context of the growing conflict between Church and state. In a prologue we find the king telling his boon companion Becket, not yet priest, of his fears that Eleanor may seek the death of Rosamond, his 'true heart-wife', and that he has built for her a bower to save her life and 'the soul of Eleanor from hell-fire'. The queen gets wind of this and schemes with Fitzurse, a former admirer of the girl, to bring her to the dust, have her 'eat it like the serpent, and be driven out of her paradise'.

In London Rosamond, not yet shut away, is saved from the pursuing Fitzurse by Becket, who has her escorted to the bower in monk's disguise. Her total innocence is gradually revealed: she thinks herself married to Henry, by whom she has an infant son Geoffrey; and she believes Eleanor still to be queen of France. When accidentally enlightened by a maidservant, she is utterly bewildered. Eleanor comes to the woods round the bower and there finds little Geoffrey straying, persuades him that she is a fairy, and has him lead her to his mother, following a silken thread. With few preliminaries other than the disclosure of her identity, she offers her rival the choice of dagger or poison or else, on the sudden appearance of Fitzurse, to surrender herself to him. Rosamond indignantly rejects him and bids Eleanor strike. The queen raises the dagger, crying:

> This in thy bosom, fool,
> And after in thy bastard's!

But at that moment her arm is caught from behind, and the dagger falls to the ground. The hand belongs to Becket, who, though now archbishop, had once been appointed by Henry as his mistress' guardian. The good man will now take her and the child to Godstow nunnery.

We are next transported to Normandy, where Eleanor has arrived with Fitzurse, aiming to kindle Henry's anger against the archbishop. Their success is marked by the king's well-known cry: 'Will no man free me from this pestilent priest?' Back in Canterbury we hear Rosamond, disguised once more as a monk, pleading with Becket to spare Henry from excommunication. Events then take their more authentic course, with the archbishop being hewn down at his altar by four knights, Fitzurse among them. But the poet has reserved one last dramatic device: the Fair Rosamond, praying in the cathedral for her holy protector, has witnessed the grim deed; and as the murderers rush out, she is left kneeling alone by the body as lightning flashes through the shrine.

Although Tennyson has developed Eleanor's character along familiar lines, he has filled it out with other traditions that had grown about her. She is very much a daughter of the south: 'I would I were in Aquitaine again – your north wind chills me.' We even see her in the prologue composing a song, 'for I am a Troubadour, you know, and won the violet at Toulouse; but my voice is harsh here, not in tune, a nightingale out of season; for marriage . . . has killed the golden violet'. Are we to feel some sympathy for a woman embittered by exile from her native land and the neglect of a truant husband? On the other hand, the cornered Rosamond reveals more knowledge of her past than we had suspected. Threatened by the dagger, she despairs of her life and her son's:

> both of us will die,
> And I will fly with my sweet boy to heaven,
> And shriek to all the saints among the stars:
> 'Eleanor of Aquitaine, Eleanor of England!
> Murder'd by that adulteress Eleanor,
> Whose doings are a horror to the east,
> A hissing in the west!' Have we not heard
> Raymond of Poitou, thine own uncle – nay,

> Geoffrey Plantagenet, thine own husband's father –
> Nay, ev'n the accursed heathen Saladdeen –
> Strike!
> I challenge thee to meet me before God.
> Answer me there.

Eleanor seems to feel less guilt than nostalgia for that murky past. When Becket declines to retrieve the fallen dagger, she picks it up herself:

> I had it from an Arab soldan, who,
> When I was there in Antioch, marvell'd at
> Our unfamiliar beauties of the west;
> But wonder'd more at my much constancy
> To the monk-king Louis, our former burthen,
> From whom, as being too kin, you know, my lord,
> God's grace and Holy Church deliver'd us.
> I think, time given, I could have talk'd him out of
> His ten wives into one.

Tennyson may have failed to bring Rosamond convincingly to life (or indeed death); but he has used all his reading to broaden and deepen Eleanor's character. Left alone after her foiled attempt to undo her rival, she questions her own intentions, reflects on her value to Henry, and resolves that Becket at least must not gain his ear on the matter:

> The world hath trick'd her – that's the King; if so,
> There was the farce, the feint – not mine. And yet
> I am all but sure my dagger was a feint
> Till the worm turn'd – not life shot up in blood,
> But death drawn in; – [looking at the vial] *this* was
>   no feint then? no.
> But I can swear to that, had she but given
> Plain answer to plain query? nay, methinks
> Had she but bow'd herself to meet the wave
> Of humiliation, worshipt whom she loathed,
> I should have let her be, scorn'd her too much
> To harm her. Henry – Becket tells him this –
> To take my life might lose him Aquitaine.
> Too politic for that. Imprison me?
> No, for it came to nothing – only a feint.

Why should I swear, Eleanor, whom am, or was,
A sovereign power? The King plucks out their eyes
Who anger him, and shall not I, the Queen,
Tear out her heart – kill, kill with knife or venom
One of his slanderous harlots? 'None of such?'
I love her none the more. Tut, the chance gone,
She lives – but not for him; one point is gain'd.
O I, that thro' the Pope divorced King Louis,
Scorning his monkery, – I that wedded Henry,
Honouring his manhood – will he not mock at me
The jealous fool balk'd of her will – with *him*?
But he and he must never meet again.

Tennyson's remains the most substantial treatment of the
Rosamond affair. The Antioch scandal had shown us legend
growing from scraps of fact and rumour. In the development of
the Rosamond story we have watched the extension of this
process: how, from shaky foundations, it evolved, shaped by
various hands, into a neat tale with the simple coherence of a
minor myth, its protagonists reduced to stereotypes. Now with
Tennyson historical time and place have been refashioned into a
setting within which the characters are manoeuvred to give the
illusion of humanity.

At the heart of this redesigned world Eleanor appears as a
woman largely at odds with it. Far from her own lands, the source
of her pride and power, foreign to her subjects, betrayed by a
husband with eyes only for her inheritance, their sons her sole
hope for the future, we can understand if not sympathize with her
jealous scheming against her rival and then Becket when her plans
were foiled. Yet she was not so intent on revenge as not to feel
scruples when confronted with Rosamond's disarming innocence;
and she is herself left uncertain as to whether she would have
steeled herself to deal the fatal stroke.

Tennyson, using the artist's privilege of devising actions and
circumstances to give them coherence, has created, not discovered,
character. The historian lacks this freedom as he practises a kind
of psychological archaeology, unearthing known deeds and proposing the most plausible motives for them. The poet's final doubt
about Eleanor's character was self-induced: the historian's is
inevitable because of the nature of his exercise. Winston
Churchill's sympathy did not, in the case of the Fair Rosamond

story, lie with the historians; and he was surely voicing popular sentiment when he wrote: 'Tiresome investigators have undermined this excellent tale, but it certainly should find its place in any history worthy of the name.'[37]

THE AMAZON QUEEN

In modern times, then, the general perception of Eleanor's personality has been prejudiced by the best-known of the legends connected with her: her supposed dealings with Rosamond Clifford. Counteracting this to some extent has been her subjection to a more flattering kind of character distortion: an idealized picture of her as a romantic figure, resulting from the too ready acceptance of certain tales, some over-enthusiastic interpretation, and a good measure of wishful thinking.

Reports of her behaviour on the crusade were not wholly unfavourable, not that is before her indiscretions in Antioch; and within her lifetime they acquired more than a touch of glamour. The wholesale participation of women in the expedition caused, it is true, the raising of clerical eyebrows in some quarters; but in others it seems that their spirit was admired. One of the first to appeal for help to defend the holy places had, after all, been a woman: the revered queen mother Melisande of Jerusalem. So, in the general fervour, why should not women respond to the call? Privately, perhaps, the ladies were excited more by the prospect of exotic travel and the accomplishment of the greatest pilgrimage than by the thought of military campaigning, of which they could see plenty at home. They had heard of the wonders of the east from those who had returned from 'Outremer', and many had relatives living there. There was, moreover, a growing cult at this time for the legends and marvels of Classical Antiquity, not least the story of Troy as passed on through medieval Latin versions. And Troy brought to mind the exploits there of Penthesilea and her Amazon warriors.

One cannot know whether such matters entered Eleanor's head as she headed east with her companions in the crusading army. It was a decade or so later that she was to be the probable dedicatee, as we saw, of Benoît de Sainte-Maure's *Roman de Troie*. There the Amazons' exploits are treated at some length.[38] Penthesilea brings them to the city to be greeted by Priam and told of Hector's death. They prepare for battle:

> In a vast square beside an ancient towered building the Amazons armed. Penthesilea donned a hauberk whiter than snow upon frost: never, I am sure, might a man see so fine an armed figure. Two maidens to whom their lady showed great honour and much love placed her helmet on her head. It must have been precious and very costly, for the circlet and nose-piece were studded with precious stones and shone more brightly than a sunbeam. Burning with fierce rage, she swiftly mounted a Spanish bay that was bigger, stronger, more mettlesome and speedy than any other horse. It was covered with a silk cloth that seemed whiter than a lily and was hung with a hundred tiny golden, tinkling bells. Without more delay she girt on the polished steel sword, with which she will strike great powerful blows. By its strap of rich brocade she took a stout shield, whiter than snow and with a pure gold boss and bordered with gems: fine, blazing rubies and lustrous green emeralds. This she hung close at her neck. A maiden passed to her a lance of ash wood with a keen steel point and a beautiful bright pennant. Then she had her company mount quickly, without more ado. Of the thousand and more there are not ten who lack armour on heads, faces, arms and flanks. Over their double-linked hauberks threaded with gold they let their lovely hair hang free, groomed to such resplendence as to make pure gold seem dark. Bold and stout-hearted and with shields at the ready, they rode their horses straight through the gates. No such company had been seen since the world began nor will be again so long as it lasts; and each one of them bore a pennant on her sturdy, steel-tipped lance.

It is no wonder if those familiar with such accounts of noble, female warriors should find an analogy with the band of ladies who rode off to the crusade. Towards the end of the century the Greek chronicler Nicetas Choniates surely had Eleanor herself in mind when he described the arrival of the crusaders at Constantinople:

> Even women travelled in their ranks, boldly sitting astride in their saddles as men do, dressed in male clothes and, with their lances and armour, looking just like men. With their warlike looks, they behaved in an even more masculine way than the Amazons. Among them there was even a second Penthesilea: a woman who, because

of the gold embroidery on the hem of her dress, was nicknamed Chrysopus (Golden Foot).[39]

So glorious a sight was apt to turn the heads of historians, who were even inclined to ascribe to the ladies much of the initiative in the crusade. Thus Joseph François Michaud, who wrote his history of the crusades in 1812–22:

> A great number of women, attracted by the example of Eleanor of Guienne, took up the cross, and armed themselves with sword and lance. A crowd of knights eagerly followed them; and indeed a species of shame seemed attached to all who did not go to fight the infidels. History relates that distaffs and spindles were sent to those who would not take arms, as an appropriate reproach for their cowardice. The troubadours and trouvères, whose songs were so much liked, and who employed themselves in singing the victories of knights over the Saracens, determined to follow into Asia the heroes and the dames they had celebrated in their verses. Queen Eleanor and Louis the Young took several troubadours and minstrels with them into the East, to alleviate the tediousness of a long journey.[40]

The prim Agnes Strickland did not approve of such goings-on:

> When queen Eleanora received the cross from St Bernard, at Vezalai, she directly put on the dress of an Amazon; and her ladies, all actuated by the same frenzy, mounted on horseback, and forming a lightly armed squadron, surrounded the queen when she appeared in public, calling themselves queen Eleanora's bodyguard. They practised Amazonian exercises, and performed a thousand follies in public, to animate their zeal as practical crusaders. By the suggestion of their young queen, this band of mad-women sent their useless distaffs, as presents, to all the knights and nobles who had the good sense to keep out of the crusading expedition.

Strickland's acceptance of the legend is plain from her very anti-feminist vituperations:

> Such fellow-soldiers as queen Eleanora and her Amazons would have been quite sufficient to disconcert the plans and impede the projects of Hannibal himself; and though king Louis conducted himself with great ability and courage in his difficult enterprise, no

prudence could counteract the misfortune of being encumbered
with an army of fantastic women . . . . .

The freaks of queen Eleanora and her female warriors were the
cause of all the misfortunes that befell king Louis and his army,
especially in the defeat at Laodicea. The king had sent forward the
queen and her ladies, escorted by his choicest troops, under the
guard of count Maurienne. He charged them to choose for their
camp the arid but commanding ground which gave them a view
over the defiles of the valley of Laodicea. . . . Queen Eleanora acted
in direct opposition to his rational directions. She insisted on her
detachment of the army halting in a lovely romantic valley, full of
verdant grass and gushing fountains. The king was encumbered by
the immense baggage which, William of Tyre declares, the female
warriors of queen Eleanora persisted in retaining in the camp at all
risks.

Our historian goes on to tell how Louis, obliged to go looking for
her, was ambushed by the Arabs and at one point forced to defend
himself from the branches of a tree.

At length, by efforts of personal heroism, he succeeded in placing
himself between the detachment of his ladies and the Saracens. But
it was not till the dawn of day that he discovered his advanced
troops, encamped in the romantic valley chosen by his poetical
queen. Seven thousand of the flower of French chivalry paid with
their lives the penalty of their queen's inexperience in warlike
tactics; all the provision was cut off; the baggage containing the
fine array of the lady-warriors, which had proved such an en-
cumbrance to the king, was plundered by the Arabs and Saracens;
and the whole army was reduced to great distress.[41]

Although there is no reliable evidence to support the notion of
these noble wives of warrior husbands seeing themselves in the
Amazon role and by their frivolous cavortings undermining the
whole enterprise, modern writers have been reluctant to dismiss it
entirely. Amy Kelly, for instance, speaks of the legend of their
transvestite antics at Vézelay, but adds: 'This dazzling dramatiza-
tion of the story of the Amazons, popular in every castle, must
have made a sensation and stimulated the recruiting notably.' And
later she affirms: 'She appears to have kept en route to her role of
Penthesilea, which, as it is said, had been such a success and
inspiration at Vézelay.'[42] But although we may sometimes suspect

Eleanor of drawing inspiration from the courtly literature of her day, our caution in this instance cannot be too extreme.

THE COURTS OF LOVE

Tennyson's depiction, following Strickland, of Eleanor as a 'troubadour' is not totally implausible, though there is no documentation to support it. We know of a handful of *trobairitz*, the female counterparts of the troubadours, noble ladies with a countess or two among them; so there were no social impediments to Eleanor's practising the art. Her family, we remember, had its exponents in the shape of her grandfather William and her favourite son Richard; and she may well have tried her hand at a tactful song or two. It is also a safe assumption that more troubadours than Bernard of Ventadour enjoyed her patronage at one time or another. Even if she did not herself compose, we can reasonably conclude that she had a lively interest in new ways of handling the eternal theme of love and in observing the social and literary posturings of its aficionados. All this had, after all, acquired in large measure the character of a refined courtly game.[43]

If these conclusions can be drawn with some confidence, they have not been enough to satisfy past generations of scholars as well as popular historians, who have magnified unreasonably Eleanor's role in this romantic revolution. She has been seen as presiding at Poitiers over actual 'courts of love' in the full juridical sense, where specific cases were debated and judgements issued. In this she would have been no mere observer, but would have played a leading part in promoting and codifying the amoral system of *fin amor* which for more than a century has been commonly known as 'courtly love'.

The whole idea stems from what is now accepted as a too literal interpretation of the treatise *De Amore* by Andreas Capellanus, or Andrew the Chaplain, which I mentioned earlier. Nothing certain is known of this Andrew, who seems to have written his provocative work between 1186 and 1196 at the court of Eleanor's daughter Marie of Champagne. It purports to be instruction offered to a young man in the ways and proper conduct of lovers. In it Andrew defines the nature of love and its various manifesta-

tions, and how it may be pursued and maintained by the discrimi-
nating; particular cases are pronounced upon, and the God of
Love's thirty-one rules are listed as vouchsafed to a British knight
at King Arthur's court. In a final section, however, Andrew calls
all his instruction into question by recommending his young friend
to turn his back on it and think rather of directing his thoughts to
God. The retraction is reminiscent of Ovid, the work's principal
inspiration; and the very brevity of this final section suggests a
conniving wink from Andrew as, living up to his nominal office,
he offers his unexpected advice to the young tyro.

   To overturn in this way his previous lessons would seem a
gratuitous snub to the fine ladies whose judgements he had just
reported. They were Marie herself, an anonymous group in
Gascony, Louis's third queen Adela of Champagne, Eleanor's
niece the countess of Flanders, Ermengarde countess of Narbonne,
and Queen Eleanor herself. The first of the latter's judgements
concerned a lover who, having obtained his lady's permission to
transfer his affections elsewhere, later returned to her claiming
that he had remained faithful, having merely wished to test her
constancy. The lady did not accept his explanation and refused
him her love.

> But the opinion of Queen Eleanor, who was consulted on the
> matter, seems to be just the opposite of this woman's. She said, 'We
> know that it comes from the nature of love that those who are in
> love often falsely pretend that they desire new embraces, that they
> may the better test the faith and constancy of their co-lover.
> Therefore a woman sins against the nature of love itself if she keeps
> back her embraces from her lover on this account or forbids him
> her love, unless she has clear evidence that he has been unfaithful to
> her.'

After this, Eleanor pronounced on two other cases:

> A worthless young man and an older knight of excellent character
> sought the love of the same woman. The young man argued that
> she ought to prefer him to the older man because if he got the love
> he was after he might by means of it acquire an excellent character,
> and it would be no small credit to the woman if through her a
> worthless man was made into a man of good character.

To this Queen Eleanor replied as follows: 'Although the young man may show that by receiving love he might rise to be a worthy man, a woman does not do very wisely if she chooses to love an unworthy man, especially when a good and eminently worthy one seeks her love. It might happen that because of the faults of the unworthy man his character would not be improved even if he did receive the good things he was hoping for, since the seeds which we sow do not always produce a crop.'

This other love affair was submitted to the decision of the same queen. A certain man who had in ignorance joined in love with a woman who was related to him, sought to leave her when he discovered his fault. But the woman was bound by the chain of love and tried to keep him in love's observances, saying that the crime was fully excused by the fact that when they began to enjoy the love it was without any sin.

In this affair the Queen answered as follows: 'A woman who under the excuse of a mistake of any kind seeks to preserve an incestuous love is clearly going contrary to what is right and proper. We are always bound to oppose any of those incestuous and damnable actions which we know even human laws punish by very heavy penalties.'[44]

It is hardly surprising that Andrew's text was seized upon by social and literary historians alike. Here is not only a manual of courtly love, that profoundly influential twelfth-century phenomenon, but also the romantic Queen Eleanor herself giving her measured opinions on sexual relationships, in which she was in more than one sense a past mistress, or so popular report had it. For good measure it was supposed that the book records the minutes, as it were, of a council of grand ladies assembled for amorous debate at Eleanor's court at Poitiers, presumably some time in the late 1160s or early 1170s. It all seems, alas, too convenient to be true.

Eleanor's own judgements could, of course, be taken as the expression of the royal conscience, especially as regards the problems of age difference between the partners and the belated discovery of consanguinity. But they could equally well have been devised as oblique comment on the marital difficulties of the Plantagenets, especially if taken together with the countess Marie's considered verdict that true love cannot exist within marriage. It is risky to take too seriously a writer schooled by Ovid who makes a show of recanting at the end of his work. It is even more rash to conclude, without any support from the text, that the ladies in question were, on this or any other occasion, assembled together for their pronouncements.

.The fact is that we have no evidence for there having been any contact after Eleanor's divorce from Louis between herself and her daughter Marie, who was seven at the time. As for the 'courts of love', they too lack any basis in recorded fact. It has even been argued that the court of Champagne should not be seen either as a centre for the promulgation of the courtly love ethic or 'as a point of literary interchange between north and south'.[45]

It is with some regret that we have to consign yet another of Agnes Strickland's romantic pages to the realm of legend:

> The political sovereignty of her native dominions was not the only authority exercised by Eleanora in 'gay Guienne'. She was, by hereditary right, chief reviewer and critic of the poets of Provence. At certain festivals held by her, after the custom of her ancestors, called Courts of Love, all new sirventes and chansons were sung or recited before her by the troubadours. She then, assisted by a conclave of her ladies, sat in judgement, and pronounced sentence on their literary merits. She was herself a popular troubadour poet. Her chansons were remembered long after death had raised a barrier against flattery, and she is reckoned among the authors of France. The decisions of the young duchess-queen in her troubadour Courts of Love, have met with the reprobation of modern French historians, on account of their immorality; they charge her with avowing the startling opinion, that no true love could exist between married persons; and it is certain, that the encouragement she gave to her sister Petronilla and the Count Raoul of Vermandois, offered too soon a practical illustration of these evil principles.[46]

Strickland situates the gatherings at the time when Eleanor was queen of France. Amy Kelly, in one of the more extravagantly imaginative chapters of her biography, allows us to eavesdrop on one such occasion at Poitiers in about 1170. There she has installed Marie of Champagne as mistress of ceremonies; and it is a pleasure for us to suspend our disbelief as we mingle with the elegant company in the queen's new hall, listening to musical preludes and a Breton lay or episode from a romance. Then the lady jurors are called to attention as a young knight puts a point of love-conduct to them, through an advocate so as himself to remain anonymous. His own case then another are debated and judgements given before the court adjourns to the moonlit terrace for a breath of air and snatches of song.

> But the April moon sets at last upon the grand assize of the ladies; and cocks call for the sun from a distant croft in the valley. Quiet falls upon the palace and the little streets of the high place where the carven saints and angels dream in the portals of the Romanesque façades; and in the stillness lauds sound faintly from the precincts of Saint Porchaire.[47]

One would wish it so and is willing, even eager, to join the author in her eavesdropping. But then one remembers that this too may be no more than legend, woven from the highly suspect evidence of a clerical ironist.

THE CANK'RED QUEEN

There is nothing romantic about Shakespeare's Eleanor in his *Life and Death of King John*, which revolves round the tragic fate of Arthur of Brittany.[48] It is Arthur's mother Constance who refers to the queen as a 'cank'red grandam' (Act II, Sc. 1); and the French ambassador is no more flattering in speaking of John's mother as 'An Ate, stirring him to blood and strife' (Act II, Sc. 1), Ate being the personification of blind folly and the loss of moral judgement. As such, we feel Eleanor's brooding presence throughout the play until her death is reported in the fourth act. She is above all a schemer, determined to protect her son's right to the throne in the face of Constance's ambitions for Arthur. On her release and Arthur's capture at Mirebeau, John assures the boy of his own and his 'grandam's' love for him; but then, as Eleanor draws Arthur aside with an endearing 'Come hither, little kinsman; hark, a word', John turns to Hubert to order his murder (Act III, Sc. 2). When we learn in quick succession of three deaths, those of Arthur, Eleanor and Constance, that of the old queen gives us least cause for regret.

In an early ballad, 'Queen Eleanor's Confession', collected by Bishop Percy, we see her in a contrite mood, thinking herself to be on her death-bed. The merry poet shows her to have little affection

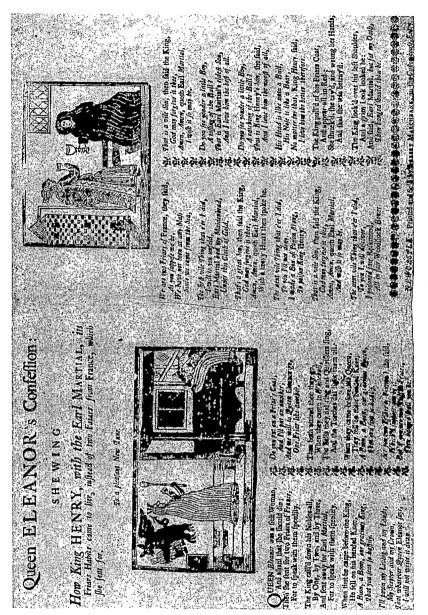

Plate 12 A crudely illustrated version of 'Queen Eleanor's Confession', the first picture apparently partially inspired by legendary elements extraneous to the ballad. (Douce Ballads 3., fol. 80r.)

for 'King Henry's youngest son' in his scurrilous account of her past misdeeds.[49]

> Queene Elianor was a sicke woman
> And afraid that she would dye:
> Then she sent for two fryars of France
> To speke with her speedilye.
>
> The king calld downe his nobles all,
> By one, by two, by three;
> Earl marshall, Ile goe shrive the queene,
> And thou shalt wend with mee.
>
> A boone, a boone, quoth earl marshall,
> And fell on his bended knee,
> That whatsoever queene Elianor saye,
> No harme thereof may bee.
>
> Ile pawne my landes, the king then cryd,
> My sceptre, crowne, and all,
> That whatsoever queen Elianor saye,
> No harme thereof shall fall.
>
> Do thou put on a fryar's coat,
> And Ile put on another;
> And we will to queen Elianor goe
> Like fryar and his brother.
>
> Thus both attired then they goe:
> When they came to Whitehall,
> The bells did ring, and the quiristers sing,
> And the torches did lighte them all.
>
> When that they came before the queene
> They fell on their bended knee;
> A boone, a boone, our gracious queene,
> That you sent so hastilee.
>
> Are you two fryars of France, she sayd,
> As I suppose you bee?
> But if you are two English fryars,
> You shall hang on the gallowes tree.

We are two fryars of France, they sayd,
As you suppose we bee,
We have not been at any masse
Sith we came from the sea.

The first vile thing that ever I did
I will to you unfolde;
Earl marshall had my maidenhead,
Beneath this cloth of golde.

That's a vile sinne, then sayd the king;
May God forgive it thee!
Amen, amen, quoth earl marshall;
With a heavye heart spake hee.

The next vile thing that ever I did,
To you Ile not denye,
I made a boxe of poyson strong,
To poison king Henrye.

That's a vile sinne, then sayd the king,
May God forgive it thee!
Amen, amen, quoth earl marshall;
And I wish it so may bee.

The next vile thing that ever I did,
To you I will discover;
I poysoned fair Rosamonde,
All in fair Woodstocke bower.

That's a vile sinne, then sayd the king,
May God forgive it thee!
Amen, amen, quoth earl marshall;
And I wish it so may bee.

Do you see yonders little boye,
A tossing of the balle?
That is earl marshall's eldest sonne,
And I love him the best of all.

Do you see yonders little boye,
A catching of the balle?
That is king Henrye's youngest son,
And I love him the worst of all.

His head is fashyon'd like a bull;
His nose is like a boare.
No matter for that, king Henrye cryd,
I love him the better therfore.

The king pulled off his fryar's coate,
And appeared all in redde:
She shrieked, and cryd, and wrung her hands,
And sayd she was betrayde.

The king lookt over his left shoulder,
And a grimme look looked he;
Earl marshall, he sayd, but for my oathe,
Or hanged thou shouldst bee.

With this ballad we have returned to the picture of the licentious
Eleanor, the 'giddy queen' as Agnes Strickland dubbed her, subject
to bouts of 'disgusting levity'. The poem, of which a Scottish
version exists, seems to have been first printed in the late
seventeenth century. Its origins, though, may go much further
back; for the theme of·the husband acting as his unsuspecting
wife's confessor was a popular one found, for instance, in an Old
French fabliau and in one of Boccaccio's tales. That it became
personalized round Eleanor is not surprising in view of her reputed
sexual misdemeanors.

Here, then, we have a further example of the continual give-
and-take between history and legend. We have seen the process
operating in different ways. With the Antioch scandal, events and
attitudes gave rise to rumours, baseless or not, from which lurid
fictions evolved. In other circumstances, historical facts could
evoke memories of well-known tales circulating at the time; and
the two sets of data might then become merged in a hybrid
account or 'tall story' in which truth was overlaid with fantasy.
The Amazon crusaders would fall into this category. I would
suggest that another instance, though not directly involving Eleanor, is found in the accounts of the future. Philip Augustus's
misadventure on his way to be crowned. It will be remembered
that, separated from his hunting party, the prince became lost in
the forest. Rigord, a monk of Saint-Denis, gave a graphic description of his encounter with a hideous, coal-black, misshapen giant
of a man, who nevertheless turned out to be amiable enough to

rescue him from his plight.[50] Unless I am mistaken, Rigord's testimony, still found in history books, had been embellished by reference to an episode in *Yvain*, one of Chrétien de Troyes's romances. Fiction has added a tasty relish to fact.

In the above cases, history has been the starting point for legendary development. With 'Queen Eleanor's Confession' the process has been reversed. There a popular tale had brought to the mind of some balladeer memories of the English queen as he understood her to have been; and he amused himself and us by casting her in the ready-made role he found there. Her 'confessions' are, of course, part of her legend; but the frame-story is from another, independent tradition.

These, then, are the main legends which can be set against the known facts of Eleanor's life and some suggestions as to the processes involved in their formation and growth. In my final chapter I shall be skating on thinner ice. The medieval narrative poets and, increasingly from the thirteenth century, writers of prose were apt to smuggle into their works disguised references to real characters or events. With this in mind, I shall explore the possibility of such largely 'incognito' appearances of Eleanor and her activities, real or imagined, in a variety of medieval texts. These will for the most part be in French, the main literary language on both sides of the Channel in and well beyond her own day. Can she even be credited with some discreetly formative influence on a wide area of Western literature? I can promise only a speculative answer.

4

Literature

History, legend, literature: let me first define these terms as I shall be using them in the following discussion. By history I shall mean reasonably certain facts: events, political and social circumstances and developments, general cultural movements. My second chapter was concerned with history as far as it can be established. The chronicles of the time are, of course, valuable repositories of historical fact, but we have found them very ready to falsify it, intentionally or by accident, and to contaminate it with elements borrowed from legend or literature.

Legend in this context is largely the stuff of oral tale-telling. It may be the popular deformation of historical fact, or mythical material of diverse origin circulating in common lore, or wholly apocryphal anecdotes, pious or profane; and as such it was liable to be taken seriously by the gullible, manipulated for particular purposes by the unscrupulous, or accepted as possible by honest people lacking the means of forming sound critical judgements. By its nature, legend in this sense remains unrecorded except when it is drawn into chronicles or used in literature.

Literature I here take to be consciously crafted compositions intended for presentation to a public. Although they have at some stage been committed to writing, in Eleanor's day they would for the most part have been delivered orally; but as literacy increased, private reading became more common, especially with a growing preference for prose over verse from about 1200. With their reverence for authority, medieval writers seldom indulged in large-scale invention; so their works are for the most part re-handlings either of earlier literature both lyric and narrative and often perpetuating stereotypes, or of oral tales that have come

162

their way, or perhaps of gleanings from other legendary material. Now and then they might stir in some elements of fact, occasionally based on personal experience but more often on hearsay. The immediate purpose of the journeyman poet or clerk was usually to secure patronage from the aristocracy or, increasingly from the thirteenth century, from wealthy bourgeois. To this end they supplied entertainment and propaganda in varying proportions.

In chapter 3 we saw various examples of literature feeding and fattening itself on legend, which there almost totally usurped the place of history. In those cases, Eleanor was the explicit subject, and no interpretation was necessary. To trawl through what purport to be fictions in search of covert references to her, or even barely conscious reminiscences, will be a more delicate and hazardous operation. It will involve an assessment of the interplay of legend and history within literature, with the aim of drawing us a little closer to Eleanor as she actually was, as she was perceived to be in her own age, and even as she may sometimes have perceived herself.

That this approach may be attempted at all is due in part to the limited informational resources of the medieval writers, of whom even the better educated lacked the means to create or truly appreciate historical perspective. This meant that although their narratives may have been notionally set, say, in Classical Antiquity or the reign of Charlemagne or the far-off days of King Arthur, they could only trace them through against a familiar background: the physical conditions, social structures and attitudes of their own times. The sophisticated Chrétien de Troyes certainly had some vague perception, albeit conventional, of the flow of history: 'Through the books we possess we learn of the deeds of the people of past times and of the world as it used to be. Our books have taught us how Greece ranked first in chivalry and learning; then chivalry passed to Rome along with the fund of transcendent learning that has now come to France.' Yet he went on to assure us of the Greeks and Romans that 'their glowing embers are dead',[1] and embarked on a romance of Byzantine intrigue and Arthurian gallantry in which he held the mirror to his own world. And when elsewhere he painted a portrait of Ovid's Philomena, he had in his mind's eye not a Roman maiden but some well nurtured daughter of the twelfth-century aristocracy.[2]

Beneath its surface narratives and conceits, then, medieval literature embraced to a greater or lesser extent contemporary reality. This was the reality within which Eleanor passed her long and varied life, and it predicated a view of the world and man's place in it which would in broad outline have been shared by her. Our search for her, or her shadow, will be conducted chiefly in the area of courtly literature; for that is where the upper classes would have found the reflection of their own style of life, more or less idealized and to that extent having an exemplary function. These works, standing at the very heart of their culture, performed a service beyond mere entertainment: they not only portrayed but also helped to reinforce the role and principles of the feudal aristocracy.

Although in Eleanor's day the writing of vernacular literature was a largely male preserve, we do know of a few early women poets and even one who turned her hand to narrative. Marie de France produced a collection of fables and translated from the Latin the legend of St Patrick's Purgatory; but she is best known for having put into verse a dozen *lais*, short tales of love and adventure mostly derived from Breton legend.[3] Despite her name, she seems to have been resident in England and probably dedicated the *Lais* to Henry II or possibly his son the Young King. This would place their composition before 1189. Her identity is uncertain: one suggestion is that she was Henry's half-sister, who became Abbess of Shaftesbury; but in any case, her considerable education and a familiarity with the aristocratic life makes it quite likely that she moved in court circles. We have no means of knowing how much, if any, of her work dates from before Eleanor's captivity or how closely she may have been associated with the queen. For us, her interest lies in the fact that she was a woman; and her *Lais* show enough personal features to let us sense the feelings and preoccupations of a woman breathing the same air as Eleanor, perhaps even to give us a vicarious glimpse into Eleanor's own mind.

Marie's stories contain many vignettes of aristocratic life on both sides of the Channel: in court and castle, journeys by land and sea, wars and tournaments, dealings between lord and vassal and between individual knights, the administration of lands and of justice and, within the social group, scenes of leisured dalliance, gossip and petty jealousies as well as loyalty and largess. Plainly, though, Marie's main concern was with the assorted love relationships and the discreet pointing of her lesson that life's greatest joy was to be experienced by lovers matched in age and rank, their devotion sealed by mutual respect and fidelity. Marriage was a bonus if those conditions were met; if not, adultery could be condoned. Worst of all are those situations resulting from arranged unions: old, jealous husbands treating their young wives as chattels. In several of her tales the wife pines behind barred doors: one is imprisoned in a tower for seven long years before a lover appears to her in bird-form. Eleanor would have cause to sympathize with these estranged ladies! Marie's call for sincerity within love is far from the posturings of the troubadours, although one story of a lady unable to choose between four suitors does contain the elements of one of those love debates promoted by Andrew the Chaplain. The lady in question pays for her harsh prevarication by being left with three corpses and one disabled lover. So even here one detects in Marie a deep sense of the vulnerability of women, at least in the affairs of the heart.

Eleanor might therefore have found food for thought as well as enjoyment in Marie's work. To anticipate a later stage of my discussion, I would suggest that her attention could well have been caught by the presentation in one *lai* of the legendary couple King Arthur and Queen Guenevere. Neither is shown in an ideal light. The story of Lanval opens at Carlisle, after Arthur has been campaigning against the Picts and the Scots. In distributing gifts and favours, the king completely overlooks the hero, a prince from a distant land come to do him service. Later in the tale, however, he does show concern both for his wife's honour and for the proper meting out of justice. There is, on the other hand, nothing good about Guenevere, who is revealed as not only lecherous, but mendacious too, when her attempted seduction of Lanval is rebuffed. The plot, though, is traditional, which would have dispensed Eleanor from taking offence at the queen's disreputable behaviour, even if winks might have been exchanged in other quarters.

ELEANOR IN DISGUISE

I mentioned in an earlier chapter the vogue among the Plantagenets of the 'Matter of Britain', including the Tristan legend, a polished version of which was produced by a certain Thomas, probably for Henry and Eleanor at some time before their estrangement. Although only the concluding episodes have survived, the outstanding German poet Gottfried von Strassburg modelled his own *Tristan* on it, so Thomas's version can be reconstructed with reasonable confidence.[4] That he was well acquainted with England, whether or not that was his home, is evident from his description of London and its port: it is the fairest city of Christendom, the mainstay of England, drawing trade from every Christian land, and full of worthy, honourable, generous and good-humoured people. Thomas also accurately traces a voyage from London through the Channel to Brittany. Of more immediate interest is that he makes Mark king not just of Cornwall but of all England. He thus invites the association of Mark with King Henry and hence of Iseut with his queen Eleanor.

One must of course beware, especially in view of the traditional roots of the story, of reading the work as a *roman à clef* on so flimsy a basis. A. T. Hatto, on the other hand, by adjusting the historical correspondences, makes an intriguing case for seeing in Mark an image of the well-meaning but ineffectual King Louis, Eleanor's first husband, and behind Tristan the more dynamic figure of Henry. In support of this he cites Mark's voluntary severance from his wife when he dismisses the lovers from court, and also the supposed conferment on Tristan of the Plantagenet armorial bearings, though this fact has been disputed. These associations as well as Thomas's use of courtly dialectic have led Hatto to see in Eleanor the poet's patron and adviser.[5]

If a modern reader finds it easy to draw such parallels between romance and reality, they are likely to have struck the poet's contemporaries even more forcibly, whatever his intention. The individuals in question could have experienced some personal involvement with the characters and their predicaments, feeling flattered or taking offence at the way in which their fictional counterparts were portrayed. They might even have been prompted to review their own behaviour and take to heart any implicit lessons, like one of Chrétien's heroines who expressed her revulsion at the thought of being taken for another Iseut. Underlying much of the discussion that follows, therefore, will be the likelihood that such parallels between fictional and historical characters and situations as seem clear to us would have been equally evident to any member of the medieval literary public who was apprised of the relevant facts.

The atmosphere in the court as evoked in Thomas's romance is one with which Eleanor would have been familiar. It was a rather claustrophobic place where rivalries festered and, despite the courtly manners, ladies were a ready prey for philandering knights. Not every amorous affair was sublimated in terms of a subtle love-debate such as was proposed by the clerkish Thomas. At one point he suspends his narrative to compare the unhappiness inflicted by love on his leading characters: Mark, Tristan, Iseut and Tristan's neglected bride Iseut of the White Hands. Whose was the greatest sorrow? Let lovers themselves, he says, be the judge. Again we recall Andrew the Chaplain and the rulings he records. Such refined speculation, one assumes, would have been to Eleanor's taste.

However, it is easy to imagine her feeling some qualms when she hears Yseult's companion Brengain berating her mistress for her loose morals: what a woman learns in her youth, unless she is rebuked for it, will stay with her all her life, should she be able to have her way; Mark has been too tolerant and should have punished her for it: 'You are shaming your lineage, your friends and your lord!'[6] Brengain's diatribe (and there is much more) is likely to have struck home with Eleanor, had she reviewed her whole life in terms of Hatto's analogies; and one is even forced to wonder if she was not already out of favour at court when Thomas loosed off his moralizing shafts against illicit love. It is perhaps safest to conclude that Eleanor's enjoyment of his work would not have been unalloyed.

With the 'Matter of Britain' we have been on the Plantagenets' home ground. To them the adaptations of Classical legend would have seemed more remote in their subject matter. The *Roman de Thebes*, probably composed, as we saw, on their territory and in the early years of Henry's reign, was less liable to evoke such personal associations. The source material had, though, been adapted by the poet to have some relevance for his courtly public.[7] His demonstration of the evils of fratricidal strife seems to carry echoes of that between the sons of William the Conqueror; and certain characters and events are marked by memories of the First Crusade. For a couple of his lines (971–2) the poet appears to have been inspired by thoughts of Eleanor herself. Speaking of the two daughters of Adrastus, he declares that their laughter and kisses were worth more than London or Poitiers: a pretty compliment, if intended, for the Queen of England and Countess of Poitiers.

Here is an illustration of a technique common among medieval poets: the infiltration into their works of historical elements, often anachronistic, to lend a spurious credibility to their fictions. Just as from the thirteenth century writers turned to prose as a medium more apt to convince their readers of the truth of their stories, however preposterous, so others contrived a sham plausibility by leavening their fables with a few recognizable facts. This process, characteristic of the writers of romance, is the reverse of that found in the epic chansons de geste, for which some threads of history formed the starting-point round which ever more elaborate tissues of fiction were woven. A glance at a few more romances from Eleanor's lifetime or a little later will reinforce this point that history, often in conjunction with credible geography, could lend a sham authentication to a fabulous plot.

Gautier d'Arras had distinguished patrons. Working between about 1170 and 1185, he dedicated his *Ille et Galeron* to Beatrice, the wife of Frederick Barbarossa, and undertook *Eracle* for Count Thibaut of Blois and Eleanor's daughter Marie of Champagne and offered it to Count Baudouin of Hainaut.[8] The first of these works is the story of a young Breton nobleman, Ille, who is robbed of his birthright before being trained and knighted at the court of France, winning the hand of Galeron, sister of the Breton duke Conan, then serving for a time with the Emperor of Rome, whose daughter he weds after Galeron's retreat to a convent. Anthime Fourrier disentangled various historical strands from the fiction, including reminiscences of the rivalry between the Greek and German emperors and of various events of past and contemporary Breton history, some involving Henry II and his sons.[9]

Of more direct interest to us is *Eracle*, which seems to date from the time of Eleanor's captivity. We are nevertheless reminded of her at the beginning of the story, when the hero is born to the wife of a Roman senator in answer to their prayers after seven childless years. Gautier's patron Marie might have reflected that it was after seven years of her mother's marriage to Louis that Eleanor appealed to Saint Bernard and her prayers were met by the conception of Marie herself. Initially called Dieudonné, like Marie's half-brother Philip Augustus, the hero was only later christened Eracle.

The years pass, and the Roman emperor Laïs enters the story. He too has enjoyed seven years of marriage: to Athanaïs, on whom he dotes. When he has to go away to the wars, and fearful that his wife might turn her affections elsewhere, he seeks Eracle's advice as to whether or not he should shut her away. Eracle argues strongly that such a virtuous woman should be left at liberty: were she imprisoned, she might react to her husband's detriment. Laïs is not convinced; and, more weak than wicked, he leaves Athanaïs confined to a tower and guarded by twenty-four knights and their own wives. Eracle's fears are shown to be well founded when the empress contrives an affair with a young harpist. When Laïs returns and discovers his betrayal, he is persuaded by Eracle not to take vengeance on Athanaïs, but instead to repudiate her in favour of her lover. Alerted by the early apparent echoes from Eleanor's past, we cannot fail to find more in the subsequent events, with the emperor reminding us now of the doting but resigned Louis, now of the sterner Henry. Could we even read into Eracle's compassionate reasoning a veiled plea on behalf of the captive mother of Gautier's patron Marie?

At about the same time and in this case on Plantagenet territory, Hue de Rotelande composed two romances, *Ipomedon* and *Protheselaus*.[10] Hailing probably from Rhuddlan in the Welsh Marches, he was living near Hereford at the time he dedicated the second of these to Gilbert Fitz-Baderon, lord of Monmouth, who died before 1191. Although his characters masquerade behind good Classical names (the influence of the *Roman de Thebes* is apparent), the action of both works takes us to lands very much in the news in Hue's day: Sicily, Calabria, Apulia, France and several of its provinces. The first tells of the love of Ipomedon, prince of Apulia, for La Fière, who has inherited Calabria; and the second recounts that of their son Protheselaus for Medea, the queen of Crete. Both feature fratricidal feuds: Ipomedon, for instance, helps Atreus the king of France in his war against his brother Daire (Darius) king of Lorraine.

All this is redolent of contemporary domestic and international affairs: the stormy relations of Henry's sons (as well as the strife between William the Conqueror's sons and, indeed, between Polynices and Eteocles in the Theban story), and events in the Norman kingdom of the Two Sicilies. In *Ipomedon* the Sicilian king Meleager was childless, as was the actual king William who, in 1174, had married Joanna, the daughter of Henry and Eleanor. She, it will be remembered, was detained in Palermo on William's death in 1189 by his usurping nephew Tancred, and was only released when Richard arrived on the island. One might see echoes of this in Ipomedon's rescue of Meleager's niece La Fière, besieged by an importunate suitor. There is in fact a wealth of associations ready for the making by Hue's fellow-subjects, for they were well aware of happenings in those southern parts: it is known, for instance, that one of his neighbours near Hereford had spent some time as chaplain to the King of Sicily.

At one point the poet, in a personal aside, makes a direct reference to an event that must have been fresh in his own memory. It is to 'the great overseas war, when Rouen was besieged by the king, which brought great trouble on the country' (*Ipomedon*, ll. 5350–52). The allusion is to Henry's siege of Rouen in that fateful year of 1174, shortly after he had brought his wife back from Normandy as a captive. Eleanor, it must be said, has left no clear mark on Hue's work. One might look for something of her personality behind the imperious features of La Fière and even, in *Protheselaus*, see Hue's unusual stress on reconciliations and their happy effects as having some relevance to Henry's treatment of his queen. But if this is a mark of his sympathy for her, his discretion was absolute.

The interest among the aristocracy in Sicilian affairs continued into the thirteenth century. It was perhaps about 1220 that a poet dedicated his romance *Guillaume de Palerne* to Yolande, daughter of the Count of Hainaut.[11] Yolande's husband had actually been on the island with the crusaders in 1190–1. The Guillaume of the title was the son of the king of Apulia and the Greek emperor's daughter Félise. Brought up near Rome, he went to Sicily to thwart the King of Spain, who had designs on his sister as a prospective daughter-in-law and was besieging his mother in Palermo. His destiny was to marry the daughter of the Emperor of Rome, whom he eventually succeeded. Alexandre Micha in his edition is inclined to see Roger of Sicily, who died in 1154, as the prototype for Guillaume, whilst the besieged Félise, like La Fière in *Ipomedon*, has much in common with Joanna, whose imprisonment had also been in Palermo. Other equations could be made, but none of them directly involving Eleanor.

Leaving the Sicilian scene with its Plantagenet associations, we may notice in passing an amusing but very different little poem which dates from about 1190 and features a number of high-born ladies of the time, all presumably known to Eleanor and including her daughter Marie. This is *Le Tournoiement des dames* by Huon d'Oisi, an otherwise unknown rhymester.[12] He gives a wry account of that imaginary tournament contested at Lagny by a company of worthy dames, who wish to experience at first hand the blows normally dealt by their lovers on their behalf. All equipped like Amazons, they joust most gallantly. In their number are 'the queen' (presumably the Queen of France) and the Countess of Champagne, a fierce contender (in a similar, anonymous, poem she carries off the honours). There is evidently some topicality here; but I mention it only as a skit in the courtly love tradition on those active, combative ladies of Eleanor's acquaintance and of whom she was surely one.

She showed those qualities throughout her life; and even as a virtual octogenarian she displayed them at Mirebeau in her confrontation with the pretender Arthur of Brittany, who was operating, it will be recalled, at the instigation of the French king. If the accounts of the besieged queens we have seen in *Ipomedon* and *Guillaume de Palerne* were at least partly inspired by her daughter Joanna's experience at Palermo, it appears that her own gallant stand at Mirebeau so impressed some later writers of romance that they used it to bolster episodes in their own tales.

Within a few years of the event, I believe it was put to such use in a most unlikely quarter by a poet who signs himself Guillaume le Clerc. In the early years of the thirteenth century he composed a romance, *Fergus*, which is on the surface a tale of fairly orthodox Arthurian adventure.[13] A unique feature is that the action takes place almost entirely in southern Scotland; and a closer examination shows the author to be heavily dependent on the work of Chrétien de Troyes and his followers, which he has parodied to produce what is in effect a skit on the first Grail story and its hero. He tells of the aspirations of Fergus, the son of a wealthy peasant, to serve King Arthur and how, in the course of their fulfilment, the lad seeks and finally weds Galiene, a princess of Lothian who has become queen of that land on her father's death.

While deriving the main lines of his story from the modish romances of his day. Guillaume amused himself by basing certain of his characters on subjects of the Scottish king William the Lion who are known to have frequented his largely French-speaking court. Guillaume's familiarity with the social scene as well as the geography of southern Scotland makes it virtually certain that he was himself a resident in the country and rubbed shoulders with its aristocracy. The most likely candidate I have found for the authorship of the romance is William Malveisin, whom we first meet as a royal clerk in the 1180s and who ended his life as Bishop of St Andrews in 1238.[14] A much travelled man of the world, he was well informed of affairs of state and even represented his king on a number of diplomatic missions to the court of King John.

Towards the end of *Fergus* Queen Galiene is besieged in her castle at Roxburgh by a hostile king and his nephew. With their armies bivouacked before the castle walls, the nephew is admitted to Galiene's presence to put in person the terms for her surrender, but only to be met with her haughty disdain. She manages to send a messenger out of the fortress to seek help in thwarting the would-be usurpers. Fergus comes to her aid with a surprise attack and succeeds in killing the nephew and forcing the king himself to renounce his claims and withdraw. Now although Guillaume le Clerc had a literary source for the broad outline of the episode, a number of features are more closely paralleled by the events at Mirebeau, not least the crucial involvement of a nephew-figure and his elimination: the ill-fated Arthur of Brittany, we remember, was actually John's nephew and also the grand-nephew of King William the Lion. As if to give us a pointer to the associations he was making, the artful poet supplies him with a name which is only found in this romance: Arthofilaus. It surely cannot be by pure chance that this apparently invented name happens to be a virtual anagram of 'Artus li faus', 'the false Arthur'. In any case, a perceptive contemporary could easily have put two and two together and drawn the analogy between Roxburgh and Mirebeau. Indeed, Eleanor's bold stand appears to have become something of a literary motif, and we shall come across further instances of its apparent exploitation.[15]

Eleanor was probably dead by the time Guillaume's romance was circulating on the Continent (it achieved some popularity in the north-east). She would have no doubt felt flattered by being equated with the gallant and beautiful Galiene. On the other hand there is streak of misogyny in the work; and Guillaume seems to have doubted the ability of women to manage public affairs. Galiene herself tells her lords that she must make a good marriage, since she cannot rule her land without a man's help; and later she asserts to King Arthur that 'A land left to a woman is badly governed' (ll. 6648–9). This poet was a sharp-eyed realist; and having evoked the memory of Eleanor, he did not miss the opportunity of making a political point.

In the epics, history or pseudo-history came increasingly to be submerged by material typical more of the romance. Our next text is an example of this hybrid genre, which often tended towards the comic. This is the anonymous *Gaydon*, dating from the first third of the thirteenth century but probably a rehandling of an earlier poem; and in it critics have long fancied they saw the figure of Eleanor lurking behind that of the heroine.[16] The events are set in the reign of Charlemagne, some time after the disaster of Ronce-vaux. Gaydon, the rather quick-tempered duke of Anjou, falls out with the emperor, who is too easily swayed by dishonest advisers. The quarrel leads to a great battle before Angers, in which Charlemagne's allies include Richard of Normandy, King Loth of England, and Gillemer of Scotland. This first part of the story is full of knockabout epic action with some courtly touches and a smattering of rough warrior humour.

Now there enters the romantic heroine: Claresme, who is on her way to pay homage to Charlemagne for her fief of Gascony. She is also bent on a meeting with Gaydon, with whom she has fallen in love purely on the basis of his gallant reputation. She sends him a message proposing marriage and promising to placate the emperor should he comply. Gaydon soon feels the pangs of love himself and responds favourably to her advances. Charles, however, has different plans. Continuing his manoeuvres against Gaydon, he has decided to have Claresme married to his weak-kneed, disreputable favourite. At one point he is concerned to know whether the hero still has the support of the English and Irish, who usually accompany him to tournaments and are excellent men. In the course of the subsequent action, Charles manages to enter Angers, Gaydon's capital, disguised as a pilgrim on his way back from a visit to the Holy Sepulchre in Jerusalem. In the end he becomes reconciled with the hero, whom he makes high seneschal of France. Gaydon's marriage to Claresme is then celebrated with due pomp in Angers. But it is short-lived: in less than a year Claresme dies, whereupon Gaydon retires from the world as a hermit.

This is another case where the poet's contemporaries are likely to make associations with recent history, beginning with the obvious parallel of the marriage of the dazzling, courtly mistress of Gascony (part of Aquitaine) to the fiery Angevin, whom she prefers to a despicable Frenchman. The suspicion that this reflects the actual Eleanor–Louis–Henry triangle is strengthened when the marriage takes place shortly after the pretended return of the French king from an expedition to the Holy Land. There is no telling where the original story was fabricated; but behind its amusing extravagances there would appear to be some pro-Plantagenet bias. The attractive heroine, who is full of initiative, makes no bones about her contempt for the flabby Frenchman, determined as she is to become the wife of the gallant young Angevin, who is in league with the stalwart chivalry of England. Their union is no marriage of convenience, but a true love-match. So it is unusual to find it not the prelude to many years of wedded bliss and a copious family, but a tragically brief affair. One might speculate that the original poet could have been composing some time after the actual marriage of Eleanor to Henry had turned sour, perhaps even while the queen was still in custody. By anchoring his fiction and its associations so firmly in the past, he might have wished to avoid any chance of giving present offence.

The use of ostensibly historical figures, identifiable or not, in the service of humour is a feature of several thirteenth-century romances. This is the case with the Provençal *Flamenca*, perhaps written by a worldly cleric from the Auvergne region.[17] The centre of the action is the Bourbonnais, where the lady Flamenca is the wife of a member of the local nobility. It is, however, at a tournament in Namur that the king of France offends his queen by bearing on his lance-tip a sleeve which she supposes to have been donated by Flamenca. This deludes the latter's husband into paroxysms of jealousy, which lead to his shutting her away in an impregnable tower, which she may leave only to go to church or to the bath-house. A valiant but lecherous knight William from Nevers contrives to effect her improbable seduction in those two localities and thereafter to continue an affair with her under the very nose of her husband. In none of this, not even in the sequestered lady motif, do we catch any glimpse of Eleanor; and I mention the work only because it was the likely inspiration of another romance where she actually makes a brief personal appearance.

The poem in question is the anonymous *Joufroi de Poitiers*, tentatively dated after 1250.[18] It is a delightful medley of history, grossly distorted, and romantic fantasy. In a series of personal interventions the poet, who may have hailed from the south-east of France, makes us privy to a courtly love affair of his own, which proceeds in counterpoint to those of his hero. But this need not concern us; so let me briefly summarize the rest of this preposterous tale.

Joufroi, son of Count Richier of Poitiers and his wife Eleanor, journeyed with his father's leave to England to seek knighthood at the hand of King Henry. He found the court at York and very quickly made a good impression on the English, not least by his defence of the honour of Queen Alice. The royal seneschal claimed he had found her in bed with a kitchen boy, which roused Henry's righteous wrath until Joufroi, challenging the seneschal to a duel, put an end to both slander and slanderer. At that point he learned of the death of his father; so pledging his eternal service to the English king and queen, he returned to Poitiers to be acclaimed as the new count. There he won great honour through his tourneying and general largess.

One day he asked his minstrel to name the fairest lady in the land. 'Agnes de Tonnerre' was the reply, but with the rider that her jealous husband held her captive in a tower. Never one to duck a challenge, Joufroi went tourneying at Tonnerre masquerading as the lord of Cockaigne; and the last of his triumphs was the surreptitious conquest of fair Agnes. When he was back in Poitiers, a messenger arrived with a casket of jewels from an anonymous lady admirer, then departed, leaving Joufroi with the hope that in the course of his travels he might learn who she was. With a companion he returned to England, where he was not recognized owing to his long absence.

At Lincoln he fought victoriously for King Henry against the Scots and Irish before leaving with him for London. There he squandered his wealth on high living and was obliged to marry the daughter of a rich bourgeois to make ends meet. Meanwhile in Poitou Count Alphonse of Toulouse had attacked his lands, and Joufroi was nowhere to be found. Among those sent to look for him was the troubadour Marcabru; and he happened to be visiting

King Henry when in walked the object of his search. Hearing Marcabru's news, Joufroi prepared to leave for home, but not before arranging the transfer of his wife, now surplus to his requirements, to a more worthy husband. He also resolved on a visit to Queen Alice, then staying in Beverley. The revelation that it was she who had sent the casket heralded a brief but passionate affair with her. When he did eventually arrive back in Poitiers, he first defeated, then made peace with Count Alphonse and, as a gesture of reconciliation, married his beautiful daughter.

At a first reading, this seems to be a farrago of fact and fiction. We catch glimpses of a whole array of historical figures, but then are left wondering whether it is not all an illusion. Here are the main identifications proposed in the past: Richier de Poitiers is Richard Coeur-de-Lion; King Henry is Henry I (if he is not Henry II); Alice is Henry I's queen (or Alice of France, Henry II's reputed mistress and Richard's spurned bride); Joufroi himself may be Gui-Geoffrey (William VI) of Poitou or perhaps Geoffrey of Brittany; Agnes de Tonnerre is one of two countesses of Tonnerre bearing that name, or conceivably the third wife of Philip Augustus or even Agnes of Burgundy, mother of Gui-Geoffrey, or else a countess of Oxford imprisoned by her husband; the Anfos de Seint Gile is commonly identified as Alphonse of Toulouse; Marcabru is the well-known troubadour; Giraud de Berri could be Gerald of Barry (that is of Wales); Robert, Joufroi's companion, might be Robert of Gloucester or even Robert d'Arbrissel, the founder of Fontevrault. Then of course there was Eleanor herself, here Countess of Poitou. We are bemused by the choices available. Then there are the authentic places, including those in England: York and Beverley, Winchester, London, and Lincoln, which was actually besieged in 1140 by Stephen of Blois.

One is tempted to see in all this an elaborate *roman à clef*. But where is the key that will unlock it? Is it out of ignorance that the poet seems to confuse at every turn the honest seeker of historical prototypes and events? I think not; and when we realize what a clever use he has made of counterpoint and reversal in his 'personal' interventions in the story, his game becomes clearer. For it is a game he is playing, and there is method in his apparent madness. His opening move is typical of this humorous strategy. Joufroi is introduced as the son of Eleanor and Richier of Poitou, identified with Richard Plantagenet: the son, that is, of Eleanor and her own son, which makes him in a sense his own brother! This comedian, then, has taken a whole pack of historical allusions, covering a couple of centuries or more, and then shuffled them thoroughly before dealing them out in his narrative. He has created a whole world of topsy-turvydom for his own and our amusement.

If he did have a single prototype for his hero, was this really Gui-Geoffrey? It is surely much more likely that his real model was not Eleanor's great-grandfather, but her rapscallion grandfather, William the troubadour. His initial inspiration, as I am not the first to point out, could have come from William's short Provençal biography quoted in chapter 1 above.[19] So can we detect anything of the historical Eleanor in the romance? We think of the lady whom her husband tries to keep out of mischief by isolating her from society; or of the queen suspected by her husband King Henry of adultery below her station, then later achieving it in his absence. We should not, I believe, look too hard; because at best any reflection we may catch will be of the Eleanor of legend, the 'giddy queen', not of the real person. I find it hard to see this poet as a would-be satirist or commentator on past history from which, we must remember, he was probably removed by a generation or so. No, despite his apparent display of familiarity with genuine people and places, he has used it in a way designed not to underpin but to undercut his fiction. His trade is in legend, not history.

Other poets followed the less reputable chroniclers in using legend to extend and glamorize history, as in what are sometimes called 'ancestral romances'. One example of this is the strange story of the Lusignans as told at the beginning of the fifteenth century by Coudrette, who may have been a native of Poitou, though he spent some years in Paris. His romance of *Mélusine*[20] was, he claims, derived from earlier records. It begins by telling how Raymond was adopted by a count of Poitiers, whom he killed accidentally while on a hunt. As he rode in great distress through the forest, he came to a fountain beside which were three ladies. The most beautiful, who knew all about him, promised him comfort and great fortune if he would marry her. She was the fairy Mélusine who, it transpires, was in the habit of becoming a serpent from the waist down every Saturday; and we learn later that her parents were the King of Albany (Scotland) and a fairy mother, her father being now dead and buried inside a mountain in Northumberland. Despite her unorthodox lineage and attributes, it was from her union with Raymond that the whole Lusignan family descended.

Although only known from the late fourteenth century, the legend is no doubt much older and is a good example of the injection of supernatural lore into family history. We are reminded of the attachment of the swan legend familiar from *Lohengrin* to the name of Godfrey de Bouillon by the middle of the twelfth century, not to mention the scandal of the demon countess in Plantagenet annals. Although the story of Mélusine evolved in Eleanor's homeland, it contains no apparent references to her, although she did have associations with the abbey of Saint-Maixent, supposedly built by Mélusine, who is also said to have constructed the towers at Niort, though history claims that Richard Coeur-de-Lion was responsible for them at the end of the twelfth century.

That brings us to another example of the weaving of legend into family history, the result being the remarkable English romance, *Richard Coer de Lyon*, which has a more direct bearing on our investigation.[21] Although we may draw an almost complete blank in our quest for Richard's mother, this in itself may not be without significance. The work, based perhaps on an earlier Anglo-Norman poem, was probably composed in the London area in about 1300. Its popularity long outlived the Middle Ages.

The author opens by saying that there are romances in both England and France about Roland, Oliver, the twelve peers, Alexander, Charlemagne, King Arthur, Gawain, Turpin, Ogier the Dane, Troy, Hector and Achilles. But Richard is the best warrior found in any 'geste'. Then his own story begins. At the age of twenty, King Henry was advised by his barons to marry; so messengers were sent forth to seek the most beautiful of all women. At sea they encountered a marvellous vessel of ivory and gold bearing the King of Antioch and his lovely daughter Cassodorien, who had been alerted by a vision to sail to England. They landed at the Tower of London; and it was not long before Henry and the princess were betrothed at Westminster Abbey. At the climax of the Mass, Cassodorien fainted, since as a result of some magic she never dared to set eyes on the host.

The royal pair were blessed with two sons and a daughter: Richard, John and their sister Topias; and the family enjoyed fourteen years together. Then one day, at the request of an earl, Cassodorien was compelled to stay in a church until the priest was about to elevate the host. That was too much for her. 'She took her daughter by the hand, nor would she be without her son. She made her way out through the roof in full view of them all. At that moment John fell from her and broke his thigh on the ground; and she fled away with her daughter, never to be seen again' (ll. 227–34).

Richard was crowned in his fifteenth year and was soon plunged into a life of chivalric adventures. One of these finds him making his way through Germany as a pilgrim and being imprisoned there. The king's daughter is able to make amorous advances to him and actually has him visit her in her room. Informed of this, the king determines to punish him by releasing a lion into his cell. Richard, however, when confronted by the beast, plunges his arm down its throat and plucks out its heart, which he presents to the king. A ransom is then demanded for his release. It is collected in England and brought to Germany, whereupon Richard is released and returns to England, while the disgraced princess remains behind to await a summons from her lover to become his queen. She waits in vain.

Eleanor has no mention in any of this; and indeed she only appears briefly in one group of manuscripts, at the point where Richard has left for the crusade and has arrived in Sicily. 'His mother sent him a fair present: Eleanor brought him Berengaria, the King of Navarre's daughter. King Roger's wife came with her then. Her name was Joan, a fair woman. King Richard, the precious one, should marry Berengaria, but said: "No, not at this time!" He did not wish to marry her among the Sicilians: after Easter, should he still be alive, he would take her as his wedded wife. Eleanor took her leave and went home, so says the book' (variant after l. 2039).

After performing many doughty deeds in the Holy Land and returning to England, Richard reigned no more than ten years before he was shot at Château Gaillard. Two versions give an expanded account of his end. When it was near, he ordered that his body be brought to be with his father at Fontevrault, and so it was: his bones now lie there beside those of his father King Harry, lord of all England.

Throughout this rip-roaring biography of her son, Eleanor is conspicuous by her almost total absence. It seems unjust that her favourite offspring, with her own hot southern blood in his veins, has been denied the support and guidance of a fond mother and been foisted instead on the demon lady of family legend. Then in his glowing account of Richard the king, the poet (or some Anglo-Norman predecessor) has ignored Eleanor's part in retrieving him from his German captivity and in finally laying his body to rest in her most favoured sanctuary. Despite his garbling of historical fact, he was surely aware of Eleanor's role as King Harry's queen and widow. So why this neglect? One wonders if by this time her reputation in England had been too sullied by the legend-mongers. We have seen how it was already suffering at the pen of Gerald of Wales, and had doubtless degenerated further by the time *Richard Coer de Lyon* was circulating among the English aristocracy. The poet may not have wished such a focus of growing scandal to have a place in his eulogistic portrayal of her son. For the people of England, it seems, her place in history was already yielding before the onslaught of her legend. What, then has happened to the memory of the dignified, wise, diplomatic queen so well versed in courtliness and the affairs of the heart? It was, I suspect, still preserved in another branch of literature; and to this I shall now turn.

ELEANOR AS GUENEVERE

I suggested earlier that Eleanor and literature as we know it virtually grew up together. In a more particular sense the same could be said of Eleanor and Queen Guenevere, leading lady of Arthurian romance.[22] We have already seen how eagerly the legend of Arthur was embraced by King Henry, bolstering as it did his image as the inheriter of a glorious tradition of British kingship fit to rival the Continental cult of Charlemagne. If Henry saw himself as the neo-Arthur, then Eleanor was necessarily cast as the neo-Guenevere. A known patron of this 'new wave' of courtly entertainment, she could not have failed to be aware of, and may well have relished, the role which it conferred on her.

Guenevere is unlikely ever to have existed in the flesh. Before Geoffrey of Monmouth she appears fleetingly in a few early Welsh texts; and in Caradoc of Llancarvan's Latin life of Saint Gildas there is reference to her abduction by Arthur's enemy Melwas, who held her captive in Glastonbury before finally surrendering her to her husband. Some version of this abduction story was represented on an archivolt at Modena fairly early in the twelfth century, which implies the circulation in northern Europe of tales about her at about the time Eleanor was born. Whether or not such tales had reached the young girl's ears from itinerant story-tellers, she is likely to have encountered her in Geoffrey's 'best seller' fairly soon after its appearance in 1136. Not that she would have learned very much about her personality from Geoffrey; but there was the matter of her extra-marital affair, which may have stirred her adolescent imagination.

Guenevere, we learn, came from a noble Roman family and was brought up by Duke Cador of Cornwall before her marriage to Arthur. She was the most beautiful woman in Britain. Geoffrey describes her crowned in state with her husband and accompanied by a retinue of attendants at a truly regal court in Caerleon. Evidently enjoying Arthur's trust, she was put in charge, together with his nephew Mordred, of the defence of Britain while he went campaigning against the Romans in Gaul. But while he was there, news reached him that Mordred had usurped his crown and was living in adultery with his wife, who had broken her marriage bond. The king hurried back to Britain to deal with Mordred. Guenevere was in York when she learned of his return. In despair she fled to Caerleon and there entered a community of nuns, taking the veil and vowing to pass the rest of her life in chastity. In a great battle by the river Camblam (Camlann) Mordred was slain; and Arthur, mortally injured, was carried to the Isle of Avalon for the healing of his wounds.

From these scanty details was to grow a vast complex of stories featuring Queen Guenevere and her sentimental entanglements. It may be that one or two later texts contain elements from native Welsh lore; but Geoffrey's *History of the Kings of Britain* was to all intents and purposes the fountain-head for the literary presentation of Guenevere and her deeds. There we have seen her as a grand courtly lady of rare beauty, enjoying her husband's trust but betraying it by living in adultery with his traitorous nephew. We may note that her own guilt in the matter does not seem to have been a feature in the primitive abduction story.

The Jerseyman Wace, as we saw, turned Geoffrey's history into French verse as *Le Roman de Brut* and allegedly presented his work to Eleanor, who had for some three years been Henry's queen. Wace adapted his material with a good deal of freedom and with an eye, one assumes, to the tastes of his courtly patrons. This is especially evident in his treatment of Arthur. He is noble, courtly, peopling his Round Table with all the best Scots, Bretons, French, Normans and Angevins, as well as nobles from Flanders, Burgundy and Lorraine. He is loved by the poor, honoured by the rich, envied and feared by foreigners, and a model of generosity and prowess (ll. 1191ff.).[23]

Wace makes some interesting changes to the account of the betrayal. Mordred, he says, had secretly loved Guenevere for a long time, and she had returned his affection, which was particularly shameful, since he was of her husband's kin. When in York she heard that Arthur had returned and Mordred was in flight, 'she was brooding and dejected, dwelling on how basely she had demeaned herself for Mordred: she had brought shame on the good king and loved his nephew Mordred, who had unlawfully taken her as his wife, to her great degradation. She would have rather been dead than alive, and her thoughts were full of grief. She fled to Caerleon, where she entered an abbey, and was there hidden away, having taken the veil as a nun. Nothing was heard or seen of her; no one found her or knew her whereabouts. The reason was her shame for her misdeed and the sin she had committed' (ll. 4637–54).

After the final battle, says Wace, Arthur had himself borne to Avalon to have his wounds tended. The poet then recalls, with some insistence, a tradition already current in his day to the effect that the king is still there, awaited by the Britons, and may yet return to live on; for Merlin was right in saying that his death would remain in doubt. Then, following Geoffrey in telling how Arthur had left his kingdom in the hands of Count Cador's son until he should return, he adds: 'It was a pity he had no children!' (ll. 4705–28). King Henry would have basked in the reflected glory of Arthur, this exemplary ruler of Britain and his predecessor; and he might have welcomed the expectation of his return as happily anticipating the new golden age of his own reign.

If we can fairly suppose that Wace was very conscious of the Arthur–Henry parallel, the assumption has as its corollary the

more delicate equation of Guenevere with Queen Eleanor. This
would have been flattering enough in the earlier episodes. Guenevere is first presented as a young, attractive, courtly figure: 'She
was full of social graces and of a noble bearing, extremely
generous and a good conversationalist: Arthur loved her with a
great affection; but they were blessed with no heir and were
unable to have any child' (1113–18). This latter remark (repeated
later as we have seen) might be taken as a partial justification for
Guenevere's turning to Mordred in her husband's absence. Her
relationship with Arthur reminds us, perhaps, of that of Eleanor
with the doting Louis, for whom she likewise could produce no
heir.

Wace could not, of course, skate over the Mordred affair, which
brings his romance to its climax. So, almost as if waving a
cautionary finger, he puts great emphasis on Guenevere's guilt and
subsequent repentance. Then, significantly, he banishes her to
total oblivion, thus strikingly dissociating her from her husband,
who remains forever in the thoughts of all. If he had earlier evoked
associations with his own queen, this should have satisfactorily
dispelled them. Some years later, in his *Roman de Rou*, as if to
ensure Eleanor's favour, he commended her wisdom and virtue
and applauded her marriage to Henry.[24]

Layamon, in his free rendering into English of Wace's *Brut*,
mentions the Jersey poet's gift of his work to the noble Eleanor,
wife of the high King Henry. He does this in terms which imply
that Henry is no longer alive, hence the usual dating of his poem
after 1189. Possibly of Scandinavian descent, Layamon lived in the
Severn valley and had little time for the courtly manners dear to
Wace and his aristocratic public. So he has rather coarsened the
presentation of Guenevere (his Wenhaver); and he blackened her
character even further when he came to describe the treason.[25]
Arthur loved her deeply. However, just before he received news of
her betrayal he had a dream in which he witnessed the demolition
of his hall by Mordred and herself, whereupon he hewed off
Mordred's head and hacked his wife to pieces before plunging her
into a black pit. Gawain later vows to him that he will destroy
Mordred and have Guenevere dragged by horses. In England the
queen was told of Arthur's imminent return; and she immediately
informed Mordred, 'the dearest of men to her'. Layamon follows
Wace in execrating the treason and banishing Guenevere from

men's memories; and he omits the possibly mitigating circumstance of her failure to give Arthur children.

Coincidence or not, it is interesting to find in these successive accounts of the Mordred affair a progressive degrading of Guenevere's character that seems to parallel the worsening of Eleanor's reputation in popular esteem. A version of the story found its way, perhaps by about 1200, into a branch of the beast epic, the *Roman de Renart*, and there the queen's behaviour is even more reprehensible in that she remains entirely unrepentant.[26] King Noble the lion sets out with his army to fight the pagans, leaving his land in the charge of Reynard the fox and Queen Fière. Reynard fakes a report saying that Noble is dead and that his last wishes were that Reynard should marry his queen. The fox loses no time in proclaiming himself king and, amid the general rejoicing, taking Fière as his very willing bride. Back from his victorious expedition, Noble finds his castle closed to him by the traitor. After a siege of fluctuating fortunes, Reynard is captured but then pardoned by Noble in recognition of past services. The lion is welcomed back into his castle by the queen who, however, maintains a tactful silence about her adultery with Reynard. Although some critics have claimed to find historical allusions in the episode, there can be no doubt about its origins in the story of Mordred and Guenevere. In this case, however, the unfaithful queen lives to love another day.

*

By the time Chrétien de Troyes laid the foundations of Arthurian romance as we know it, other tales of the legendary monarch, his queen and his illustrious knights must have been circulating in the Celtic world and beyond. Some of them had probably bypassed Geoffrey's *History* and kept Guenevere's reputation unsullied. Certainly in most of Chrétien's romances she appears as the model queen; and given the fact that for at least part of his career he enjoyed the patronage of Eleanor's daughter Marie of Champagne, it would not be surprising if in his portrayal of the British queen he glanced occasionally in the direction of Queen Eleanor. It has been suggested that he at some time visited the Plantagenet court himself, but there is no strong evidence for this. It may therefore not be entirely irrelevant to look briefly at his presentation of Guenevere.

Chrétien's first romance, *Erec et Enide*, is normally dated about 1170.[27] That was the year which saw the coronation of the Young King and the installation of Richard as Duke of Aquitaine. More significantly, Henry had spent the Christmas of 1169 at Nantes, where it is supposed that he invested the young prince Geoffrey with the lordship of Brittany, having secured his betrothal to its heiress Constance three years earlier. We have no record of Eleanor's attendance at this court. Now the climax of Chrétien's romance is the crowning of Erec and his wife Enide at a splended ceremony arranged by King Arthur at Nantes on Christmas Day; and it is usually assumed that for this Henry's court of 1169 was the model (there seems no other reason for the choice of Nantes). It has also been claimed that Chrétien deliberately described each coronation throne as bearing the Plantagenet armorial beast, the leopard, and moreover that the name of their donor, Bruiant (Brian) of the Isles, was that of one of Henry's closest companions. The conclusion is that the romance was intended for Plantagenet consumption.[28]

As it seems likely that in the coronation episode at least Arthur is cast in the role of Henry, we are justified in examining Guenevere as a possible Eleanor-figure. Her portrait in *Erec* is in fact entirely flattering. She is courteous to the hero, whom she encounters on the way to the royal hunt. Then, when he returns to court with Enide, his prospective bride, she is all care and attention, lavishing on the girl her own finery and supervising the preparation of the marriage chamber. At Nantes she likewise takes charge of the robing of Enide for her coronation. Throughout she appears as a dutiful and considerate queen, generous and motherly towards the young couple, and acting in perfect harmony with Arthur.

That Chrétien was interested in seasoning his romances with topical material is shown even more clearly in *Cligés*, in the second half of which there are unmistakable allusions to certain matrimonial negotiations between the German emperor, Frederick Barbarossa, and the Byzantine Manuel Comnenus. Also involved was Henry the Lion, Duke of Saxony, the husband of Eleanor's daughter Matilda. Guenevere, however, does not appear in this part of the work; and it is hard to see any influence of Eleanor, who would have been in custody by the time the negotiations broke down in 1174.

In the first section of the romance, however, Guenevere plays a vital and wholly admirable role, despite the fact that Chrétien based much of the action on Wace's account of Mordred's treason. For here, far from being an accomplice to treason, the queen sails with Arthur when he leaves on his expedition to Brittany. On the same ship are her niece Soredamors and Alexander, a young Greek, both of whom exhibit the symptoms of what she takes to be sea-sickness. Realizing later that their pallor and tremblings were caused by the onset of love, she shows all the motherly care we discerned in *Erec* and first encourages, then extracts the young pair's admission of, their feelings. She also takes the opportunity of giving them a short lecture on the mutual responsibilities involved in an honourable marriage. That such is her relationship with Arthur is made plain as, for instance, when he offers Alexander any reward he might ask, other than his crown and his queen. We do, though, see one moment of discord between them, when she objects to Arthur's harsh treatment of some captive traitors, though without managing to persuade him to show clemency. Again our thoughts turn to Eleanor and the severe punishment Henry was exacting at the very time Chrétien was writing. Could this have been a hint dropped for Plantagenet ears and calculated, perhaps, to meet with the approval of Eleanor's daughter, the Countess Marie?

It was to her that he dedicated, a year or so later, his romance of *Lancelot (The Knight of the Cart)*, saying that it was she who provided him with its subject. The fact that he left it for a colleague to complete is sometimes taken to indicate his disapproval of its theme, which is the abduction of Queen Guenevere and her rescue by her lover Lancelot, with whom she commits adultery when still far from Arthur's court. The tale's origins are to be sought in the primitive abduction legend mentioned above, although the ingredient of adultery could have been inspired by the Mordred story. Its appeal for Marie could have had something to do with her own mother's incarceration. Perhaps too she saw in it a chance for her favoured poet to treat it as a troubadour-style courtly love affair in action, involving, that is, a worshipping lover seeking the favour of a stand-offish lady. Be that as it may, that is the way Chrétien handled the subject; but instead of turning it into a straight adventure romance, he infused it with a good deal of parodic humour.

Arthur's court is disturbed by an intruder, who demands that the queen be handed over to him; and then, should any knight succeed in winning her back, he would surrender all the prisoners he has taken from the king. Arthur cuts a sorry figure: he forbids Kay to take up the challenge and even has Guenevere fall at the seneschal's feet to dissuade him from acting on her behalf. As she is led off by the aggressor, she laments the absence of one knight who would not have allowed this. Her thoughts, as we learn much later, are on Lancelot. Arthur may command her obedience: he does not rule her heart.

Lancelot is ultimately successful in his quest and wins Guenevere's freedom. She, however, feigns offence at his having once deigned to travel in a hangman's cart. The distraught hero attempts suicide, whereupon the queen, thinking him dead, reveals her true feelings and makes an assignation which leads to a night of love in her apartment. Arthur rejoices when she returns to her own land, though without Lancelot, who has been treacherously imprisoned by her abductor. As Guenevere presides at a tournament, a knight shows up incognito. Suspecting this may be Lancelot, she puts her hunch to the test by ordering him to do by turns his worst and his best. It is indeed her lover, out on parole, and he obeys. So here is Guenevere still behaving like the capricious, haughty lady of the lyric poets. Chrétien abandons the story with Lancelot back in captivity, leaving his continuator to stage his triumphant return to court. Perhaps Chrétien preferred not to contemplate the resulting reunion of Guenevere, her lover, and her cuckolded husband. It was left notably to the later prose writers to explore that delicate situation.

It appears that Chrétien's concern in this romance was not to deepen his earlier characterization of Arthur and Guenevere but slyly to caricature them in a set of parodic variations on a traditional theme. If Plantagenet associations were still at the back of his mind, we can only assume that he was cocking a snook at Henry through the sadly debilitated Arthur, but without intending any comment on his by then estranged queen. In that case it could be significant that in his last two romances he did not totally rehabilitate Arthur.

Yvain (*The Knight of the Lion*) seems to have been composed concurrently with *Lancelot*, since it contains allusions to Guenevere's abduction. It opens with Arthur offending his court

by dallying at his queen's side in his apartment during the high
festivities one Whitsuntide. Guenevere plays only a secondary
role: at the beginning she intervenes in a squabble to put the
spiteful Kay in his place; and at the end of the romance we find her
back in court after her enforced absence and present at a climatic
judicial combat.

Perceval or *Le Conte du Graal* probably dates from about 1182.
There she again appears as the sympathetic first lady of the royal
court as she joins with Arthur in consoling a group of wounded
prisoners. Then, though, her dignity is affronted and she is
plunged into a fit of suicidal wrath when a hostile knight contrives
to spill a cupful of wine over her. Later she is glimpsed at table
with Arthur before a feast, and once more during festivities at
Caerleon. Finally, she is present at another grand occasion in the
city of Orkney; and the romance breaks off during that scene, just
as she is asking one of her ladies the cause of her distress.

So in Chrétien's last two romances Guenevere is portrayed in
her former role as a sensitive, charitable royal spouse concerned
with the harmonious conduct of court life. When treated seriously
by the poet, then, she is an attractive figure and well cut out to be a
model for Eleanor, whether or not her portrait has caught any of
the features of the contemporary, real-life queen. With *Lancelot*,
on the other hand, he opened the way for the development of a
new and less idealized, indeed largely tragic Guenevere.

The debt to Chrétien of later practitioners of romance was
immense. Some of them, introducing Guenevere as a secondary
figure in their plots, stuck to the image of the kind-hearted queen,
counsellor of and even go-between for lovers, but not herself one
of their number. This is the case in *Gliglois*, an anonymous text of
the early thirteenth century.[29] With Arthur she has just participated in a ceremonial crowning when a maiden, Beauté, arrives at
court and is put in her care. Her nephew Gawain, a born
philanderer, quickly succumbs to the girl's charms and asks
Guenevere for advice. She chides his impetuosity in wanting
Beauté for himself at once, but promises to put in a good word for
him provided he seeks to win her by acts of chivalry. Complica-
tions arise when Gliglois, Gawain's squire, also falls in love with
Beauté; and at this point matters pass beyond Guenevere's control.
It is interesting to find that in the course of the romance the poet
never names her, but simply refers to her as 'the queen'. The
implication is that, rather than having a personality in her own

right, she is fulfilling the recognized duty of a queen in the royal court, namely to ensure the observance of the rules of civilized behaviour and so keep potential trouble at bay.

Again unnamed, she performs this function even more forthrightly in *Meraugis de Portlesguez*, a romance of the same period by another northern French poet, Raoul de Houdenc.[30] For Raoul reserves for her the role of official adjudicator in amorous affairs, perhaps under the influence of Andrew the Chaplain. Meraugis and Gorvain Cadrut are both in love with Idoine, who suggests that rather than fight a duel for her, they should ask Arthur's barons to resolve the issue at his Christmas court. There the matter is discussed. 'And after a good deal of talk, the queen comes to ask for her own court, whereupon the king orders her to be quiet; but she refuses. She put her request to him very proudly, saying: "Sir King, it is well known that all judgements in matters of love are mine: that is no business of yours!"' (ll. 886–93). Others support her; and she tells the king to clear the hall for her and her maidens. She opens the proceedings; and a long discussion ensues in which, among others, the Duchess of Gloucester takes part. Should a suitor love the girl for her beauty as Gorvain does, or for her courtliness like Meraugis? The verdict eventually goes for Meraugis; and then the queen sends for Arthur, to have it proclaimed in open court.

Here, then, is Guenevere in what one might think an exemplary role, asserting her authority as a great courtly lady in the mould of Eleanor. And if we think of Eleanor in this context, it is because Raoul de Houdenc's queen is seen dispensing her judgement just as Eleanor did in Andrew the Chaplain's *De Amore*, though not in a formally constituted court like Guenevere's. So in this way our thoughts are drawn to the legendary rather than the real Eleanor.

Raoul's episode depicts the rational side of courtly love, with Guenevere exercising her mind, not her heart. But after Chrétien's *Lancelot* her image became more and more frequently that not of a wise observer and mediator but of a full participant in a passionate, and tragic, love affair. Her appearance as a typed role model yields increasingly to that of Guenevere the fallible human being deeply and desperately divided in her loyalties. However, in the next work to be considered it appears that an attempt has been made to restore her innocence.

Yder,[31] an anonymous romance apparently composed on Plantagenet soil and possibly in England in the reign of King John, seems inspired by some early version of Guenevere's extra-marital activities. If so, she is seen partly as herself, but partly masquerading under the name of Queen Guenloie, whose full identity is never clearly established. In this guise she is loved and eventually won by the hero Yder, a native of Carlisle. For us, though, the main interest lies in the characterization of King Arthur and the actual Guenevere.

Arthur early appears in an unfavourable light. The young hero saves his life and hopes to receive knighthood at his hand, but is then neglected by him. The snub persuades Yder to help Arthur's enemy, besieged by the king in his castle of Rougemont. Queen Guenloie, as a spectator, is impressed by Yder's prowess, of which she wants proof before fully reciprocating his love. Among the youth's feats is his unhorsing of Kay three times, which goads the seneschal into treacherously thrusting his sword into Yder's back. This act so disgusts both sides that they cease hostilities. The grievously wounded hero is taken to be tended in a convent recommended by Guenloie; and on learning of this, Guenevere pleads with Arthur to take her to see Yder and then enlist him in his company of the Round Table. Her request rouses Arthur's jealousy, but quite without cause, since we are assured more than once of his wife's great love for him; and she treats him with the utmost deference. Nevertheless, he reluctantly complies; and Yder, now recovered, comes to the court. While there, he has occasion to rescue Guenevere from a marauding bear.

After further episodes, in which Arthur again appears in a far from ideal light, his jealousy surfaces once more and prompts the poet into a diatribe against the evil of this destructive passion. Though assured of Guenevere's love, the king demands to know whom she would marry should he die. When, under his pressure, she admits it would be Yder, he decides that the young man must be destroyed. Despite his hopes, however, Yder emerges unscathed from a fight with two giants, which took place near Worcester in the forest of Malvern, and thereby wins Guenloie's consent to their marriage. Immediately afterwards he also survives an attempt by Kay to poison him, although at one point the king believes him to be dead. Arthur then has a change of heart, arranges Yder's marriage to Guenloie, and has him also crowned king.

It is intriguing to find a version of the fight with the giants in William of Malmesbury's *De antiquitate Glastoniensis ecclesiae*.[32]

One Christmas at Caerleon, Ider, son of King Nuth (as in *Yder*), was knighted by Arthur, who then took him to a certain mount to fight with three wicked giants. Ider slew them, but fell into a deep faint from his wounds. Arthur supposed him to be dead and himself to be responsible. In his contrition he established at Glastonbury twenty-four monks to pray for Ider's soul; and he supplied them with much wealth and land for their subsistence. William's work is dated 1129–35; but the passage in question is probably a late interpolation serving as propaganda for Glastonbury. On the other hand, Arthur's belated clemency in *Yder* might suggest its author's acquaintance with some similar tale.

Several English place-names in *Yder* as well as its somewhat uncourtly tone could well indicate an insular home for the romance, which may have pre-dated the surviving text. Consequently, the presentation of Arthur there is of considerable interest. He is not a very honourable figure; he does not manage his sometimes conflicting duties well or achieve notable success in his enterprises; and above all, he is consumed by irrational jealousy. We might hazard the explanation that the originator of the romance started from a story of Guenevere's adultery in which she was the guilty and Arthur the innocent party. Wishing to restore the good name of Guenevere, he split her into two and made her alter ego, Guenloie, the object of Yder's love and ultimately his wife. This would allow him to retain, indeed stress, Guenevere's true love for her husband, any adultery being now only a figment of his jealous imagination. The author has evidently been at pains to rehabilitate Guenevere while blackening the character of Arthur. If now one assumes that he was conscious of the Plantagenet dimension of the Arthurian story, his work could be read as a studied defence of Eleanor and a disparagement of her blundering and suspicous husband Henry. This would charge the whole romance with political meaning, especially if it originated in Henry's lifetime.

Durmart le Galois, a long verse romance composed before 1244, perhaps on the Norman–Picard border,[33] provides a striking contrast to *Yder*, which seems to have been one of its sources. Its action, which takes place within the Plantagenet domains, tells of the love-quest of Durmart, a Welsh prince, for the Irish queen Fenise after hearing a report of her great beauty. It includes an account of a most gentlemanly abduction. On a royal hunt, Guenevere finds herself in the care of Yder, having become separated from Arthur and his company. Yder, however, is unable to prevent her being carried off by an old admirer of hers, Brun de Morois. He, though, in a spirit of true chivalry, promises not to violate her while the sun is still up and will hand her back should any knight defeat him in combat. Durmart learns of this and makes for Brun's castle, where he finds Guenevere in a beautiful orchard sitting on a silken cloth opposite her captor. Yet he is merely gazing at her, not daring to so much as kiss her hand, 'for noble love makes him timid before the queen and forbids him to do so' (ll. 4546–7). As he dare not even be alone with her, she is accompanied by a group of ladies-in-waiting. Once Brun is defeated by Durmart, Guenevere politely asks his leave before quitting his castle!

Later in the romance, Durmart, still pursuing his quest for Fenise, arrives at Glastonbury in the middle of King Arthur's Christmas celebrations. He is warmly welcomed by Guenevere, who commends him to Arthur for his prowess and nobility. He sits beside the king throughout the feasting, which only ends after Guenevere has retired to her room with her usual posse of attendants. In contrast to the state of affairs in *Yder*, all is sweetness and light in the royal household.

Eventually, Durmart learns that Queen Fenise is besieged by an enemy in her castle at Limerick. The citadel and castle can only be attacked from one side; but the enemy force is lodged in the suburbs of the town. Durmart arrives to rescue his beloved; and with some companions he makes his first attack early in the morning while the besiegers, as when John came to his mother's aid at Mirebeau, are still occupied with domestic affairs (here they are watering their horses). After a complex series of incidents, Fenise is liberated; and the lovers, married in Arthur's presence, embark on a wise and happy reign in Limerick.

The besieging of Fenise in her fortress seems inspired by the siege of Rougemont in *Yder*; but several of the details are strongly reminiscent of Eleanor's celebrated stand at Mirebeau. That, as I suggested earlier (and we shall come across another instance), would seem to have provided authors of romance with a model for their descriptions of beleaguered queens. As for the rest of the poem, we are struck in particular by its almost exaggeratedly courtly atmosphere and setting, within which Guenevere is cast in her charmingly virtuous role. In similarly stark contrast to *Yder* is the complete rehabilitation of Arthur. The anonymous author, whose refinement is tinged with piety, was no scandal-monger or lover of sordid intrigue and base passions. If he was looking back to the reign of Henry and Eleanor, he was doing so through rose-tinted spectacles.

*

After chasing Eleanor's shadow through the verse romances, let us now see if it becomes any more substantial in the corpus of prose texts, which are the main vehicle for the portrayal of Guenevere to Malory and beyond. The first work to consider does not belong to the main group, the so-called Vulgate cycle, which it may well precede. This is *Perlesvaus*,[34] a strange mixture of courtliness, piety and brutality which links the Lancelot story to the Grail quest. There has been much debate over its place and date of composition; but the most plausible suggestion is that it was written in the first decade of the thirteenth century, possibly in England. Two manuscripts carry a colophon asserting that it was translated into French from a Latin work in the possession of the monks of the abbey on the Isle of Avalon (that is Glastonbury), where lie the bodies of King Arthur and his queen. Whether or not we take that claim seriously, Glastonbury does have an important place in the romance, as will be seen; so let us recall the events which led to its identification as the last resting place of the royal couple.

After the abbey there was destroyed by fire in 1184, King Henry ordered it to be reconstructed on a grand scale. The Lady Chapel was completed by 1186; but the whole work was still unfinished at the time of Henry's death three years later. Then in 1191 the monks claimed to have discovered the bones of Arthur and Guenevere in a sarcophagus with an identifying inscription. Gerald of Wales, who visited Glastonbury a year or so later, even speaks of a lock of Guenevere's golden hair, which sadly disintegrated in the hand of one of the monks.[35] But let us return to the romance.

Moving on as it does from the earlier stories of Perceval (Perlesvaus here) and Lancelot, Guenevere's past adultery with the latter is assumed but discreetly veiled. We first meet her at the

Plate 13 Glastonbury, with the monastery ruins bottom right.

court of a lethargic Arthur, whom she has to goad into action. He meekly accepts her advice and sets out to seek adventure, cutting a dashing figure which wins her admiration. It later emerges that his court at Carlisle had lost its reputation for chivalry because his fear of losing her had made him a stay-at-home. This establishes the pattern of their relationship throughout the rest of the romance: Arthur the doting husband whose thoughts, we are told, remain on Guenevere wherever he may be; and she the dutiful queen, a charming hostess and benevolent counsellor who enjoys real authority in the court. To Arthur she acts as a loyal companion; for though her love for Lancelot is not denied, it is presented here as purely platonic. Lancelot himself sins only in thought and without any active encouragement from the queen. It is through his eyes that we see her virtues most clearly. He confesses his sin to a hermit: 'I truly love my lady, who is a queen, more than any living person, though she is the wife of one of the best kings in the world' (ll. 3657–8); nor will he repent, for 'in her there is so much beauty and worth and sense and courtliness that no man she was prepared to love should abandon her' (ll. 3670–1). All this, says the hermit, is the devil's work and a mortal sin for which Lancelot will be denied the sight of the Holy Grail.

In *Perlesvaus* Arthur and Guenevere have a son, Loholt, who is treacherously slain by Kay. One Whitsuntide the king is holding court at Carlisle when a maiden arrives, bearing the boy's head in a silver casket. Both parents are distraught with grief. Arthur takes the head to be interred in the Lady Chapel at Glastonbury, then leaves on a pilgrimage to the Grail Castle, while Guenevere remains in Carlisle to nurse her sorrow. This is increased when she receives a false report of Arthur's death; and those about her realize that her grief is so deep it will bring about her own end. The king is now far away with a large company, assembled after a knight has appeared with a white charger and a golden crown. These, he says, are to be the prize for a tournament, the victor in which will have the duty of defending the land of a dead queen, whose crown this is. Arthur wins the day, whereupon the knight announces that it is he who must defend the land of this best of queens who is no more. It was the realm of King Arthur, the finest of all kings; and the crown was that of Guenevere, now dead and buried.

Arthur is grief-stricken, whilst Lancelot, who is present, 'does not know what he can do; and he says under his breath that his joy is gone and his chivalry is at an end now that he has lost the noble queen who gave him heart and comfort and the inspiration to do good' (ll. 7158–61). Amid his tears he asks to be allowed to return to Carlisle to defend the land while Arthur completes his pilgrimage. His wish is granted; and his sorrow now becomes a leitmotif in the narrative. At last he comes to Avalon or Glastonbury and enters the chapel beside which are three large, well-appointed buildings. In the middle of the chapel are two richly adorned tombs: one of them is for King Arthur and Queen Guenevere; and there the queen already lies. The other contains the head of her son. A hermit tells Lancelot that though Arthur is still alive, 'the queen said that on his death his body should be put beside hers. We have her letters with her seal to that effect. She had this place and chapel restored to its present state before her death' (ll. 7599–602). Later in the work, Arthur, when wooed by a pagan queen, declared that he would never take another wife unless she was equal in worth to the good Queen Guenevere.

Perlesvaus seems a key text. Whether or not it was composed in England, its atmosphere as well as its action are strongly evocative of the insular scene. Here Guenevere is cast in her entirely sympathetic role as the loyal, wise and capable wife of a basically good king. There is a hint of possessiveness about his love for her, but this is not the paranoid jealousy he displayed in *Yder*; and although it initially sapped his chivalric energy, Guenevere herself persuaded him of his error.

It has been proposed that *Perlesvaus*, with its markedly Benedictine content, may have originated in Glastonbury as a piece of monkish propaganda for the abbey. Although doubts have been expressed on this score, the fact remains that the romance patently reflects the Plantagenet interest in the establishment and its renovation as initiated by Henry. As Guenevere's last refuge it has taken the place of the convent at Caerleon found in the Mordred tradition. It is significant that *Perlesvaus* gives her a new reason for abandoning the world. No longer is she overcome by guilt and shame: now it is by grief for her husband and her dead son, Loholt, whom the author may have borrowed from early Welsh legend. So in keeping with her virtuous image in this romance, she dies with honour and is interred with due reverence at Glastonbury in the chapel whose restoration she herself had ordered. The writer has thus ascribed to her the work on the abbey he surely knew to have been the responsibility of King Henry.

In this account of Guenevere's last days we become very conscious of the unseen presence of Queen Eleanor. We cannot say whether she shared her husband's personal interest in Glastonbury: she was, after all, only just emerging from her seclusion when he put it to practical effect; and certainly there had been no

question of her wishing to have him and her son buried in the
abbey there. What, though, of that other religious house of which
she had long been a patron: Fontevrault? It was there that her
dead husband was buried and that she had the remains of her
cherished son Richard entombed; and there she was herself finally
laid to rest beside them. All this must have been in the *Perlesvaus*-
author's mind as he described the end of good Queen Guenevere.
Her image must for him have been fused in at least this part of his
romance with that of Queen Eleanor; and if here, why not
elsewhere in the work? It might appear likely that he was writing
after Eleanor's death and certainly after that of Richard in 1199.
So we must suppose that any portrait of her behind that of
Guenevere would have been based on distant memories of his own
or on a living tradition. Whatever the truth, it is a sympathetic
picture he has painted for us.

I have mentioned the main body of French Arthurian prose
romances, usually known as the Vulgate cycle.[36] An alternative
name is the Pseudo-Map cycle, since two of its constituent texts
carry the name of Walter Map as author, one asserting that he was
writing at the command of his lord King Henry. The claim is not
usually taken seriously: for one thing the romances are commonly
dated a full generation after Henry's death, though Map himself
lived until about 1209. But it does at least show that these
thirteenth-century writers had the Plantagenet connection very
much in mind. As published in H. O. Sommer's edition, the cycle
consists of five romances: the *Estoire del Saint Graal*, the *Merlin*,
the lengthy *Lancelot*, the *Queste del Saint Graal*, and the *Mort
Artu*. Of these the *Estoire*, telling the early story of the Grail and
probably the last to be written, does not concern us here. Nor
would it be profitable to venture into the thorny thickets of
datings, relationships and sources, which have long been an area
of scholarly exploration but are still not reliably charted. There is,
however, one theory which has a direct bearing on our investigation, attempting as it does to determine whether the cycle was
organized according to a preconceived plan.

J. Neale Carman, after a detailed study of the geography and
possible historical allusions in the texts, states: '. . . as I see it,
Eleanor of Aquitaine was the initial patron and planner of the
whole pseudo-Map Cycle, the close supervisor of a limited section
at the beginning of the *Lancelot*, responsible also for many

detailed features until the hero should become established as the best knight in the world.'[37] Later patrons, he believes, may have included King John's second wife Isabella of Angoulême. Many of his proposed identifications of locations and of fictional with historical characters are based on evidence too slender to carry conviction. Yet his ample demonstration that the adventurers range freely through former Plantagenet Continental territories as well as Britain shows how readily associations could have been called to mind with the real people who walked that stage under King Henry and his successors. So while Eleanor's involvement in planning the whole project or any part of it must remain only a remote possibility, it is far from unreasonable to imagine the authors drawing on memories of her to lend credibility to this or that episode.

As a relatively late addition to the cycle, *Merlin* presents a retrospective rather than a new view of Guenevere. Here she is still the innocent young woman before her amorous involvement with Lancelot, since this work covers Arthur's career only to the high point of his reign. She is the legitimate daughter of King Leodegan of the fictional land of Carmelide. However, she was born on the same day as her double, the 'False Guenevere', whom the same king had fathered on his seneschal's wife, and who was destined to add a surplus angle to the celebrated love triangle of the Lancelot story.

As a girl the real Guenevere was as dazzled by King Arthur's feats of arms as he was by her beauty, on which the author expands: 'How could I describe the maiden's beauty? And even greater than her beauty were her goodness, generosity and courtliness, her good sense and merit, sweetness and good breeding' (II, p. 158). She was the wisest, most attractive and best loved woman in Britain, apart from the daughter of Pelles, the Grail King. After her marriage to Arthur, we see her quickly assuming the responsibilities of first lady at his court. She accepts her nephew Gawain and his companions as 'her knights'. They are in duty bound to tell her of all their adventures, and are widely known as 'les chevaliers de la reine Guenièvre'. She is already a valued counsellor. On one occasion, after exercising her diplomatic talents on Gawain, he praises her precocious prudence: 'If you live long, you will be the wisest woman alive: indeed, you already are, in my opinion' (II, p. 333). Here and elsewhere we see her acting in harmony with

Arthur, giving and accepting advice, even at one point using her authority to prohibit a tournament; and throughout, Arthur is shown both enjoying and returning her deep love and finding in her an inspiration for his chivalry. So on the one hand she provides a model for any Queen of England; and on the other she may well reflect some of the circumstances of Eleanor's own life during the better days of her relationship with Henry.

Lancelot, the longest of the romances, continues Guenevere's story and leads us through her love for and guilty association with this paragon of knights until her dismissal of him for having slept with the Grail King's daughter, although he had been deceived into believing that it was the queen herself who shared his bed. First, however, we learn of Lancelot's birth and upbringing. His father, King Ban of Benoic, a fictional kingdom somewhere in western France, meets his death at the hand of King Claudas, whose ancestral lands have been identified with Berry. The infant Lancelot is abducted from under his mother's nose and subsequently brought up by the Lady of the Lake. No sooner has he been carried off than his bereft mother retires to a nearby convent on the urging of its abbess. She dedicates her wealth to the construction there of a church, where prayers might always be offered for her dead husband's soul. 'News spread throughout the land that Queen Elaine of Benoic had become a nun. This place was consequently known as the Royal Minster. It grew great in size and renown; and the noble ladies of the land went there in throngs for God and the love of the queen' (III, p. 16). There King Ban himself was laid to rest until his own church was completed; and Elaine's sister also took the veil there and was accorded queenly honours. During the rest of her very long and pious life, Elaine's outstanding beauty did not fade. As Carman has seen, the Royal Minster, patronized by a queen, under the rule of an abbess and a fashionable retreat for many aristocratic ladies, has surely been patterned on the abbey of Fontevrault. Even the name of its benefactress and most noble inmate, the long-lived Queen Elaine, reminds us forcibly of that of Queen Eleanor. With *Lancelot* we figuratively as well as literally find ourselves on Plantagenet territory.

The heart of the romance, the love of Guenevere and Lancelot, is handled by the author with the utmost delicacy. When of an age, the young man is sent by the Lady of the Lake to Arthur's court at

Camelot, there to be knighted by the king; and that is where his first meeting with Guenevere takes place. Whereas for him it is love at first sight and a love so intense that he becomes virtually witless in her presence, her own feelings are initially passed off as a kindly interest in this tongue-tied novice knight. We have watched the queen continuing to perform her courtly duties as, for example, when she entertains and rewards knights who have been successful in a joust. But from now on our interest will be held more by the developing relationship, indicated in the case of Lancelot as often as not by his tendency to lapse into love-trances, but for Guenevere's part more by discreet authorial hints than her overt behaviour.

Lancelot puts his prowess to the test in a series of adventures throughout England, which culminate in his winning of his castle, the enchanted Douloureuse Garde, which lies on Humberside. There he is visited by Arthur and Guenevere before its enchantments are brought to an end, after which a further meeting with the queen takes place in the court at Camelot. A little later, Arthur encounters a holy man who refuses to greet him, saying he is the worst of sinners and on the point of losing all honour. Not only was he born out of wedlock, but he has neglected the lower orders for the rich and faces damnation unless he makes humble confession. This Arthur does and is given instruction in humility, generosity, and the other regal virtues, which Guenevere likewise must practise towards those of her sex.

Eventually Lancelot's friend Galehot contrives for him an assignation with the queen for which he is too timid to ask. It takes place and, on Galehot's urging, Guenevere grants Lancelot her love, sealed by a kiss. Now their meetings become more frequent until, on the very night when Arthur lies in the embrace of a Saxon sorceress, the young knight is admitted to her chamber, and their love is consummated. It is plain that the author's sympathy for the lovers has caused him embarrassment when their guilty relationship is put into direct practice. So he has been at pains to invent on their behalf some extenuating circumstances: firstly Arthur's own honour is impugned by a man of God, and then their sinful union is timed to coincide with the king's own rather weakly motivated adultery. At the same time our writer is not above having an ironic chuckle at the gullibility of the royal cuckold. After Lancelot has shown great valour in rescuing him from his enemies, Arthur wishes him to join his company of the Round Table. The hero agrees, but only on condition that he has the queen's approval. Guenevere consents in full court, and with an enthusiasm that might seem excessive: she flings her arms round his neck and with a kiss declares that for the love of her husband she grants him her own love and herself. Poor Arthur, we are told, is delighted by the spontaneity of her gesture.

The plot is now complicated by the sudden appearance of the False Guenevere pretending that she is the true queen, whereas the other is an impostor. The life of the court is at once disrupted. Not only is the real Guenevere called upon to find a knight to defend her cause (fortunately Lancelot is at hand), but Arthur is kidnapped in the course of the intrigue. In this turmoil the portrayal of character has to take second place to the twists and turns of the plot; but no great violence is done to the natures of the main figures as we have come to know them. Guenevere still plays a leading role at court during Arthur's absence; and she grieves sincerely at his loss, which means the end of all true chivalry and joy. We find on his return that his love for her remains, though he is said to have more affection for the one he now believes to be his wife. All of the three chief protagonists retain their honour in the circumstances as they perceive them. Thus, when the False Guenevere is unmasked, Lancelot advises the queen to remain with Arthur. Then, having been told of his wife's adultery, the incredulous king asserts that even if it were true, he would let Lancelot have Guenevere, if that was her wish, rather than lose the services of his noble knight.

There follows a version of Chrétien's account of Guenevere's abduction. Once back in court, she continues her liaison with Lancelot and pines for him when she mistakenly thinks him dead. But now a new side to her character is fleetingly revealed: she dreams of her jealousy at seeing him lying in the arms of a beautiful damsel and of his losing his wits when she reproaches him for it. Her dream will prove prophetic when, unknown to her, Lancelot is tricked into sleeping with Helaine, the Grail King's daughter, believing her to be the queen. For the time being their relationship is not disturbed; although Guenevere does begin to feel the prick of conscience, telling Lancelot of her regret that their carnal passion will prevent him from achieving the great Grail adventure. This grieves her, she says, at least as much as him, 'for it is a great sin, when God has made you the best, most handsome and gracious of all men and granted you the joyful possibility of seeing openly the mysteries of the Holy Grail, for that now to be lost to you because of your union with me' (V, p. 193).

On a second occasion Lancelot is tricked into Helaine's bed; and this time it is in Guenevere's own apartments. She discovers them together, dismisses her lover, then soon repents, but not before madness has seized him. For a long time he wanders in this state; but then, by chance, he is vouchsafed a brief sight of the Grail and at once recovers his sanity. He eventually returns to the court, where no one is as glad to see him as the queen. His son Galahad is placed in a convent near Camelot until he shall come of age. And the romance ends with King Arthur preparing to hold a great court there to receive the youth with due honour, for he is now ready to undertake and achieve in full the high adventure of the Holy Grail.

The author of *Lancelot* has treated Guenevere kindly. He has mitigated her sin as far as his story allowed and has shown her not untouched by conscience, while retaining for her husband her affection and such loyalty as remains at her disposal. Arthur himself is not faultless; but as with his wife, he retains a sense of honour. In this he stands in strong contrast to the Arthur we encountered in *Yder*. We find a similarly sharp distinction between the sympathetic treatment of Guenevere by this author and the short shrift she receives in the next romance of the cycle, the finely crafted *Queste del Saint Graal*. Its writer, a man of great piety and an overriding concern for the spiritual aspect of the Grail quest, has been shown to be imbued with the mysticism of the Cistercians and of Saint Bernard himself. It is not in his nature to condone the sins of the flesh.

For him the chaste Galahad is the true hero; and he begins by showing us Guenevere reconciled to the fact that the youth was fathered by Lancelot in ignorance. She is full of grief when her lover leaves on the great quest. To one of the numerous hermits who inhabit this romance, Lancelot makes his confession: the queen has been his continual inspiration; but for this, he realizes, he is in a state of mortal sin; and on the hermit's insistence he pledges to renounce her love. Another hermit is equally forthright in his advice to Lancelot: Guenevere, who had never made true confession since her marriage, had through her eager glances seduced him into the sin of lust; and that had lost him to God and put him in the clutches of the Devil; it had turned all his virtues into vices. The hermit's lengthy harangue causes the knight to burst into tears and renew his vow to sin no more. At the end of his quest, Lancelot was privileged to see the Grail; but before the revelation of its divine mysteries, he fell into a trance, in which he remained for fourteen days.

The man who wrote the *Queste* stands out from the other authors of the cycle. Zealot that he was, he had no interest in the human dilemmas and struggles of conscience of a noble woman who succumbed to temptation. For him Guenevere was herself the temptress, Eve under another name and fit only for expulsion from the enclosed garden of his faith. It is no surprise to find that the adventures he recounts are divorced from any precise geography, and that he has shed all details suggestive of a Plantagenet connection. Unless, that is, one takes as his own the final passage of the work, which states that a record of those adventures had been kept in the library at Salisbury and was used by Master Walter Map, who had translated the story for King Henry from Latin into French. But Map was no friend of the Cistercians; and this curious attribution could well have been made by the man who used his name at the beginning of *La Mort Artu* (or *La Mort le Roi Artus*).

There we read: 'After Master Walter Map had treated the adventures of the Holy Grail as far as he thought fit, his lord King Henry was of the opinion that what he had done would not suffice unless he told of the end of those he had mentioned earlier and of how the ones whose deeds of prowess he had recorded in his book had met their deaths. He therefore set about this last part' (VI, p. 203). After his Grail experience, Lancelot returned to court; and within a month he had resumed his passionate relations with Guenevere who, though no longer young, was 'so beautiful a woman that her like was not to be found in the entire world; and this led some to say that as her loveliness never faded she was the fountain-head of all beauty' (VI, p. 205).

The lovers were no longer as discreet as before; and the nature of their association soon became clear to all but Arthur. Guenevere, however, now found cause to show herself once more capable of feeling jealousy. Believing unjustly that Lancelot had returned the hopeless passion of the fair maid of Escalot (or

Plate 14 King Henry and Walter Map. (MS Royal 14 E III, fol. 140.)

Astolat), she flew into a frenzy compounded of grief, repentance and jealousy, vowed revenge, and declared that she would never be reconciled with Lancelot, for whom 'she had such mortal hatred that there is no shame or dishonour in the world that she would not have wished on him' (VI, p. 230). Only when the maid has died of love and her body is brought to Camelot does

Guenevere recognize her error, and her relationship with Lancelot is resumed.

Arthur is at last convinced of his wife's adultery when the lovers are surprised *in flagrante delicto*. Despite his feelings of pity, which are shared by all his people, he determines to have Guenevere judicially convicted and burnt for her crime. It is time for Lancelot to come once more to the rescue; and he carries her off to his castle, the renamed Joyeuse Garde. Arthur moves with his army to besiege them there; and in the course of the fighting, he is unhorsed and finds himself at his rival's mercy. But Lancelot's sense of honour does not allow him to harm his lord. Hostilities end with the intervention of the pope, who orders the king to take back his wife, for whom he still feels genuine love. Guenevere considers her position; and it is Lancelot who persuades her to return to Arthur, while he himself will go unforgiven into exile.

The time has come for the author to bring the whole affair to a close; and for this he turns to the old story of Mordred's treason. Arthur invades Gaul and leaves the disconsolate queen in the charge of Mordred, who loves her passionately and schemes to take her for himself. To this end he has a letter forged purporting to come from the king. In it Arthur declares that he has been mortally wounded by Lancelot; and as his successor he nominates Mordred, saying that he should take Guenevere as his wife, lest she should be abducted by Lancelot. Preparations for this are put in train in the midst of universal grief. The desolate queen, however, refuses to take another husband and plans to escape from Mordred's clutches.

She shuts herself with a garrison of her supporters in the Tower of London. Then from its battlements she rails at Mordred, accusing him of the betrayal of Arthur's trust. When siege is laid to the Tower, it is stoutly defended; and Guenevere manages to have a message smuggled out calling on Arthur, if alive, or otherwise Gawain to come to her rescue. The defenders manage to hold out until news is received of the king's arrival in England, which causes Mordred to break off the siege in order to confront him. Now free, Guenevere goes to a nearby abbey, intending to take the veil within its walls. Its abbess says that she would be welcome, but only after Arthur's death: then the community would accept her as their superior, though she might find the strictness of their order hard to endure.

Plate 15 *The Tower of London. (15th century: MS Royal 16 F II, fol. 73.)*

Events then take their familiar course. After a great battle on Salisbury Plain the king, who is now indeed mortally wounded, is borne away in a boat crewed by ladies. Shortly afterwards his tomb is seen in the Black Chapel, whither the ladies had taken him. On being informed of her husband's death, Guenevere loses no time in carrying out her intention to take the veil. Time passes; and Lancelot, who had honourably survived renewed hostilities with Arthur, learned of his beloved lady's death when he was at Winchester, ridding the world of Mordred's sons. He came to a chapel where he found two priests, one of whom was the Archbishop of Canterbury; and in their company he spent the rest of his life as a hermit. When he died in his turn, angels were seen to descend for his soul. Then, as he had wished, his mortal remains were taken for burial to the Joyeuse Garde.

With *La Mort Artu* we have returned to familiar territory, the heartland of the Plantagenets, where once again the ghost of Eleanor seems to roam. Apart from the inherited detail of the widowed queen retiring from the world to end her days in an abbey of nuns, there are two main episodes where we are encouraged to see fiction rubbing shoulders with history. First there is the case of the queen, estranged from her loving husband on grounds of adultery, and on whose behalf a well-meaning pope intervenes in an attempt to restore the security of the marriage. The parallels here with the events following the rift between Eleanor and her first husband Louis at Antioch need no stressing. Then, equally striking, are the similarities between the siege of the Tower of London and that of Mirebeau: in each case the crown is under threat from a usurper, against whom the gallant queen personally hurls her scorn before defending her position until help arrives. Significantly, this event did not figure in the original account of Mordred's betrayal, which showed Guenevere as his consenting partner in the high treason.

Our conclusion must be that throughout this great cycle of prose romances, with the exception of the heavily didactic *Queste*, their authors, however many may have been involved, depicted the world of King Arthur with their eyes lingering now and then on that of his renowned 'successor' Henry II and his wayward wife Queen Eleanor. Is it possible that for the latter, through her surrogate Queen Guenevere, they showed genuine sympathy and not a little admiration? I believe it is. That she had a hand in commissioning, or even advising on, their joint project is only a slender possibility. Nevertheless, they are likely to have remembered her as a patron of their predecessors in the field of courtly romance and even, through Andrew the Chaplain, as a supreme authority in matters of the heart.

By the late fourteenth century, when English romances using this French material first appeared, the historical Eleanor had faded in people's memories, so that to search through them or the later writings of Malory in the hope of finding some reminiscence of Henry's queen is a vain task. The earliest of these works is probably the alliterative *Morte Arthure*, which combines romance and chronicle elements; and in it the character of Guenevere seems to change according to the demands of the plot.[38] As Lancelot does not have a place in the story, her only adultery is with Mordred, and to her are credited the traitor's children mentioned in earlier texts. That she cares more for her own safety than for theirs is not a fault that can conceivably be attributed to Eleanor. Thus while in the French romances we find little in Guenevere's psychological make-up that could not be a faint reflection of the actual personality of Eleanor, that can scarcely be the case here.

By way of a light-hearted postscript I shall mention two French verse texts which treat the question of Queen Guenevere's infidelity in a less than serious way. The first is the Anglo-Norman *Lai du cor*, which may have been composed in Eleanor's lifetime.[39] One day Arthur is presented with a horn inscribed with a message, which is read aloud to the court. It states that no man can drink from the horn without spilling its contents if he is a cuckold, or harbours jealousy, or has a wife who has coveted other men in her thoughts. This causes a considerable stir among the ladies present; and even the queen (who is unnamed) bows her head when she hears it. Arthur himself takes the first drink, but the wine spills down to his feet. Enraged, he seizes a knife and makes to stab the queen to the heart; but Gawain and the others relieve him of the weapon, assuring him that there is no married woman alive who has not entertained foolish thoughts. The queen declares that since her marriage she has always been perfectly content with her husband: let her be cast on a fire and, should she show any signs of burning, be put to death. As an afterthought she admits that she did once present a ring with her love to a young man who had just killed a giant (this must be Yder, though he too is unnamed); but she would never have gone further than that. Arthur then orders all his knights to drink in turn. Only one, Caradoc, manages to do so without spilling the contents of the horn. This puts the king in a better humour; and he freely forgives his queen. Caerleon was the scene of the testing; and the horn is in safe keeping at Cirencester.

Another version of this story is found at about the same period in the First Continuation of Chrétien's *Perceval*.[40] A knight arrives at Arthur's court in Caerleon with a horn which, he claims, will turn water into wine, but will spill its contents if either the drinker or his wife has been unfaithful. Guenevere pleads with Arthur not to try to drink, since this is all a magic trick designed to bring shame on people. Arthur, however, insists that he will put the horn to the test, whereupon Guenevere prays God that if he does try he may be drenched. The king raises the horn to his lips; and its contents do indeed spill over him. But instead of being angry, he is delighted with his wife, thinking how well she must be loved by God to have her prayer answered in this fashion! As in the *Lai du cor*, Caradoc is the only one to pass the test.

Though probably dating from Eleanor's lifetime, neither of these amusing anecdotes could have given any offence. By then Guenevere's conduct with Lancelot was well known; and in any case of all the lords and ladies at the royal court, only one knight comes out of the test with an untarnished reputation. The poets may have been taking a sly dig at the social behaviour of the aristocracy, but they were also indulging a popular taste for comedy on the theme of women's inconstancy.

*

Our pursuit of our quarry through some of the highways and byways of medieval literature is over; and it is time to assess what we have discovered about the writers' covert use of Eleanor and her deeds in their works. Our aim has been to learn by this indirect method something of the way in which she was perceived by her literate contemporaries or near-contemporaries. Having seen in the early chapters what the historical sources could tell us about the real woman, we then turned to the caricature of her presented by legend. Our hope now is to find something of Eleanor as she really was, although masquerading behind various pseudonyms. Our justification has been the writers' habitual concern to give credence to their fictions by leavening them with what their public could recognize as reality: in this case by using the well-known Queen Eleanor as a model for their own royal ladies.

We did not expect to find any direct references to her in their works; but in fact her name turns up three times. The first occurrence is in *Joufroi de Poitiers*, where she is merely mentioned as the hero's mother. In view of that rapscallion's behaviour, this is no compliment to Eleanor. In any case, the work is simply a piece of fun in which historical reality is deliberately garbled; so it can shed no light for us on the queen as she was or even on her public image. The second mention of her by name is in one or two manuscripts of the English *Richard Coer de Lyon*; otherwise the poet has banished her from history as he conceived it. Perhaps by the time he was writing, her reputation had deteriorated to the point where it might detract from her son's glory. But whatever his reasons, he too has held truth at arm's length and so has no value for us as a witness. The same applies to Layamon's statement that Wace had offered her his *Brut*; for whether or not this actually happened, we hardly need corroboration of her patronage of literature.

Of the other works we have reviewed, we can say with reasonable confidence that some half-dozen introduce Eleanor under another name, and that name is often Guenevere. The anonymous writer of *Perlesvaus* took advantage of the fact that Arthur's queen was said to have ended her life in a convent by patterning his account of Guenevere's withdrawal on that of Eleanor to Fontevrault, where she lived in at least semi-retirement from 1194. Particularly interesting is the way in which, while nominally referring to Glastonbury and using authentic information on that establishment, he contrived to evoke memories of the great French abbey which, unlike Glastonbury, did serve as a mausoleum for the king and queen of England and their beloved son. Like *Perlesvaus*, the prose *Lancelot* was almost certainly written within a decade or two of Eleanor's retirement; and it too contains evident reference to Fontevrault. For there can be little doubt that, located as it is in western France, the Royal Minister (Moustier Royal) of that romance was conceived in imitation of the favoured retreat and burial place of the Plantagenets. This time it is the hero's mother and aunt who are said to have sought their final refuge there: Guenevere is still alive at the end of the romance.

Another event in Eleanor's later life made, to all appearances, a strong impact on the writers. This was her stand against her grandson Arthur and his French allies at the castle of Mirebeau. Although a besieged lady may be thought a common motif of romance, we have found two examples containing unusual details that recall the Mirebeau incident with some insistence. The first is in *Fergus*, where the name of the insolent aggressor Arthofilaus may have been intentionally devised as a pointer; and the other occurs at the end of *La Mort Artu*, fancifully dedicated to King Henry, but where we had already thought we caught Guenevere rehearsing in one episode the part of his queen. To these two likely recollections of Mirebeau we could add, if with slightly less conviction, the case of the later *Durmart le Galois*.

Eleanor's relations with Louis may have had some influence on a number of works, but in the case of two there are particularly strong grounds for suggesting it. In both there are other details that can be called on to support the contention. In *Gaydon* she would be represented, logically enough, by the lady of Gascony, and Louis by her intended husband, Charlemagne's insipid favourite. It is on the king's return from the Holy Land that his candidate is rejected for the Angevin Gaydon, the counterpart of Henry of Anjou. In *La Mort Artu* Arthur, it might be thought, lays aside his usual role as Henry's surrogate in order to represent Louis at the point where he becomes estranged from his wife on the grounds of her infidelity and it needs an intervention from the pope to restore his marriage to an uneasy equilibrium. It is hardly a coincidence that the same romance also carries echoes of Eleanor at Mirebeau and Fontevrault.

Thoughts of Eleanor, then, seem to have occupied the minds of the authors of these texts at some point during their composition. Other works, as we have seen, were composed if not for her, then for her immediate circle. Wace may have dedicated his *Brut* to her. Gautier d'Arras was patronized by her daughter Marie, as was Chrétien de Troyes for at least one of his romances. Both include elements in one of their stories that seem to relate to circumstances of Eleanor's life: to her first marriage and then to her imprisonment by Henry in the case of Gautier's *Eracle*; and in Chrétien's

Erec to her son's investment at Nantes. So for these men too she was a familiar figure, readily available as a model for their portraits of noble wives of illustrious kings.

The parallels we have discovered in these fictions have all necessarily been with Eleanor's known activities; and prudence might counsel us to stop there. We might legitimately add that in more general terms they help to paint in the background to those activities: a courtly, cultured society at least on the surface, but subject to all the tensions and rivalries of an unsettled age. We move about with a peripatetic court, in England and on the Continent; and within that court we recognize the responsibilities of the feudal queen. She should concern herself with preserving domestic harmony as well as supporting the king and providing him with heirs; and she might even venture advice beyond purely domestic matters, though without taking offence if she was overruled. Writers like Marie de France and Chrétien back their improbable plots with a rich store of details which provide a convincing picture of twelfth-century life, at least among the aristocracy.

To that extent, we are helped to see the world as it would have appeared to Eleanor. But do the particular works we have looked at carry us further and give us some impression of the woman herself? Literature of this kind, even when it attempts in ways we have noticed to give the illusion of truth, still views reality through a distorting lens. There are the demands of the story that may have to be met at the expense of logical motivation; and there is also the natural tendency to idealize the characters for whom the authors feel sympathy. Can it be possible, faced by these obstacles, to peer back through the mists of time and catch so much as a glimpse of the real Eleanor?

5

Portrait of a Queen

In the absence of reliable contemporary descriptions of Eleanor the person, I would suggest that the nearest we could come to seeing her as she was perceived in her heyday might be to assemble a composite picture of Henry's queen from the more sympathetic of the portrayals of Guenevere in courtly romance. As an exquisitely beautiful young girl, of noble southern blood according to the chroniclers, she had made an ideal match by marrying the most illustrious of kings, who ruled over Britain and territories beyond the Channel. The great mutual love between the couple was to become eroded, though never entirely disappear, in the course of their long reign. Even when her own affections were divided, she continued to perform to the best of her ability her duties as mistress of the royal court: to be the confidante and counsellor of its younger members, acting as intermediary, when the need arose, between them and the king, encouraging chivalric practice, while being prompt with sensible advice on wider matters of state. She saw her special domain as the arbitration of sentimental issues, which were always a potential source of discord in the close-knit social unit of the royal entourage. She helped to make it a more civilized place by encouraging the arts, including literature, which itself served as a mirror of refined social intercourse; and she shared with her husband the role of Maecenas. Generous in thought and deed, she usually managed to control her personal feelings except under the pressure of grief and, on rare occasions, of jealousy. Her virtues earned for her universal affection; and her long life ended in pious seclusion.

If we find such a portrait too bland and vague, then we must exercise our privilege, as have most writers on Eleanor, of creating our own picture by accommodating our personal vision of her to the known facts of her life. Not only must we avoid the stereotypes of her legend (fairy princess, devil's daughter, scheming witch and so forth), but allowance must be made for the development of her character over the course of her long life as it suffered the stress of circumstances and personal relationships. So, in the guise of a conclusion, I shall offer a sketch of my own, on the understanding that its authenticity is limited to the skeleton of fact that underlies it.

Let us accept that the young Eleanor was beautiful, but not with the blonde radiance favoured by the medieval poets and rhetoricians: dark-haired rather, and with a sparkle in her eyes. She had inherited the family intelligence and interest in the arts that flourished around her; and as heiress-apparent to her father's great duchy, she was well schooled too in more practical matters. Passionate and adventurous as a girl, when she was suddenly wrenched from the relaxed life of her native south she took some time to adjust to the more sober atmosphere of King Louis's Paris. But once she had found her feet as queen, she was not content to remain the passive ornament of her adoring husband's court. Leaned on by political favour-seekers on the one hand and by men of the Church on the other, she quickly gained a shrewd knowledge of and interest in state affairs, while being inclined to leave excessive devoutness to her pious husband.

When the crusade was called, she was only too eager to be free of tiresome political intrigue and participate in its adventure. But this turned out to be quite different from the romantic jaunt of her dreams; and the trials and disasters of the journey were for her a maturing experience. Yet they did not efface her nostalgia for the cultured gaiety of her childhood; and this was reawakened by the hospitality at Antioch of her dashing uncle Raymond of Poitiers. It made her restive under Louis's heavy-handed restraint, and especially resentful of the authority he so sternly imposed. On their homeward journey, she bore with the pope's well-intentioned admonitions, which reinforced her growing sense of inadequacy at her failure to produce a royal heir to the crown of France. By now, both she and her husband were becoming increasingly aware that their temperaments were seriously incompatible and that their continued partnership was in the best interests of neither themselves nor the French kingdom. Then Eleanor's natural inclinations towards romance, adventure and active statecraft led her to seize the chance of marriage to a more dynamic but potentially equally powerful man.

A foreigner even in France, she viewed the prospect of Anglo-Norman England as no less attractive than Paris. Its reputation for learning may have been lower, but it was no cultural backwater. In any case, as a hardened traveller, she had no qualms about returning across the Channel as opportunity offered; so when, after spending the first eighteen months of her marriage on her native soil, she left for England and the crown, she was assured of the possibility of going back there from time to time. By then she had realized one of her dearest ambitions with the birth of her first son, William. True, he survived barely three years; but by now she had another boy, Henry, so although the loss hurt, she felt only passing sorrow, as when she had had to leave her daughters behind with Louis. Indeed, in thirteen years she presented Henry with eight children: five sons and three daughters. This fully satisfied her maternal instincts, which were strong; and she continued to care deeply for the welfare of her children, although the girls' marriage potential did not leave them under her wing for long.

Her early years as queen of England were fulfilling for her in other ways. Despite her frequent pregnancies, her existence was far from sedentary. Apart from several visits to the Continent, she was often found travelling about England with her restless husband. She retained too a lively interest in domestic and international affairs and always with an eye to her children's prospects. For she was not one to dwell on the past, but showed as much concern for the future as the present. Even her continuing interest in Fontevrault was not entirely altruistic: it was only prudent in her day to prepare for some unfortunate contingency which would call for a secure refuge from the storm. In the meantime, though, she could not be bored when she had such an ambitious and dynamic husband; and besides, she found pleasure in receiving visitors at her court, patronizing its cultural life, and bringing some southern sparkle to what she must sometimes have felt as the dour materialism of Anglo-Norman society.

However, as with Louis though for different reasons, she had to reconcile herself to a slow deterioration in her marital relations with Henry. It was not just his notorious bouts of temper: she had soon learnt to side-step or otherwise deal with them. Nor was it his equally well-known infidelities which, as the much older partner, she had to tolerate. It was more that whereas he seemed to live mainly in a frantic present, the romantic dreams of her youth had now given way to long-term dynastic ambitions for her sons. While he acted, she planned her strategy for a more distant future. Although her patience with Henry became increasingly strained, she would not have contemplated making a break with him (the convent was still for her an unthinkable alternative) had he not caused the disaffection of her sons. For once, though, her plans misfired and she became her husband's captive.

Her frustration now was not as total as it might have been. Although her energies had not waned, confined as they now were by the restrictions on her movements, the time had come to harbour them until her freedom returned. In the meantime, she had become an interested spectator, kept in touch with affairs, but not participating in them. The change was not as drastic as it might seem, since she had long lost her influence over Henry in public matters. So for her this was a time for contemplation, refining her political judgement and waiting for a favourable turn of events. Feeling herself the widow of a still living husband, she could only look beyond him to a life still full of possibilities. During these long years her native intelligence matured into wisdom. And when at last he gradually allowed her back on the public scene, she was content to be used by him as a pawn until such time as she would be needed again to play an active role.

Her relief was tempered by tragedy with the deaths of her sons the young Henry and Geoffrey, with that of Matilda soon to follow. Perhaps the knighting of John heralded happier days to come; and there was still the promise of Richard, her favourite. Then came the further death, that of her husband, over which she found fewer tears to shed. Now in her late sixties, she felt herself revitalized; and indeed her remaining years were to be full of activity. It was not over calm seas that she was to sail to that long prepared last haven of Fontevrault. She felt keenly the deaths of more of her children: Marie her first-born, Alice, Richard, Joanna, but especially Richard. Yet she used her reserves of energy to the full, perhaps even relishing her last adventures as much as her first. As a final pleasure she was able to visit her dear Poitiers once again, and possibly even died there before resting for ever in her equally cherished abbey of Fontevrault.

Few people of her age, and certainly few women, could have experienced more, learnt more of the ways of their pulsating world. A legend in her own lifetime, Eleanor of Aquitaine may not have been one of the great makers of history, but she was certainly one of the great livers of it.

Chronology

781	Louis the Pious crowned king of Aquitaine.
877	Aquitaine ceases to be a kingdom.
951	It passes to William I of Poitiers = III of Aquitaine.
993–1030	Ruled by William V 'the Great' (= III of Poitiers); and
1086–1127	by William IX (= VII of Poitiers), Eleanor's troubadour grandfather.
1100	Foundation of Fontevrault.
1122 (?)	Eleanor born at Poitiers or Belin, near Bordeaux, to William (tenth and last Duke 1127–37) and Aenor of Châtellerault.
1137	Easter: Eleanor inherits Poitou and Aquitaine on her father's death.
	July: married to Louis, the French heir, at Bordeaux. Louis VI dies.
	August: Louis and Eleanor enter Paris as King and Queen of France.
1142–3	Louis's ravaging of Champagne and the burning of Vitry.
1144	December: the fall of Edessa.
1145	Birth of Marie.
	Christmas: Louis declares his intention to take the cross.
1147	11 June: he takes the cross at Saint-Denis and leaves on crusade with Eleanor.
	4–16 October: at Constantinople.
1148	February: at Attalia (Antalya).
	19–28 March: in Antioch, whence Eleanor is taken under duress to Jerusalem.
1149	Early summer: Louis and Eleanor leave Palestine; are separated at sea. Eleanor is taken to Palermo (Sicily).
	29 July: Louis arrives in Calabria, where he is later joined by Eleanor before leaving overland for France.

218

9–10 October: with Pope Eugenius at Tusculum (Rome).

November: they return to Paris.

1150 Birth of Alice (Alix).

1151 January: Suger dies.

August–September: Geoffrey of Anjou and his son Henry visit Paris. Geoffrey dies on the return journey.

1151–2 Louis with Eleanor in Aquitaine, dismantling royal administration.

1152 21 March: annulment of their marriage at Beaugency. Eleanor returns to Poitiers, foiling kidnap attempts by Thibaut of Blois and Henry's brother Geoffrey.

18 May: marriage of Henry and Eleanor, probably at Poitiers.

Eleanor's first visit to Fontevrault.

1153–4 Henry campaigning in England.

1153 17 August: birth of William (died 1156).

Death of Bernard of Clairvaux (canonized 1174).

1154 April: Henry returns to the Continent.

Louis remarries.

25 October: death of King Stephen.

8 December: Henry and Eleanor to England.

19 December: their coronation at Westminster.

1155 February: birth of Henry at Bermondsey.

Thomas Becket chancellor.

1155–6 Eleanor regent while Henry is on the Continent securing Anjou and Maine.

1156 June: birth of Matilda in London.

Eleanor takes the children to Normandy; joins Henry in Anjou.

October: progress with Henry through Aquitaine.

Christmas at Bordeaux.

1157 February: with the children to London. Henry returns to England in the spring.

8 September: birth of Richard at Oxford.

Christmas: ceremonial crowning at Lincoln.

1158 Easter (?): crowns laid aside after a ritual coronation at Worcester.

August: Henry returns to the Continent; negotiates with Louis the betrothal of Prince Henry to Margaret Capet. Eleanor remains in England as regent.

23 September: birth of Geoffrey.

December: Eleanor to Normandy. Christmas with Henry at Cherbourg.

1159 Henry's abortive attempt to revive Eleanor's claim to Toulouse.

  Christmas: Eleanor with Henry at Falaise.

1160 early: Eleanor returns to England. Perhaps brief visit to Normandy.

  September: to Normandy with Matilda and Prince Henry.

  November: marriage of Prince Henry to Margaret.

  Christmas: Eleanor with Henry at Le Mans.

1161 September: birth of Eleanor at Domfront.

  Christmas: Eleanor with Henry at Bayeux.

1162 3 June: Becket consecrated Archbishop of Canterbury.

  Christmas: Eleanor with Henry at Cherbourg.

1163 January: they cross with the princesses to Southampton.

  Christmas court at Berkhamsted.

1164 January: Henry with Prince Henry at the Council of Clarendon.

  Eleanor probably spends Easter in London, summer in southern England, and Christmas with the court at Marlborough.

  Marriage of Marie and Alice, her daughters by Louis, to Henry of Champagne and Thibaut of Blois.

1165 Lent: Henry to the Continent to negotiate marriages for the princesses Matilda and Eleanor.

  May: Eleanor to Normandy with Matilda and Richard. Brief reunion with Henry, who then crosses to England, leaving her at Angers as regent over Anjou and Maine.

  Birth of Joanna at Angers, where Eleanor probably spends Christmas.

  August: birth of Louis's son Philip (= Philip Augustus).

1166 March: Henry to Maine; rejoins Eleanor. They spend Easter at Angers.

  June: betrothal of Geoffrey to Constance of Brittany.

  October or November: Eleanor probably to England with Matilda.

  24 December: birth of John at Oxford. Henry spends Christmas at Poitiers with Prince Henry.

1167 Eleanor stays in England, with Henry occupied on the Continent.

  September: death of Henry's mother, the 'Empress' Matilda.

  September: Eleanor supervises the departure of Princess Matilda for her marriage to Duke Henry the Lion of

Saxony. She spends some weeks in Winchester before crossing to Normandy.

Christmas: she rejoins Henry at Argentan.

1168   She accompanies Henry to Poitou.

About Easter she escapes an ambush by Guy de Lusignan near Poitiers while Henry is negotiating an accord with Louis.

Christmas: Henry at Argentan, Eleanor apparently at Poitiers.

1169   January: Henry and Louis ratify their accord at Montmirail, whereby the princes Henry and Richard do homage to Louis, and Richard is betrothed to Alice of France.

Christmas: Henry at Nantes with Geoffrey, now invested as Count of Brittany.

Eleanor probably spends the whole year in Poitou.

1170   January: Henry to Normandy, then England.

May–June: Eleanor supervises Richard's installation as Duke of Aquitaine, then goes to Normandy.

14 June: Prince Henry crowned as king presumptive at Westminster while Eleanor detains papal messenger at Caen. Henry returns to the Continent.

29 December: Becket murdered at Canterbury (canonized 1172).

1171   Henry in Brittany, then Normandy and, in October, to Ireland, spending Christmas in Dublin.

Eleanor's movements unknown.

1172   April–May: Henry to England, then Normandy with the Young King (= Prince Henry) and Margaret.

27 August: Henry in Brittany when the Young King is re-crowned with Margaret at Winchester.

Eleanor may have visited England briefly.

September: Henry to Normandy.

November: the Young King and Margaret join him briefly on their way to the French court.

Christmas: Henry at Chinon with Eleanor, Richard and Geoffrey.

1173   January: the Young King is summoned to Anjou; and they all travel south for negotiations at Limoges concerning John's betrothal and the status of Toulouse.

March: they head north, Eleanor, Richard and Geoffrey going to Poitiers, Henry and the Young King making for

Normandy.

5 March: the Young King absconds from Chinon to Paris, where he is joined for a time by Richard and Geoffrey.

Eleanor leaves Poitiers in secret for Paris (date unknown), but is apprehended and held (in Normandy?) by Henry.

1174   July: Henry crosses to England to foil the Young King's plans, taking Eleanor to captivity, perhaps at Old Sarum (Salisbury).

August: he returns to Normandy and raises the siege of Rouen.

End of sons' rebellion.

Eleanor remains in captivity in England for the next decade, her whereabouts being largely unrecorded.

1175   May: Henry and the Young King to England. They spend Christmas at Windsor.

Eleanor is said to have rejected a proposal to accept divorce and retire to Fontevrault.

1176   Easter: Henry at Winchester with the Young King, Richard and Geoffrey.

Michaelmas: Eleanor perhaps at Winchester with Joanna before her depature to marry King William of Sicily.

Death of Rosamond Clifford, Henry's mistress.

1177   The Young King and Richard campaigning in Poitou.

August: Henry to Normandy.

1178   July: he returns to England.

1179   1 November: the English princes attend Philip's crowning at Reims as French king presumptive.

1180   September: Louis dies and is succeeded by Philip 'Augustus'.

Henry goes with the Young King to Normandy.

1181   Henry returns to England.

1182   Back in Normandy, he spends Christmas at Caen with the Young King, Richard and Geoffrey.

1183   Richard feuding with the Young King and Geoffrey. Henry to Limoges.

11 June: the Young King dies at Martel. He is buried at Rouen.

Late summer (?): from Normandy Henry summons Eleanor to visit her dower lands there, after which she returns to England.

1184   Eleanor's movements are less restricted; at Berkhamsted (Easter), Woodstock, Winchester with the exiled Duke of Saxony and Matilda, then back with them to Berkhamsted.

November: she meets Richard, Geoffrey and John at Westminster.

Christmas: at Windsor court with Richard, John, Matilda and her grandchildren.

1185   early: Eleanor at Winchester.

March: perhaps at John's knighting by Henry at Windsor. Restrictions on her movement lifted.

April: Henry to Normandy. Summons Eleanor to receive Richard's surrender of Aquitaine. She goes to Normandy with Matilda.

1186   April: Henry and Eleanor return to England.

19 August: Geoffrey killed at a tournament in Paris. Buried in Notre-Dame.

Eleanor spends some time in Winchester.

Christmas: Henry at Guildford with John.

1187   February: Henry crosses to Normandy. Hostilities against Philip, who is then joined by Richard.

March: birth of Geoffrey's posthumous son Arthur.

October: Jerusalem falls to Saladin. Richard takes the cross, as do Henry and Philip.

Eleanor often in Winchester.

1188   early: Henry returns to England.

July: he crosses to the Continent. Meets with Philip at Gisors and renews hostilities with him, abetted by Richard.

Eleanor perhaps again under surveillance.

Christmas: Henry at Saumur.

1189   Philip resumes hostilities; Henry accepts terms near Tours.

6 July: Henry dies at Chinon. Buried at Fontevrault.

July: death of Matilda.

13 August: Richard and John return to England. John marries Isabelle of Gloucester.

3 September: coronation of Richard.

12 December: Richard to France.

Eleanor is very active after Henry's death and travels widely in southern England.

1190   early: Richard visits southern territories.

February: Eleanor crosses to Normandy.

March: with John, attends Richard's council at Nonan-court.

late June: Richard leaves on crusade.

14 September: he arrives at Messina, two days before Philip.

Eleanor sends for (fetches?) Berengaria from Navarre and

	leaves with her for Sicily.
1191	30 March: they arrive at Messina.
	2 April: Eleanor leaves and travels to Rouen (arrives late June) by way of Rome, where she meets the pope.
	12 May: Richard marries Berengaria in Cyprus.
	Christmas: spent by Eleanor at Bonneville-sur-Touques.
1192	February: she returns to England to counter John's plans to league with Philip.
	9 October: Richard leaves Palestine.
	December: he is captured by Duke Leopold of Austria.
1193	January: Eleanor is informed of Richard's captivity.
	January–March: John plotting in Normandy. Eleanor thwarts him.
	She raises Richard's ransom.
	December: she sails for Germany.
1194	January: she travels via Cologne to Speyer.
	2 February: the Emperor Henry's council at Mainz is attended by Richard and Eleanor. Richard is released.
	March: Richard and Eleanor return to London via Cologne, Louvain, Brussels, Antwerp, Sandwich and Canterbury.
	17 April: Richard's second crowning.
	mid-May: he and Eleanor leave England for the last time and land in Normandy.
	Reconciliation with John at Lisieux.
	Eleanor retires to Fontevrault.
1194–8	Richard holds Christmas courts at Rouen, Poitiers, Bur-le-Roi (unidentified), Rouen, Domfront. No records for Eleanor.
1196	The widowed Joanna marries Raymond VI of Toulouse.
	Arthur of Brittany is taken to Paris.
1197 (?)	Death of Eleanor's daughter Alice.
1198	Death of Marie of Champagne.
1199	6 April: Richard dies of a wound received at siege of Châlus. Eleanor is present at his death and his burial at Fontevrault.
	John's succession disputed by Arthur with Philip's support.
	25 April: John is proclaimed Duke of Normandy at Rouen.
	Eleanor and Mercadier capture Angers and John Le Mans from Arthur's allies. Arthur to Paris.
	25 May: John crowned at Westminster. Only briefly in England.

April–July: Eleanor visits her domains in Aquitaine, for which she pays homage to Philip at Tours.

September: she names John heir to her duchy; visits him in Rouen.

September: Joanna dies with her new-born son at Fontevrault.

1200   early: Eleanor travels to Castile to fetch her granddaughter Blanche for betrothal to Philip's son Louis. She is briefly captured by the Lusignans.

Easter: she spends at Bordeaux, where Mercadier is murdered.

She returns to Fontevrault.

May: Louis marries Blanche.

Summer: John marries Isabella of Angoulême, having had first marriage annulled.

8 October: he has Isabella crowned queen at Westminster.

1201   Spring: Eleanor ill.

June: John returns to the Continent.

1202   April: Philip knights Arthur and grants him John's Continental lands except Normandy.

Late July: Eleanor leaves Fontevrault for Poitiers. Besieged by Arthur in Mirebeau. Rescued by John; Arthur captured. Eleanor comes to Poitiers.

1203   Arthur is transferred from Falaise to Rouen and apparently murdered.

late: John returns to England.

1204   March: Philip takes Château Gaillard.

1 April: Eleanor dies at Poitiers or Fontevrault, where she is buried.

Abbreviations
Used in the Notes and
Bibliography

ANTS   Anglo-Norman Text Society
BFR   Bibliothèque Française et Romane
CCM   *Cahiers de Civilisation Médiévale*
CFMA   Classiques français du moyen âge
DNB   *Dictionary of National Biography*
EHR   *English Historical Review*
JMH   *Journal of Medieval History*
PL   Patrologia Latina
RS   Rolls Series
SATF   Société des Anciens Textes français
SHF   Société de l'Histoire de France
TLF   Textes Littéraires Français
ZRP   *Zeitschrift für Romanische Philologie*

Notes

Chapter 1 Lineage

1   *The Song of Roland*, tr. D. D. R. Owen (London, 1972), ll. 1062–4.
2   Ibid., ll. 3684–7.
3   For the early Dukes of Aquitaine, see R. R. Bezzola, *Les Origines et la formation de la littérature courtoise en occident (500–1200)* (5 vols, Paris, 1944–63), vol. II. 2 (1960), pp. 254ff.
4   It was in fact Eleanor, not her mother, who became Duchess of Normandy.
5   Translated from Jean Boutière and A.-H. Schutz, *Biographies des troubadours: textes provençaux des XIIIᵉ et XIVᵉ siècles* (Paris, 1964), pp. 7–8.
6   See below, pp. 175–7.
7   For William's verse see Alfred Jeanroy (ed.), *Les Chansons de Guillaume IX*, 2nd edn (CFMA, Paris, 1927). Contemporary and other medieval references are given by Bezzola, *Les Origines*, vol. II.2, pp. 268ff.
8   See Rita Lejeune, 'The Troubadours', in Roger Sherman Loomis (ed.), *Arthurian Literature in the Middle Ages* (Oxford, 1959), pp. 393–9; also Bezzola, *Les Origines*, vol. II.2, pp. 318–20.
9   See Charles Homer Haskins, *The Renaissance of the Twelfth Century* (Harvard University Press, 1927; reprinted in Meridian Books, New York, 1957); Christopher Brooke, *The Twelfth Century Renaissance* (London, 1969); Colin Morris, *The Discovery of the Individual, 1050–1200* (London, 1972).

Chapter 2 Life

1   See, for instance, Bezzola, *Les Origines*, vol. III.2 (1963), pp. 353ff.
2   Ed. Ernest Langlois (CFMA, Paris, 1925). English translation by

D. G. Hoggan in *William of Orange: Four Old French Epics*, ed. Glanville Price (Everyman, 1975), pp. 1–59.

3   See Jean Frappier, *Les Chansons de geste du cycle de Guillaume d'Orange*, vol. II (Paris, 1965), pp. 58–9.

4   On medieval Paris see Jacques Boussard, *Nouvelle histoire de Paris de la fin du siège de 885–886 à la mort de Philippe Auguste* (Paris, 1976).

5   F. J. E. Raby, *A History of Christian-Latin Poetry from the Beginnings to the Close of the Middle Ages*, 2nd edn (Oxford, 1953). See especially chs X and XI.

6   *Philomena, conte raconté d'après Ovide par Chrétien de Troyes*, ed. Ch. de Boer (Paris, 1909), ll. 124–204.

7   Marcel Pacaut, *Louis VII et son royaume* (Paris, 1964), p. 36.

8   For these events, see ibid., pp. 42–5, and Amy Kelly, *Eleanor of Aquitaine and the Four Kings* (Harvard University Press, Cambridge Mass. and London, 1950), pp. 21–4.

9   *Raoul de Cambrai*, ed. Sarah Kay (Oxford, 1992). I translate from ll. 1303–28.

10 *Recueil des historiens des Gaules et de la France*, ed. Léopold Delisle (24 vols, Paris, 1869–1904), vol. XIII (1869), p. 331.

11 Pacaut, *Louis VII*, pp. 46ff.

12 Joseph Bédier and Pierre Aubry, *Les Chansons de croisade avec leurs mélodies* (Paris, 1909; Slatkine Reprints, Geneva, 1974), pp. 3–16 (my translation).

13 See, e.g., Henry Treece, *The Crusades* (New York, 1964), p. 125. William of Newburgh makes the point forcibly, declaring that, what with the wives and their maidservants, 'in that Christian camp where chastity should have prevailed, a horde of women was milling about. This in particular brought scandal upon our army' (William of Newburgh, *The History of English Affairs*, Book I, ed. and tr. P. G. Walsh and M. J. Kennedy (Warminster, 1988), p. 129).

14 See Bezzola, *Les Origines*, vol. III.1 (1963), pp. 256–7.

15 For John of Salisbury's version of events in Antioch, see his *Historia Pontificalis*, ed. and tr. Marjorie Chibnall (Oxford, 1986), pp. 52–3. On this episode and the accounts and rumours to which it gave rise, see also Kelly, *Eleanor of Aquitaine*, pp. 52ff., and ch. 3 below.

16 *The Pilgrimage of Charlemagne (Le Pèlerinage de Charlemagne) and Aucassin and Nicolette (Aucassin et Nicolette)*, ed. Anne Elizabeth Cobby and Glyn S. Burgess (New York and London, 1988).

17 For this incident and subsequent events in Italy, see *Historia Pontificalis*, ed. and tr. Chibnall, pp. 60–2.

18 *The History of English Affairs*, Book I, ed. and tr. Walsh and Kennedy, p. 129.
19 See C. N. L. Brooke, 'The Marriage of Henry II and Eleanor of Aquitaine', *The Historian*, no. 20 (1988), pp. 4–5.
20 Richard Barber, *Henry Plantagenet. A Biography* (London, 1964). See especially ch. 1 for the Angevin background.
21 Marion Meade, *Eleanor of Aquitaine, A Biography* (New York, 1977), p. 146. See also Kelly, *Eleanor of Aquitaine*, p. 77. Gerald tells the story in his *De Principis Instructione* (ed. George F. Warner, *Giraldi Cambrensis Opera*, vol. VIII (RS 21, London, 1891), p. 300).
22 For the strategic implications and advantages for both parties see W. L. Warren, *Henry II* (London, 1973), pp. 42–5.
23 See Jean-Marc Bienvenu, 'Aliénor d'Aquitaine et Fontevraud', *CCM*, XXIX (1986), pp. 15–27.
24 See Ralph V. Turner, 'Eleanor of Aquitaine and her Children: An Inquiry into Medieval Family Attachment', *JMH*, 14 (1988), pp. 321–35.
25 *De Nugis Curialium: Courtiers' Trifles*, ed. and tr. M. R. James, revised by C. N. L. Brooke and R. A. B. Mynors (Oxford, 1983), pp. 476–7.
26 Bezzola, *Les Origines*, vol. III.1, pp. 271–91.
27 Geoffrey of Monmouth, *Historia Regum Britanniae*, ed. A. Griscom (New York, 1929); variant version, ed. J. Hammer (Cambridge, Mass., 1951); tr. Lewis Thorpe, *The History of the Kings of Britain* (Penguin Books, 1966). Wace, *Le Roman de Brut*, ed. I. Arnold, 2 vols (SATF, Paris, 1938–40); tr. Eugene Mason, *Wace and Layamon: Arthurian Chronicles* (Everyman, 1912, new edn 1962).
28 Wace, *Le Roman de Rou*, ed. A. J. Holden (SATF, Paris, 1970). On Henry's interests see Walter F. Schirmer and Ulrich Broich, *Studien zum literarischen Patronat im England des 12. Jahrhunderts* (Cologne and Opladen, 1962).
29 For a discussion and analysis of this text see Bezzola, *Les Origines*, vol. III.1, pp. 126–39.
30 Boutière and Schutz, *Biographies des troubadours*, pp. 20–1 (my translation).
31 The relevant allusions are discussed by Bezzola, *Les Origines*, vol. III.1, pp. 261–3.
32 Perhaps by a 'wandering scholar', this has been preserved in the *Carmina Burana* (ed. A. Hilka and O. Schumann (Heidelberg, 1930–70), vol. I: Text 2, *Die Liebeslieder*, no. 145a). The translation is my own. For the identity of the queen see Cyril Edwards, 'The Magnanimous Sex-Object: Richard the Lionheart in the

Medieval German Lyric', in Keith Busby and Erik Kooper (eds), *Courtly Literature: Culture and Context* (Amsterdam and Philadelphia, 1990), pp. 159–77.

33 See Kelly, *Eleanor of Aquitaine*, pp. 94–5, citing Walter Map.

34 See Turner, 'Eleanor of Aquitaine and her Children'.

35 William Stubbs has a note on the date of John's birth in his edition of *The Historical Collections of Walter of Coventry* (RS 58, London, 1873, vol. II, pp. xvii–xviii). He says it was established by Robert de Monte (= de Torigny), whose authority he trusts, as 1167. But Ralph de Diceto, 'who may be regarded as correcting Robert de Monte', gives 1166, a date followed by later annalists. Stubbs sees as deriving from Robert de Monte (Torigny) the further information in the margin of Robert of Gloucester's chronicle to the effect that the birth was on 24 December and accompanied by the sighting of two meteors, the year being the thirteenth of Henry's reign, 'i.e. 1166 instead of 1167'. Is it possible that the confusion arises from the use for the first dating of the by that time conservative practice (still favoured by the Benedictines) of beginning the new year at the Nativity? The year 1167 would still have been anticipated by a day; but disregarding this, the later chroniclers would have made the correction to 1166 to accord with the new calendar. Difficulties arising from the coexistence of the two systems are illustrated in C. R. Cheney, *Handbook of Dates for Students of English History* (London, 1945), p. 4. Many modern historians (W. L. Warren is an exception) opt for 24 December 1167, despite R. W. Eyton's entry, referring to Matthew of Westminster, under 1166: 'Dec. 24. Queen Elianor, now in England, gave birth to Prince John, at Oxford' (*Court, Household, and Itinerary of King Henry II* (London, 1878; reprinted Hildesheim and New York, 1974), p. 103). Kelly, without discussion, gives 1166, but 'on the day after Christmas' (*Eleanor of Aquitaine*, p. 152). It is difficult to reconcile Eleanor's subsequent activities with the later dating.

36 Walter Map, *De Nugis Curialium*, pp. 478–9 and 494–5.

37 For the movements of Henry and Eleanor see Eyton, *Court, Household, and Itinerary*.

38 *Henry II*, p. 120.

39 *Materials for the History of Thomas Becket, Archbishop of Canterbury*, ed. J. C. Robertson and J. B. Sheppard, 7 vols (RS 67, London, 1875–85), vol. V (ed. Robertson), p. 197 (quoted by Meade, *Eleanor of Aquitaine*, p. 230).

40 Eyton, *Court, Household, and Itinerary*, p. 108.

41 Meade, *Eleanor of Aquitaine*, pp. 234–8.

42 *L'Histoire de Guillaume le Maréchal, comte de Striguil et de Pembroke*, ed. Paul Meyer (SHF, Paris, 1891–1901), ll. 1614ff. The

biographer, unlike other chroniclers, ascribes the ambush to Guy de Lusignan's brother Geoffrey.

43 Turner, 'Eleanor of Aquitaine and her Children', p. 327.
44 H. G. Richardson, 'The Letters and Charters of Eleanor of Aquitaine', *EHR*, CCXCI (1959), pp. 193–213: see p. 198 n. 2.
45 Chrétien's *Lancelot* was probably composed in about 1177 and Andreas's treatise *De Arte honeste amandi (De Amore)* some time later. The latter was translated as *The Art of Courtly Love* by John Jay Parry (Columbia University Press, 1941) from the edition by E. Trojel (Copenhagen, 1892).
46 On Marie see Edmond-René Labande, 'Les filles d'Aliénor d'Aquitaine: étude comparative', *CCM*, XXIX (1986), pp. 101–4.
47 Meade, *Eleanor of Aquitaine*, pp. 270–2.
48 Gervase of Canterbury, *Opera Historica*, ed. William Stubbs, 2 vols (RS 73, London, 1879–80). See vol. II, p. 80, and vol. I, pp. 242–3.
49 On the whole of this episode and probable literary contamination in the chroniclers' accounts see my article, 'The Prince and the Churl: The Traumatic Experience of Philip Augustus', *JMH*, 17 (1992), pp. 141–4.
50 Meade, *Eleanor of Aquitaine*, p. 289, quoting Ralph of Coggeshall.
51 Ibid., p. 279. The original is in L. Delisle (ed.), *Recueil des historiens des Gaules et de la France*, vol. XII (Paris, 1877), p. 420.
52 Benedict of Peterborough, *Gesta Regis Henrici Secundi (the Chronicle of the Reigns of Henry II and Richard I, A. D. 1169–1192)*, ed. William Stubbs, 2 vols (RS 49, London, 1867). See vol. II. pp. 160–1.
53 Ibid., vol. I, p. 305.
54 Meade, *Eleanor of Aquitaine*, pp. 290–1.
55 Gerald of Wales (Giraldus Cambrensis), *De Principis Instructione*, p. 295.
56 *L'Histoire de Guillaume le Maréchal*, ll. 8803–49.
57 For Henry's last days see Barber, *Henry Plantagenet*, pp. 230–3 and Appendix III. The details of Richard's reign are given in Lionel Landon, *The Itinerary of King Richard I* (London, 1935). See also John Gillingham, *The Life and Times of Richard I* (London, 1973).
58 *L'Histoire de Guillaume le Maréchal*, l. 9510 ('plus a ese k'el ne sout estre').
59 *The Poems of the Troubadour Bertran de Born*, ed. William D. Paden Jr, Tilde Sankovitch and Patricia H. Stäblein (University of California Press, 1986), pp. 416–17 (my translation).
60 Frederick Goldin, *Lyrics of the Troubadours and Trouvères* (New York, 1973), pp. 376–9 (my translation). The lady of Chartres was Alice, Richard's other half-sister, for whom he had little affection.
61 *L'Histoire de Guillaume le Maréchal*, ll. 11833–908.

62 Quoted from Kelly, *Eleanor of Aquitaine*, p. 353.
63 Peire Vidal, *Poesie*, ed. D. S. Avalle (Milan, 1960).
64 Roger of Hoveden, *Chronica*, ed. William Stubbs, vol. IV (RS 51, London, 1871), pp. 114–15.
65 See Kelly, *Eleanor of Aquitaine*, pp. 360–1.
66 Ibid., p. 363.
67 Quoted by Meade, *Eleanor of Aquitaine*, p. 344.
68 *Histoire des ducs de Normandie*, ed. Francisque Michel (Paris, 1840), p. 93.
69 Ibid., p. 94.
70 See W. L. Warren, *King John* (2nd edn, London, 1978), pp. 81–4; also Kelly, *Eleanor of Aquitaine*, pp. 374–80.
71 Quoted by Kelly, *Eleanor of Aquitaine*, p. 380.
72 For the whole obituary see Bienvenu, 'Aliénor d'Aquitaine et Fontevraud', p. 26 n. 98.
73 Richard of Devizes, *Chronicle*, ed. and tr. John T. Appleby (London, 1963), pp. 25–6.

Chapter 3 Legend

1 Other references to Eleanor's behaviour at Antioch are studied by Ruth E. Harvey, *The Troubadour Marcabru and Love* (London, 1989), pp. 131–9.
2 *Historia Pontificalis*, ed. Chibnall, pp. 52–3.
3 See Harvey, *The Troubadour Marcabru*, pp. 131ff.
4 William of Tyre, *A History of Deeds Done Beyond the Sea*, tr. E. A. Babcock and A. C. Krey (New York, 1976), vol. II. pp. 179–81.
5 Gervase of Canterbury, *Opera Historica*, vol. I, p. 149; Gerald of Wales, *De Principis Instructione*, p. 299.
6 *Récits d'un Ménestrel de Reims*, ed. Natalis de Wailly (Paris, 1876), pp. 3–7 (my translation).
7 Richard of Devizes, *Chronicle*, pp. 59–60.
8 Wace, *Roman de Rou*, ll. 24–36 (my translation).
9 *L'Histoire de Guillaume le Maréchal*, ll. 9507–10, 9872–6.
10 Walter Map, *De Nugis Curialium*, pp. 475–7.
11 Helinant de Froidmont, *Chronicon*, ed. J.-P. Migne (PL 212, Paris, 1855), cols 1057–8.
12 Quoted by Pacaut, *Louis VII*, p. 59.
13 Gerald of Wales, *De Principis Instructione*, pp. 298–303.
14 Ibid., pp. 300–1.
15 See Gerald of Wales, 'The Journey through Wales' and 'The Description of Wales', tr. Lewis Thorpe (Penguin Books, 1978), Appendix B ('Gerald of Wales and King Arthur').

16 Richard le Poitevin in Delisle (ed.), *Recueil des historiens*, vol. XII, p. 419; Merlin's prophecies in Geoffrey of Monmouth, *The History of the Kings of Britain*, tr. Lewis Thorpe, pp. 174–5.

17 Benedict of Peterborough, *Gesta Regis Henrici Secundi*, vol. I, p. 42.

18 On Rosamond Clifford and her legend see the article by T. A. Archer in *Dictionary of National Biography*, ed. Leslie Stephen, vol. XII (London, 1887), pp. 75–7; and Virgil B. Heltzel, *Fair Rosamund: A Study of the Development of a Literary Theme* (Evanston, 1947).

19 Gerald of Wales, *De Principis Instructione*, pp. 165–6. A variant reading is given in *DNB*, p. 75.

20 Benedict of Peterborough, *Gesta Regis Ricardi* in *Gesta Regis Henrici Secundi*, vol. II, pp. 231–2 (my translation).

21 Ranulf Higden, *Polychronicon*, vol. VIII, ed. Joseph Rawson Lumby (RS 41, London, 1882), pp. 52–5. Trevisa's translation is given on facing pages.

22 *Croniques de London*, ed. G. J. Aungier (London, 1844), pp. 3–5.

23 *DNB*, vol. XII, p. 76.

24 Chrétien de Troyes, *Arthurian Romances*, tr. D. D. R. Owen (Everyman, 1987), pp. 168–9.

25 Thomas Percy, *Reliques of Ancient English Poetry*, ed. R. A. Willmott (London, n.d.), pp. 251–2.

26 Ibid., pp. 252–7.

27 Samuel Daniel, *The Complete Works*, ed. A. B. Grosart, vol. I (n.p., 1885), pp. 79–113.

28 Joseph Addison, *The Miscellanous Works*, ed. A. C. Guthkelch, vol. I (London, 1914): *Rosamond. An Opera* is on pp. 293–332; see pp. xvii–xviii for Tickell's preface.

29 Sir Thomas More, Michael Drayton, Thomas Hearne, &c., *The Unfortunate Royal Mistresses, Rosamond Clifford, and Jane Shore, Concubines to King Henry the Second and Edward the Fourth, with Historical and Metrical Memoirs of those Celebrated Persons* (London, 1825?). See pp. iii–iv and 7 for my quotations from the introductory remarks.

30 Ibid., pp. 34–40.

31 Ibid., pp. 41–7.

32 Ibid., pp. 48–54.

33 Ibid., pp. 60–4.

34 Agnes Strickland, *Lives of the Queens of England*, vol. I, 4th edn (London, 1854). The biography of Eleanor is on pp. 237–93.

35 Algernon Charles Swinburne, *The Tragedies*, vol. I (London, 1905). *Rosamond* is on pp. 227–88.

36 Alfred Lord Tennyson, *The Life and Works*, vol. XI (*The Works*, vol. VII: London, 1899). *Becket* is on pp. 1–155.

37 Winston S. Churchill, *A History of the English-Speaking Peoples*, vol. I: *The Birth of Britain* (London, 1956), p. 160.
38 Benoît de Sainte-Maure, *Le Roman de Troie*, ed. Léopold Constans, 6 vols (SATF, Paris, 1904–12). See vol. IV, ll. 23357ff. for the episode of the Amazons; my translation is of ll. 23426–79.
39 *Die Krone der Komnenen: Die Regierungszeit der Kaiser Joannes und Manuel Komnenos (1118–1180) aus dem Geschichtswerk des Niketas Choniates*, tr. Franz Grabler (Byzantinische Geschichtsschreiber VII: Graz–Vienna–Cologne, 1958), p. 95 (my translation).
40 Michaud's *History of the Crusades*, tr. W. Robson, 3 vols (London, 1852), vol. I, p. 343.
41 Strickland, *Lives of the Queens*, pp. 246–8.
42 Kelly, *Eleanor of Aquitaine*, pp. 35, 38.
43 See D. D. R. Owen, *Noble Lovers* (London, 1975).
44 Andreas Capellanus, *The Art of Courtly Love*: Eleanor's judgements are on pp. 168–70.
45 John F. Benton, 'The Court of Champagne as a Literary Center', *Speculum*, XXXVI (1961), pp. 551–91 (p. 589).
46 Strickland, *Lives of the Queens*, p. 243.
47 Kelly, *Eleanor of Aquitaine*, ch. 15 (p. 167).
48 William Shakespeare, *King John*, ed. E. A. J. Honigmann (The Arden Shakespeare, London, 1954).
49 Percy, *Reliques*, pp. 257–9.
50 For Rigord's account see Guillaume le Breton, *Gesta Philippe Augusti. Philippide*, ed. H. F. Delaborde, 2 vols (Paris, 1882–5), vol. II, p. 11.

Chapter 4 Literature

1 *Cligés*, ll. 27–44: see my translation in Chrétien de Troyes, *Arthurian Romances*, p. 93.
2 See above, p. 17.
3 Marie de France, *Lais*, ed. A. Ewert (Oxford, 1944). See Paula Clifford, *Marie de France: Lais* (Critical Guides to French Texts, London, 1982).
4 Thomas, *Les Fragments du Roman de Tristan, poème du XIIe siècle*, ed. Bartina H. Wind (TLF, Geneva and Paris, 1960); translated by A. T. Hatto, *Gottfried von Strassburg, Tristan, with the Surviving Fragments of the Tristan of Thomas* (Penguin Books, 1960). See also Tony Hunt, 'The Significance of Thomas's Tristan', *Reading Medieval Studies*, VII (1981), pp. 41–61, esp. pp. 52–3.

5 Hatto, *Gottfried von Strassburg*, pp. 355ff.

6 Ed. Wind, fragment Douce, ll. 235–98. For Thomas's discussion of the sorrows love has brought the characters, see fragment de Turin, ll. 71–151.

7 See Aimé Petit's doctoral thesis, *L'Anachronisme dans les romans antiques du XIIᵉ siècle* (Centre d'Études Médiévales et Dialectales de l'Université de Lille III, 1985).

8 Gautier d'Arras, *Ille et Galeron*, ed. Frederick A. G. Cowper (SATF, Paris, 1956); *Eracle*, ed. Guy Raynaud de Lage (CFMA, Paris, 1970).

9 Anthime Fourrier, *Le Courant réaliste dans les romans courtois en France au moyen-âge*, vol. I: *Les Débuts (XIIᵉ siècle)* (Paris, 1960).

10 Hue de Rotelande, *Ipomedon*, ed. A. J. Holden (Paris, 1979); *Protheselaus*, ed. A. J. Holden, 2 vols (ANTS XLVII and XLVIII, London, 1991).

11 *Guillaume de Palerne. Roman du XIIIᵉ siècle*, ed. Alexandre Micha (TLF, Geneva, 1990).

12 Published by A. Jeanroy in 'Notes sur le tournoiement des dames', *Romania*, 28 (1899), pp. 232–44.

13 Guillaume le Clerc, *The Romance of Fergus*, ed. Wilson Frescoln (Philadelphia, 1983); tr. as *Fergus of Galloway, Knight of King Arthur* by D. D. R. Owen (Everyman, 1991).

14 See Appendix B to *Fergus of Galloway* and my study 'The *Fergus*-Poet' in *Medieval Codicology, Iconography, Literature and Translation: Studies for Keith Val Sinclair* (Leiden, 1994), pp. 233–9.

15 In *Durmart le Galois* and *La Mort Artu* (see below, pp. 192 and 205–7).

16 *Gaydon*, ed. F. Guessard and S. Luce (Les Anciens Poètes de la France, Paris, 1862). See also William Calin, *The Epic Quest: Studies in Four Old French Chansons de Geste* (Baltimore, 1966), ch. III.

17 *The Romance of Flamenca: A Provençal Poem of the Thirteenth Century*, revised text by Marion E. Porter, tr. Merton Jerome Hubert (Princeton University Press for the University of Cincinnati, 1962).

18 *Joufroi de Poitiers, roman d'aventures du XIIIᵉ siècle*, ed. Perceval B. Fay and John L. Grigsby (TLF, Geneva and Paris, 1972). See also Owen, *Noble Lovers*, pp. 122–7.

19 Pp. 7–8.

20 Coudrette, *Le Roman de Mélusine ou Histoire de Lusignan*, ed. Eleanor Roach (Paris, 1982).

21 *Der Mittelenglische Versroman über Richard Löwenherz*, ed. and tr. Karl Brunner (Wiener Beiträge zur Englischen Philologie XLII, Vienna and Leipzig, 1913).

22 For the whole Arthurian legend see Loomis (ed.), *Arthurian Litera-ture*. Guenevere in early Welsh tradition, the chronicles and me-dieval English romance is studied by Peter Korrel, *An Arthurian Triangle: A Study of the Origin, Development and Characterization of Arthur, Guinevere and Modred* (Leiden, 1984).

23 All line references are to the text published by I. D. O. Arnold and M. M. Pelan in *La Partie arthurienne du Roman de Brut* (BFR, Paris, 1962).

24 See above, p. 109.

25 See Korrel, *An Arthurian Triangle*, pp. 146–72.

26 *Le Roman de Renart*, ed. and tr. Jean Dufournet, 2 vols (Paris, 1985). The relevant branch (XI) is summarized in vol. II, pp. 280–5.

27 All the romances are translated in my Chrétien de Troyes, *Arthurian Romances*, which may be consulted for editions and select bibliography.

28 See Beate Schmolke-Hasselmann, *Der arthurische Versroman von Chrétien bis Froissart* (Beihefte zur ZRP 177, Tübingen, 1980), pp. 190–9.

29 *Gliglois: A French Arthurian Romance of the Thirteenth Century*, ed. Charles H. Livingston (Harvard University Press, Cambridge, Mass., 1932).

30 Raoul de Houdenc, *Sämtliche Werke*, ed. Mathias Friedwagner, vol. I: *Meraugis von Portlesguez: altfranzösischer Abenteuerroman* (Halle, 1897).

31 *The Romance of Yder*, ed. and tr. Alison Adams (Arthurian Studies VIII, Woodbridge, 1983).

32 See Edmond Faral, *La Légende arthurienne – Études et documents*, vol. II (Paris, 1929), §IX: 'L'Abbaye de Glastonbury et la légende du roi Arthur'.

33 *Durmart le Galois*, ed. Joseph Gildea, 2 vols (Villanova, Pennsylva-nia, 1965–6).

34 *Le Haut Livre du Graal: Perlesvaus*, ed. William A. Nitze and T. Atkinson Jenkins, 2 vols (University of Chicago Press, 1932–7). For the circumstances of composition see Thomas E. Kelly, *Le Haut Livre du Graal: Perlesvaus. A Structural Study* (Geneva, 1974), ch. I.

35 See Leslie Alcock, *Arthur's Britain: History and Archaeology AD 367–634* (Penguin Books, 1971), pp. 73–80.

36 *The Vulgate Version of the Arthurian Romances*, ed. H. O. Sommer, 7 vols (Washington, 1908–16): volume and page refer-ences are to this edition. See also Loomis (ed.), *Arthurian Literature*, chs 22 (by Jean Frappier) and 23 (by Alexandre Micha); Korrel, *An Arthurian Triangle*, pp. 175–207.

37 J. Neale Carman, *A Study of the Pseudo-Map Cycle of Arthurian*

Romance (University Press of Kansas, 1973), p. 111.
38 Korrel, *An Arthurian Triangle*, ch. III, studies her character in these romances.
39 *The Anglo-Norman Text of 'Le Lai du cor'*, ed. C. T. Erickson (ANTS XXIV, Oxford, 1973).
40 *The Continuations of the Old French Perceval of Chrétien de Troyes*, vol. I: *The First Continuation*, ed. William Roach (University of Pennsylvania Press, Philadelphia, 1949): MSS TVD, ll. 8493–734.

Bibliography

Addison, Joseph, *The Miscellaneous Works*, ed. A. C. Guthkelch, vol. I, London, 1914.

Alcock, Leslie, *Arthur's Britain: History and Archaeology AD 367–634*, Penguin Books, 1971.

Andreas Capellanus, *The Art of Courtly Love*, tr. John Jay Parry, Columbia University Press, 1941.
    De Amore Libri Tres, ed. E. Trojel, Copenhagen, 1892.

The Anglo-Norman Text of 'Le Lai du cor', ed. C. T. Erickson, ANTS XXIV, Oxford, 1973.

Arnold, I. D. O. and Pelan, M. M., *La Partie arthurienne du Roman de Brut*, BFR, Paris, 1962.

Barber, Richard, *Henry Plantagenet. A Biography*, London, 1964..

Bédier, Joseph and Aubry, Pierre, *Les Chansons de croisade avec leurs mélodies*, Paris, 1909; Slatkine Reprints, Geneva, 1974.

Benedict of Peterborough, *Gesta Regis Henrici Secundi (the Chronicle of the Reigns of Henry II and Richard I, A. D. 1169–1192)*, ed. William Stubbs, 2 vols, RS 49, London, 1867.

Benoît de Sainte-Maure, *Le Roman de Troie*, ed. Léopold Constans, 6 vols, SATF, Paris, 1904–12.

Benton, John F., 'The Court of Champagne as a Literary Center', *Speculum*, XXXVI, 1961, pp. 551–91.

Bertran de Born, *The Poems of the Troubadour Bertran de Born*, ed. William D. Paden Jr, Tilde Sankovitch and Patricia H. Stäblein, University of California Press, 1986.

Bezzola, R. R., *Les Origines et la formation de la littérature courtoise en occident (500–1200)*, 5 vols, Paris, 1944–63.

Bienvenu, Jean-Marc, 'Aliénor d'Aquitaine et Fontevraud', *CCM*, XXIX, 1986, pp. 15–27.

Boussard, Jacques, *Nouvelle histoire de Paris de la fin du siège de 885–886 à la mort de Philippe Auguste*, Paris, 1976.

Boutière, Jean, and Schutz, A. -H., *Biographies des troubadours: textes provençaux des XIIIe et XIVe siècles*, Paris, 1964.

Brooke, C. N. L., 'The Marriage of Henry II and Eleanor of Aquitaine', *The Historian*, no. 20, 1988, pp. 3–8.

Cahiers de Civilisation Médiévale, XXIX, 1986: X^e–XIIe Siècles; pp. 1–147 are devoted to Plantagenet studies.

Calin, William, *The Epic Quest: Studies in Four Old French Chansons de Geste*, Baltimore, 1966.

Carman, J. Neale, *A Study of the Pseudo-Map Cycle of Arthurian Romance*, University Press of Kansas, 1973.

Carmina Burana, ed. A. Hilka and O. Schumann, Heidelberg, 1930–70.

Cheney, C. R., *Handbook of Dates for Students of English History*, London, 1945.

Chrétien de Troyes, *Arthurian Romances*, tr. D. D. R. Owen, Everyman, 1987.

Churchill, Winston S., *A History of the English-Speaking Peoples*, vol. I: *The Birth of Britain*, London, 1956.

Clifford, Paula, *Marie de France: Lais*, Critical Guides to French Texts, London, 1982.

The Continuations of the Old French Perceval of Chrétien de Troyes, vol. I: *The First Continuation*, ed. William Roach, University of Pennsylvania Press, Philadelphia, 1949.

Coudrette, *Le Roman de Mélusine ou Histoire de Lusignan*, ed. Eleanor Roach, Paris, 1982.

Le Couronnement de Louis, chanson de geste du XIIe siécle, ed. Ernest Langlois, 2nd edn, CFMA, Paris, 1925.

Croniques de London, ed. G. J. Aungier, London, 1844.

Daniel, Samuel, *The Complete Works*, ed. A. B. Grosart, 5 vols, n.p., 1885–96.

Delisle, Léopold (ed.), *Recueil des historiens des Gaules et de la France*, 24 vols, Paris, 1869–1904.

Dictionary of National Biography, ed. Leslie Stephen, vol. XII, London, 1887.

Durmart le Galois, ed. Joseph Gildea, 2 vols, Villanova, Pennsylvania, 1965–6.

Edwards, Cyril, 'The Magnanimous Sex-Object: Richard the Lionheart in the Medieval German Lyric', in Keith Busby and Erik Kooper (eds), *Courtly Literature: Culture and Context*, Amsterdam and Philadelphia, 1990.

Eyton, R. W., *Court, Household, and Itinerary of King Henry II*, London, 1878; reprinted Hildesheim and New York, 1974.

Faral, Edmond, *La Légende arthurienne–Études et documents*, vol. II, Paris, 1929.

Flamenca, The Romance of: A Provençal Poem of the Thirteenth Century, revised text by Marion E. Porter, tr. Merton Jerome Hubert, Princeton University Press for the University of Cincinnati, 1962.

Fourrier, Anthime, *Le Courant réaliste dans les romans courtois en France au moyen-âge,* vol. I: *Les Débuts (XIIe siècle),* Paris, 1960.

Frappier, Jean, *Les Chansons de geste du cycle de Guillaume d'Orange,* vol. II, Paris, 1965.

Gautier d'Arras, *Ille et Galeron,* ed. Frederick A. G. Cowper, SATF, Paris, 1956.

    Eracle, ed. Guy Raynaud de Lage, CFMA, Paris, 1970.

Gaydon, ed. F. Guessard and S. Luce, Les Anciens Poètes de la France, Paris, 1862.

Geoffrey of Monmouth, *Historia Regum Britanniae,* ed. A. Griscom, New York, 1929; variant version, ed. J. Hammer, Cambridge, Mass., 1951.

    The History of the Kings of Britain, tr. Lewis Thorpe, Penguin Books, 1966.

Gerald of Wales, *De Principis Instructione,* in George F. Warner (ed.), *Giraldi Cambrensis Opera,* vol. VIII, RS 21, London, 1891.

    'The Journey through Wales' and 'The Description of Wales', tr. Lewis Thorpe, Penguin Books, 1978.

Gervase of Canterbury, *Opera Historica,* ed. William Stubbs, 2 vols, RS 73, London, 1879–80.

Gillingham, John, *The Life and Times of Richard I,* London, 1973.

Gliglois: A French Arthurian Romance of the Thirteenth Century, ed. Charles H. Livingston, Harvard University Press, Cambridge, Mass., 1932.

Goldin, Frederick, *Lyrics of the Troubadours and Trouvères,* New York, 1973.

Guillaume IX Duc d'Aquitaine (1071–1127), Les Chansons de, ed. Alfred Jeanroy, 2nd edn, CFMA, Paris, 1927.

Guillaume le Breton, *Gesta Philippe Augusti, Philippide,* ed. H. F. Delaborde, 2 vols, Paris, 1882–5.

Guillaume le Clerc, *The Romance of Fergus,* ed. Wilson Frescoln, Philadelphia, 1983.

    Fergus of Galloway, Knight of King Arthur, tr. D. D. R. Owen, Everyman, 1991.

Guillaume le Maréchal, comte de Striguil et de Pembroke, L'Histoire de, ed. Paul Meyer, 3 vols, SHF, Paris, 1891–1901.

Guillaume de Palerne, Roman du XIIIe siècle, ed. Alexandre Micha, TLF, Geneva, 1990.

Harvey, Ruth E., *The Troubadour Marcabru and Love,* London, 1989.

Haskins, Charles Homer, *The Renaissance of the Twelfth Century,*

Harvard University Press, 1927; reprinted in Meridian Books, New York, 1957.

Le Haut Livre du Graal: Perlesvaus, ed. William A. Nitze and T. Atkinson Jenkins, 2 vols, University of Chicago Press, 1932–7.

Helinant de Froidmont, *Chronicon,* ed. J.-P. Migne, PL 212, Paris, 1855.

Heltzel, Virgil B., *Fair Rosamund: A Study of the Development of a Literary Theme,* Evanston, 1947.

Higden, Ranulf, *Polychronicon,* 9 vols: vol. VIII, ed. Joseph Rawson Lumby, RS 41, London, 1882.

Histoire des ducs de Normandie, ed. Francisque Michel, Paris, 1840.

Hue de Rotelande, *Ipomedon,* ed. A. J. Holden, Paris, 1979.

     Protheselaus, ed. A. J. Holden, 2 vols, ANTS XLVII and XLVIII, London, 1991.

Hunt, Tony, 'The Significance of Thomas's Tristan', *Reading Medieval Studies,* VII, 1981, pp. 41–61.

Jeanroy, A., 'Notes sur le tournoiement des dames', *Romania,* 28, 1899, pp. 232–44.

John of Salisbury, *Historia Pontificalis,* ed. and tr. Marjorie Chibnall, Oxford, 1986.

Joufroi de Poitiers, roman d'aventures du XIIIᵉ siècle, ed. Perceval B. Fay and John L. Grigsby, TLF, Geneva and Paris, 1972.

Kelly, Amy, *Eleanor of Aquitaine and the Four Kings,* Harvard University Press, Cambridge, Mass. and London, 1950.

Kelly, Thomas E., *Le Haut Livre du Graal: Perlesvaus. A Structural Study,* Geneva, 1974.

Korrel, Peter, *An Arthurian Triangle: A Study of the Origin, Development and Characterization of Arthur, Guinevere and Modred,* Leiden, 1984.

Die Krone der Komnenen: Die Regierungszeit der Kaiser Joannes und Manuel Komnenos (1118–1180) aus dem Geschichtswerk des Niketas Choniates, tr. Franz Grabler, Byzantinische Geschichtsschreiber VII, Graz–Vienna–Cologne, 1958.

Labande, Edmond-René, 'Les filles d'Aliénor d'Aquitaine: étude comparative', *CCM,* XXIX, 1986, pp. 101–4.

Landon, Lionel, *The Itinerary of King Richard I,* London, 1935.

Loomis, Roger Sherman (ed.), *Arthurian Literature in the Middle Ages,* Oxford, 1959.

Map, Walter, *De Nugis Curialium: Courtiers' Trifles,* ed. and tr. M. R. James, revised by C. N. L. Brooke and R. A. B. Mynors, Oxford, 1983.

Marie de France, *Lais,* ed. A. Ewert, Oxford, 1944.

Materials for the History of Thomas Becket, Archbishop of Canterbury, ed. J. C. Robertson and J. B. Sheppard, 7 vols, RS 67, London, 1875–85.

Meade, Marion, *Eleanor of Aquitaine, A Biography*, New York, 1977.
Michaud's History of the Crusades, tr. W. Robson, 3 vols, London, 1852.
More, Sir Thomas, Drayton, Michael, Hearne, Thomas, &c., *The Unfortunate Royal Mistresses, Rosamond Clifford, and Jane Shore, Concubines to King Henry the Second and Edward the Fourth, with Historical and Metrical Memoirs of those Celebrated Persons*, London, 1825?
Morris, Colin, *The Discovery of the Individual, 1050–1200* (London, 1972).
Owen, D. D. R., 'The *Fergus*-Poet', in *Medieval Codicology, Iconography, Literature and Tradition: Studies for Keith Val Sinclair*, ed. Peter Rolfe Monks and D. D. R. Owen, Leiden, 1994, pp. 233–9.
    Noble Lovers, London, 1975.
    'The Prince and the Churl: The Traumatic Experience of Philip Augustus', *JMH*, 17, 1992, pp. 141–4.
Pacaut, Marcel, *Louis VII et son royaume*, Paris, 1964.
Peire Vidal, *Poesie*, ed. D. S. Avalle, Milan, 1960.
Percy, Thomas, *Reliques of Ancient English Poetry*, ed. R. A. Willmott, London, n.d.
Petit, Aimé, *L'Anachronisme dans les romans antiques du XIIᵉ siècle*, doctoral thesis, Centre d'Études Médiévales et Dialectales de l'Université de Lille III, 1985.
Philomena, conte raconté d'après Ovide par Chrétien de Troyes, ed. Ch. de Boer, Paris, 1909.
The Pilgrimage of Charlemagne (Le Pèlerinage de Charlemagne) and Aucassin and Nicolette (Aucassin et Nicolette), ed. Anne Elizabeth Cobby and Glyn S. Burgess, New York and London, 1988.
Price, Glanville (ed.), *William of Orange: Four Old French Epics*, Everyman, 1975.
Raby, F. J. E., *A History of Christian-Latin Poetry from the Beginnings to the Close of the Middle Ages*, 2nd edn, Oxford, 1953.
Raoul de Cambrai, ed. Sarah Kay, Oxford, 1992.
Raoul de Houdenc, *Sämtliche Werke*, ed. Mathias Friedwagner: vol. I, *Meraugis von Portlesguez: altfranzösischer Abenteuerroman*, Halle, 1897.
Récits d'un Ménestrel de Reims, ed. Natalis de Wailly, Paris, 1876.
Richard of Devizes, *Chronicle*, ed. and tr. John T. Appleby, London, 1963.
Richard le Poitevin, *Ex chronico*, in Delisle (ed.) *Recueil des historiens*, vol. XII.
Richard Löwenherz, Der Mittelenglische Versroman über, ed. and tr. Karl Brunner, Wiener Beiträge zur Englischen Philologie XLII, Vienna and Leipzig, 1913.

Richardson, H. G., 'The Letters and Charters of Eleanor of Aquitaine', *EHR*, CCXCI, 1959, pp. 193–213.

Roger of Hoveden, *Chronica,* ed. William Stubbs, vol. IV, RS 51, London, 1871.

Le Roman de Renart, ed. and tr. Jean Dufournet, 2 vols, Paris, 1985.

Schmolke-Hasselmann, Beate, *Der arthurische Versroman von Chrétien bis Froissart,* Beihefte zur ZRP 177, Tübingen, 1980.

Shakespeare, William, *King John,* ed. E. A. J. Honigmann, The Arden Shakespeare, London, 1954.

The Song of Roland, tr. D. D. R. Owen, London, 1972.

Strickland, Agnes, *Lives of the Queens of England,* vol. I, 4th edn, London, 1854.

Swinburne, Algernon Charles, *The Tragedies,* vol. I, London, 1905.

Tennyson, Alfred Lord, *The Life and Works,* vol. XI (*The Works,* vol. VII), London, 1899.

Thomas, *Les Fragments du Roman de Tristan, poème du XIIe siècle,* ed. Bartina H. Wind, TLF, Geneva and Paris, 1960.

   Tristan, tr. A. T. Hatto in *Gottfried von Strassburg, Tristan, with the Surviving Fragments of the Tristan of Thomas,* Penguin Books, 1960.

Treece, Henry, *The Crusades,* New York, 1964.

Turner, Ralph V., 'Eleanor of Aquitaine and her Children: An Inquiry into Medieval Family Attachment', *JMH*, 14, 1988, pp. 321–35.

The Vulgate Version of the Arthurian Romances, ed. H. O. Sommer, 7 vols, Washington, 1908–16.

Wace, *Le Roman de Brut,* ed. I. Arnold, 2 vols, SATF, Paris, 1938–40.

   Le Roman de Rou, ed. A. J. Holden, SATF, Paris, 1970.

Walter of Coventry, The Historical Collections of, ed. William Stubbs, RS 58, vol. II, London, 1873.

Warren, W. L., *Henry II,* London, 1973.

   King John, 2nd edn, London, 1978.

William of Newburgh, *The History of English Affairs,* Book I, ed. and tr. P. G. Walsh and M. J. Kennedy, Warminster, 1988.

William of Tyre, *A History of Deeds Done Beyond the Sea,* tr. E. A. Babcock and A. C. Krey, 2 vols, New York, 1976.

Yder, The Romance of, ed. and tr. Alison Adams, Arthurian Studies VIII, Woodbridge, 1983.

Index

Not all names of minor fictional characters or places are indexed, and references to the Chronology are not included.